THE OFFICIAL  GUIDE

GRAND PRIX 2010»

This edition published in 2010 by
Carlton Books Limited
20 Mortimer Street
London W1T 3JW

10 9 8 7 6 5 4 3 2 1

itv SPORT |

A CIP catalogue record for this book is available from
the British Library.

The publisher has taken reasonable steps to check
the accuracy of the facts contained herein at the
time of going to press, but can take no responsibility
for any errors.

ISBN: 978-1-84732-497-9

Project Art Editor: Katie Baxendale
Designer: Luke Griffin
Picture Research: Paul Langan
Production: Kate Pimm

Printed in the United Kingdom
by Butler Tanner & Dennis, Frome

**Formula One had a topsy turvy and hugely exciting season in 2009. Going into 2010, there
has been much change, and the team shown at the front here at Sepang in 2009, Toyota, is no
longer part of the show, with BMW also quitting, but four new teams have taken their place.**

THE OFFICIAL itv SPORT GUIDE

GRAND PRIX 2010>>

BRUCE JONES

CARLTON
BOOKS

CONTENTS

ANALYSIS OF THE 2010 SEASON 6

MERCEDES GP 8
Nico Rosberg 10
Michael Schumacher 11

RED BULL RACING 12
Sebastian Vettel 14
Mark Webber 15

McLAREN 16
Jenson Button 18
Lewis Hamilton 19

FERRARI 20
Felipe Massa 22
Fernando Alonso 23

WILLIAMS 24
Rubens Barrichello 26
Nico Hulkenberg 27

RENAULT 28
Robert Kubica 30
Bertrand Baguette 31

FORCE INDIA 32
Adrian Sutil 34
Vitantonio Liuzzi 35

TORO ROSSO 36
Sebastien Buemi 38
Jaime Alguersuari 39

CAMPOS META 40
Pedro de la Rosa 42
Bruno Senna 43

LOTUS F1 RACING 44
Jarno Trulli 46
Heikki Kovalainen 47

SAUBER 48
Nick Heidfeld 50
Kamui Kobayashi 51

TEAM US F1 52
Jonathan Summerton 54
Jose Maria Lopez 55

VIRGIN RACING 56
Timo Glock 58
Lucas di Grassi 59

TALKING POINTS
Technical changes for 2010............. 60
The Return of Cosworth 62

KNOW THE TRACKS 2010 64
Bahrain 66
Melbourne 67
Sepang 68
Shanghai 69
Barcelona 70
Monaco 71
Istanbul 72
Montreal 73
Valencia 74
Silverstone 75
Hockenheim 76
Hungaroring 77
Spa-Francorchamps 78
Monza 79
Singapore 80
Suzuka 81
South Korea 82
Interlagos 83
Yas Marina 84

REVIEW OF THE 2009 SEASON 86
Australian GP 88
Malaysian GP 90
Chinese GP 92
Bahrain GP 94
Spanish GP 96
Monaco GP 98
Turkish GP 100
British GP 102
German GP 104
Hungarian GP 106
European GP 108
Belgian GP 110
Italian GP 112
Singapore GP 114
Japanese GP 116
Brazilian GP 118
Abu Dhabi GP 120

FINAL RESULTS 2009 124

2010 FILL-IN CHART 126

Jenson Button and Brawn GP made a mighty splash in 2009, winning both the drivers' and constructors' titles, but the English driver has moved on to join Lewis Hamilton at McLaren, while the team has changed colours again, and will race in the colours of new owner Mercedes.

ANALYSIS OF
THE 2010 SEASON

The topsy-turvy nature of the 2009 World Championship and the establishment of a new order after comprehensive rule changes will make it a hard act to follow, but with four new teams and a driver merry-go-round, it has all the right ingredients and the outcome ought to be spiced up all the more by a new points scoring system.

There can be no mistaking the fact that these are times of considerable flux in Formula 1. Last year was a time of great technical change. This year the change is more procedural, but the potential for a further shake-up of the order is still there as both mid-race refuelling and the use of KERS are banned.

Furthermore, you might not at first recognise all of the teams with cars on the grid. Out has gone Toyota, BMW has quit Sauber, and in have come four new teams: Campos Meta, Team Lotus F1, Virgin Racing and Team US F1.

The FIA had grand aims for cost-cutting for 2010, looking to impose an optional $40m budget cap. The teams, under the FOTA umbrella, rejected this as they didn't want to have a two-tier F1, with the teams spending more than $40m having to run to more restricted technical rules. All 10 of last year's teams announced that they would withdraw and the rules were duly amended. Eventually, three new teams were selected from a pool of aspirants, and a fourth sought to be added to fill the gap left by BMW's withdrawal, with this team being its erstwhile partner Sauber that hadn't been

in position to sign the Concorde Agreement and so had to reapply for entry. All the new teams have been offered free air transport by Formula One Management for two cars and 10,000kg of freight each to every race, plus $10m

There has been a fair old spin of the driver merry-go-round too, with the main changes being Jenson Button quitting Brawn for McLaren, Fernando Alonso moving from Renault to Ferrari, Nico Rosberg from Williams to Brawn, which is now known as Mercedes, to be joined by Michael Schumacher, with Rubens Barrichello going the opposite way. Perhaps it will prove telling that Red Bull Racing has kept continuity, with Sebastian Vettel and Mark Webber, and are starting the season as many people's favourites.

If the new teams and faces in new places confuse initially, then there will be the further twist of the Canadian GP being back on the calendar. Furthermore, F1 will be visiting an all-new circuit for the inaugural Korean GP at South Jeolla.

Full details on the technical and sporting amendments for 2010 are covered on page 60, but the key points are: the use of narrower front tyres; the increase in minimum weight from 605 to 620kg to negate the disadvantage of heavier drivers; and most importantly the banning of refuelling. This will mean an increase in the size of the fuel tanks and the bodywork to accommodate them. But it's more complicated than that, as designers will have to consider the effect of the weight of this extra fuel on the car's balance and so move their ballast around accordingly. Another factor this year will be the dropping of KERS. This isn't a rule change, but an agreement between last year's teams, and this too will affect weight distribution.

One of the reasons behind the banning of refuelling is to encourage the engine builders to make their engines as fuel-efficient as possible. However, the other main reason is for viewers not to be confused any more by commentators having to say that a driver in, say, seventh place on the grid had actually set "fuel-adjusted pole." This year, though, the car lining up on pole position will be the out-and-out fastest as the third and final qualifying session will now be contested with a low fuel load rather than with a fuel load that has to be carried into the race and so affecting when the cars pitted for their first refuelling stop. As a consequence, all cars will start the race with a full race fuel load, and the drivers will have to remember that when they brake for the first corner and their cars are (160 kilos) heavier and require that vital amount more stopping distance...

There's a new points system to contend with, too, this time with the top 10 finishers scoring on the basis 25-20-15-10-8-6-4-3-2-1, thus increasing the advantage for the podium finishers.

So, it really is all change for 2010 and F1 fans the world over will be fortunate indeed if it can match 2009 for excitement.

MERCEDES GP

It was thought they didn't write scripts like this outside Hollywood, but disaster turned to triumph after Honda quit F1 and Ross Brawn took over and came away with both titles. Now, money troubles are over as Mercedes has bought the team.

Jenson Button has moved on, but he left the team a winning legacy.

Yes, that's right, Brawn GP rose like a phoenix from the flames and not only guided Jenson Button to the drivers' championship last year but beat the collected might of Ferrari and McLaren to become constructors' champions at the first attempt.

In short, 2009 was quite a year for the team that was called Brawn GP simply because "they had to call it something" according to team principal Ross Brawn. And now, 12 months later, it has become Mercedes GP, its future ensured.

It wasn't all happy for Brawn as he was torn early in the year when he had to do some considerable pruning of the

staff at Brackley to keep the team going, with 200 being made redundant at a time when the world economy wasn't going to make it easy for them to find another job. It was a difficult time for everyone, and one hopes that many of those who lost their jobs have been re-employed now that Mercedes is bringing in new money.

Their legacy remained, though, for all had been involved from early in 2008 in focusing on the 2009 challenger once Brawn had decided that the 2008 car was not going to become competitive – and it certainly wasn't – and reckoned their efforts would bear more fruit if aimed at tackling the myriad

KEY MOMENTS & KEY PEOPLE

TEAM HISTORY
It's become increasingly hard to define teams, as many change hands and continue with a new name. Honda raced in F1 in the 1960s, but that had nothing to do with the Honda Racing team that was spawned in 2006 from the BAR team that had run from 1999 after taking an increasing role in the set-up. The leading personnel remained the same, and Honda Racing took its first win, with Button driving, in Hungary 2006, before hundreds of staff had to be shed to keep it afloat into 2009.

ROSS BRAWN
It's been a long climb from machinist at Williams in 1976 when Ross was 24. He became chief aerodynamicist by 1979, then chief designer at Arrows in 1986. After a spell in sports cars with Jaguar, he returned to F1 with Benetton, where he teamed up with Michael Schumacher and they won titles together, both there and at Ferrari. He moved to Honda Racing as technical director, then had to pull the team around him as Honda walked out.

technical changes due for 2009. Their time, and so Honda's investment, was successful as they opted for the double-deck diffuser that would give they and two other teams – Toyota and Williams – an early-season advantage that would set them up for the titles.

For this season, it's unlikely that the order will be shaken as it was in 2009, when it was shaken like almost never before, with the status quo adjusting literally from race to race. However, to stand a chance of repeating the team's feats of their first year, the team will have to make a car that gets heat into its tyres better and thus is able to qualify at the front of the grid.

At least, with KERS banned, the drivers won't have to face up to rivals blasting away from them on the run to the first corner every race.

The major change for 2010, though, is that Mercedes-Benz has taken over the team, buying 75% of its shares after being inspired by the team's success with their engines last year and also wanting control over a team, which is something that it has never had fully over long-time partner McLaren.

The German manufacturer's involvement didn't necessarily mean that a German driver ought to be in one of the seats, but Nico Rosberg was thrust forward as a favoured candidate to come in and partner Button, although last year's World Champion eventually decided not to stay on, leaving the way clear for Michael Schumacher to be courted to come out of retirement after three years watching both from the sidelines and, occasionally, from the pit wall in his capacity as an advisor to Ferrari. Michael passed the necessary checks then upped his training.

This duo will be interesting to compare, with Rosberg knowing that he must not only adjust to being the newcomer in the team after years of leading the Williams attack, but also start delivering the regular podium finishes and wins that he said he now should be scoring.

Rosberg's speed next to Schumacher's remains to be seen, but it would take a fool to reckon that as Michael has hit 40 his amazing natural speed will have deserted him.

Welcome back silver arrows.

FOR THE RECORD

Country of origin:	England
Team base:	Brackley, England
Telephone:	(44) 01280 844000
Website:	www.brawngp.com
Active in Formula One:	From 1999 (as BAR until 2005, then as Honda Racing until 2008)
Grands Prix contested:	188
Wins:	9
Pole positions:	8
Fastest laps:	4

2009 DRIVERS & RESULTS

Driver	Nationality	Races	Wins	Pts	Pos
Rubens Barrichello	Brazilian	17	2	77	3rd
Jenson Button	British	17	6	95	1st

THE TEAM

Team principal:	Ross Brawn
Chief executive officer:	Nick Fry
Head of aerodynamics:	Loic Bigois
Head of race & test engineering:	Steve Clark
Head of vehicle engineering:	Craig Wilson
Operations director:	Gary Savage
Chief test engineer:	Simon Cole
Sporting director:	Ron Meadows
Test driver:	tba
Chassis:	Mercedes
Engine:	Mercedes V8
Tyres:	Bridgestone

Ross Brawn has two drivers new to the team to deal with in 2010.

NICO ROSBERG

Nico knows that this is the season in which he must become a grand prix winner. He has served his apprenticeship across four years with Williams and must now make his presence felt on the podium this year and secure that first grand prix victory.

Every now and again, Formula 1 drivers play musical chairs. And so it is for 2010, except the drivers were in the fortunate position that even with the departure of several manufacturers, there were more new teams coming in and so actually more seats to aim at rather than less. Nico Rosberg was keen to move on after four years with Williams failed to yield the first win he so craved. And so he has.

For 2010, look for Nico at the team that was last year Brawn GP, placed there at the behest of the team's new stakeholder Mercedes-Benz and expecting race wins at the very least.

His partnership and associated rivalry with multiple World Champion Michael Schumacher will be fascinating to watch and Nico will have to really deliver as he has never delivered before if he is to make his mark with the team. It will be novel to have a team-mate who has considerably more experience than him. However, if he really uses his brain, he will look, listen

Nico will be hoping that Mercedes can use the momentum the team built up as Brawn.

and learn from Schumacher and ensure that he picks up every point of which he and the car combined can achieve. This year really ought to be a case of "cometh the hour, cometh the man."

Looking back to last year, after Nico's six-race run of fourth, fifth and sixth place finishes, Nico's one chance of a podium finish came in the Singapore GP when he was heading for second place, only to lose concentration for a second and cross the curving white line at pit exit when leaving a pit stop. This hit him very hard, as the drivethrough penalty wrecked his race, especially with the timing of a safety car period, and he ended up out of the points in 11th place. It was a cruel misfortune.

GROOMED FOR STARDOM

As the son of a World Champion – Keke with Williams in 1982 – Nico was always likely to have a go at racing. And so he did, being team-mate for most of that time to Lewis Hamilton, thus usually being confined to being runner-up at best, as he was in the 2000 European Formula A kart series. Trying car racing when he turned 17, Nico took a different course to Lewis and won the Formula BMW title in 2002 and carried this experience to F3, outscoring Lewis when he ranked fourth in 2004. Keeping one step ahead of Lewis, who stayed on in F3, Nico had his best season in winning the 2005 GP2 crown, pipping Heikki Kovalainen in the final round. Williams signed him for 2006 and Nico shocked everyone by setting fastest lap on his debut in Bahrain, but the team hasn't provided him with a car capable of winning, although some have said a more feisty driver might have achieved more.

MICHAEL SCHUMACHER

When Mercedes took over Brawn GP for 2010, there was considerable excitement that one of its new silver arrows might be driven by a certain seven-time World Champion who had been coaxed out of retirement. Yes, Michael Schumacher...

Some drivers can walk away from F1, but Michael was never going to be one of those. He'd been so totally wrapped up in F1 as he gathered his seven world titles that you knew where his heart lay and, pretend as he did over three years, so did he. So, enter a 41-year-old who will be as enthused as a teenager. In the case of which driver would fill the second Mercedes GP seat, all fingers pointed to Michael Schumacher. Perhaps it was wishful thinking, with F1 ringmaster Bernie Ecclestone certainly licking his lips at the possibility.

F1 fans too were enthralled by the idea of having today's stars such as Lewis Hamilton and Sebastian Vettell judged against the ultimate yardstick.

Michael, too, was excited by the thought of racing again, having retired at the end of the 2006 season. Don't forget that he came close to rejoining Ferrari last year as substitute for the injured Felipe Massa, before he failed to get medical clearance, due to not recovering from injuries suffered

Michael won't be returning to F1 just to take part. He'll be aiming for his 100th victory.

falling from his racing motorbike. In light of the struggle the other replacements faced, the F60 was a tricky beast, and perhaps it was just as well he hadn't come back then.

TRACK NOTES

Nationality:	GERMAN
Born:	3 JANUARY 1969, KERPEN, GERMANY
Website:	www.michael-schumacher.de
Teams:	1991 JORDAN, 1991-1995 BENETTON, 1996-2006 FERRARI, 2010 MERCEDES

CAREER RECORD

First Grand Prix:	1991 BELGIAN GP
Grand Prix starts:	250
Grand Prix wins:	91

1992 Belgian GP, 1993 Portuguese GP, 1994 Brazilian GP, Pacific GP, San Marino GP, Monaco GP, Canadian GP, French GP, Hungarian GP, European GP, 1995 Brazilian GP, Spanish GP, Monaco GP, French GP, German GP, Belgian GP, European GP, Pacific GP, Japanese GP, 1996 Spanish GP, Belgian GP, Italian GP, 1997 Monaco GP, Canadian GP, French GP, Belgian GP, Japanese GP, 1998 Argentinian GP, Canadian P, French GP, British GP, Hungarian GP, Italian GP, 1999 San Marino GP, Monaco GP, 2000 Australian GP, Brazilian GP, San Marino GP, European GP, Canadian GP, Italian GP, US GP, Japanese GP, Malaysian GP, 2001 Australian GP, Malaysian GP, Spanish GP, Monaco GP, European GP, French GP, Hungarian GP, Belgian GP, Japanese GP, 2002 Australian GP, Brazilian GP, San Marino GP, Spanish GP, Austrian GP, Canadian GP, British GP, French GP, German GP, Belgian GP, Japanese GP, 2003 San Marino GP, Spanish GP, Austrian GP, Canadian GP, Italian GP, US GP, 2004 Australian GP, Malaysian GP, Bahrain GP, San Marino GP, Spanish GP, European GP, Canadian GP, French GP, British GP, German GP, Hungarian GP, Japanese GP, 2005 US GP

Poles:	68
Fastest laps:	75
Points:	1369
Honours:	2004, 2003, 2002, 2001, 2000, 1995 & 1994 F1 WORLD CHAMPION, 1990 GERMAN F3 CHAMPION, 1988 GERMAN FORMULA KONIG CHAMPION

WIN, WIN, WIN

Having a father who ran a kart circuit certainly gave Michael a head start for his racing career. He was the man to beat and there was much excitement when he stepped up to cars as soon as he was old enough. He cleaned up in entry-level Formula Konig to such an extent that he advanced before the year was out to Formula Ford and nearly took the German title in that as well. F3 was next and he was pipped to the 1989 German title, but bounced back to be champion in 1990. Without the backing to continue in single-seaters, he jumped at a ride with Mercedes in sports cars and then shocked with his speed in a one-off ride in Japanese F3000 and was snapped up to make his F1 debut with Jordan. Benetton snaffled him and he was World Champion in 1994 and 1995, then joining Ferrari and turning the team back into a winning machine before going on to win the world title every year from 2000 to 2004, then retiring at the end of 2006.

RED BULL

It was a case of poor season followed by great season as Red Bull Racing bounced back from a weak 2008 campaign and started scoring wins in such a way in 2009 that it might have toppled Brawn GP to be number one. For 2010, it must be feared.

Last year's RB5 was very competitive. This year's should be faster still.

There were times late last year when it seemed that Red Bull Racing might manage to land a deal with Mercedes for engines for 2010. Imagine how dangerous that would have made them: potentially the best chassis allied with what's reckoned to be the strongest engine and debatably the strongest driver line-up.

The deal didn't hold together, though, and the team couldn't afford to delay further if it wanted to focus on its chassis design, so signed on the dotted line for Renault engines to be retained for this season. The other Mercedes-powered teams will have heaved a sigh of relief. Why so? Because Adrian Newey's

Red Bull chassis was the best around for all but the opening seven races last year and with no technical changes for this year, the same should be true this time around. Unless, that is, McLaren or Ferrari can produce superior cars when they've had a full winter to design their 2010 challengers around the double-deck diffusers that they had to adopt during last year.

Red Bull will want Renault to produce engines of greater reliability than they did last year, as going racing in the final rounds under the threat of a 10-place grid penalty if they changed one more engine was certainly not the sort of background the team wanted as

KEY MOMENTS & KEY PEOPLE

TEAM HISTORY
This is one of several teams to have changed its identity. Having started as Stewart Grand Prix in 1997, set up by former World Champion Jackie Stewart and son Paul, it enjoyed a surprise second place for Rubens Barrichello at Monaco in 1997 and an even more surprise one-two headed by Johnny Herbert at the Nurburgring in 1999. Jaguar bought it for 2000, but it was often in disarray and achieved little. Mark Webber raced for it then and rejoined in 2007 after it had become Red Bull Racing.

CHRISTIAN HORNER
Here is a team boss who really understands his drivers. Why? Because he was one himself, dreaming of glory in F3000. He knew he wasn't the fastest, so started a team, Arden when he was 23. He kept on racing until 1998, then focused on team management and his team became the top one between 2002-04, after which Christian joined Red Bull Racing, settling in effortlessly into F1. By the following year, he was team principal.

it took a tilt at the world titles for the first time. They did get away without either driver having to take the penalty, but it was an added pressure that the team didn't need.

So, Red Bull's chassis is likely to be a development rather than an all-new creation. This will help the team, as will retaining the same drivers in Sebastian Vettel and Mark Webber, who finished second and fourth last year respectively. They have worked well together so far, but it will be interesting to see how either copes if the other starts to impose superiority and tries to assume the number one driver's role.

In such a circumstance, team principal Christian Horner will have to use his political skills to soothe the situation. As a former racer, though, the drivers know that he will have a better understanding of their predicament than most team principals. Team owner Dietrich Mateschitz has long been backing Vettel, though, and their shared tongue, German, binds them together further, so there is the potential there for schism, even though Webber is extraordinarily level-headed and won't want to rock the boat lest it reduces his considerable focus on the task in hand.

When looking at Red Bull Racing's challenge, one has to remember that this is a team that isn't accustomed to winning. It did so once, in freak circumstances in 1999 when it was Stewart Grand Prix, then never looked likely to do so again through its subsequent life as Jaguar Racing and then through its first four years as Red Bull Racing. So, last year was a steep learning curve for the team from Milton Keynes and there were, understandably, a few glitches as they fought at the sharp end of the field, such as the lollipop being raised early after pit stops to hit the drivers with penalties that cost points.

That said, Horner and his crew are the sort who look to learn and you can be sure that every element of their act will have been tightened up for 2010 which will make them an even more formidable outfit.

After such a stellar season, it's hard to imagine Red Bull's junior team, Scuderia Toro Rosso, outscoring it as it did in 2008. Last year, Red Bull ended up second overall, Toro Rosso 10th and last.

FOR THE RECORD

Country of origin:	England
Team base:	Milton Keynes, England
Telephone:	(44) 01908 279700
Website:	www.redbullracing.com
Active in Formula One:	From 1997 (as Stewart until 2000 then Jaguar Racing until 2004)
Grands Prix contested:	223
Wins:	7
Pole positions:	6
Fastest laps:	6

2009 DRIVERS & RESULTS

Driver	Nationality	Races	Wins	Pts	Pos
Sebastian Vettel	German	17	4	84	2nd
Mark Webber	Australian	17	2	69.5	4th

THE TEAM

Chairman:	Dietrich Mateschitz
Team principal:	Christian Horner
Chief technical officer:	Adrian Newey
Head of race engineering:	Ian Morgan
Chief designer:	Rob Marshall
Head of vehicle performance:	Mark Ellis
Head of aerodynamics:	Peter Prodromou
Team manager:	Jonathan Wheatley
Team co-ordinator:	Gerrard O'Reilly
Test driver:	tba
Chassis:	Red Bull RB6
Engine:	Renault V8
Tyres:	Bridgestone

Christian Horner brings a racer's perspective to his team management.

SEBASTIAN VETTEL

Here's a driver who has future World Champion written all over him. Many hailed him as the best in F1 last year when he hunted down points leader Jenson Button, but the season ahead could be the one in which he proves if he is or isn't.

Sebastian is a dream in the F1 paddock. Sure, he's blindingly quick and he's with a top team that can and does challenge for victories. What marks him out, though, is his personality, which is irreverent at times when he doesn't have to be focused. He's funny, good company, smiles a lot and, when he talks, talks of team effort. He's part of the gang and as far from the monosyllabic Kimi Raikkonen as could be.

Mistake Sebastian for a joker at your peril, though, as his desire to be World Champion burns bright and was clear for all to see last autumn at the Brazilian GP when Button wrapped it up and Sebastian simply couldn't conceal his disappointment.

For long-time backer Red Bull, he's helped the energy drinks company score first wins for both of its teams, Toro Rosso in 2008 and then Red Bull Racing last year. His aim for 2010 must be Red Bull's first title.

With four wins to his name last year, the most notable being his domination of the British GP after scoring that first Red Bull

Sebastian showed not just winning speed last year but a steely determination.

win in torrential conditions at Shanghai, he is more than likely to be in a winning car this year. This can be predicted with more accuracy than 12 months ago, as this

year's changes are procedural rather than technical and Adrian Newey's RB5 chassis from which this year's will evolve was the class of the second half of 2009.

Should everything come together in 2010, and Sebastian manages to become World Champion, he will be doubly delighted, as he will no longer be referred to as 'Germany's new Michael Schumacher'.

TRACK NOTES

Nationality:	GERMAN
Born:	3 JULY, 1987, HEEPENHEIM, GERMANY
Website:	www.sebastianvettel.de
Teams:	BMW SAUBER 2007, TORO ROSSO
	2007-08, RED BULL RACING 2009-10

CAREER RECORD	
First Grand Prix:	2007 UNITED STATES GP
Grand Prix starts:	43
Grand Prix wins:	5
	2008 Italian GP, 2009 Chinese GP, British GP,
	Japanese GP, Abu Dhabi GP
Poles:	5
Fastest laps:	3
Points:	125
Honours:	2006 EUROPEAN FORMULA 3
	RUNNER-UP, 2004 GERMAN FORMULA BMW
	CHAMPION, 2003 GERMAN FORMULA BMW
	RUNNER-UP, 2001 EUROPEAN & GERMAN JUNIOR
	KART CHAMPION

HELPED BY VILLENEUVE'S DEPARTURE

Germany was in racing's wilderness for years. Then Michael Schumacher came along. But there were few others. Now, the scene is awash with German drivers, and Sebastian was the pick of this crop, a winner at European level in karts then instantly a hit in the junior single-seater categories, scoring an incredible 18 wins from 20 starts in Germany's Formula BMW ADAC series in 2004. Then Red Bull snapped him up and invested in him from there. Top rookie in European F3 in 2005, Sebastian was pipped to the 2006 crown by Paul di Resta, but showed his speed by winning on two of his three outings in the more powerful World Series by Renault. Sebastian stayed on in the World Series in 2007 and was leading the way when, mid-season, he was gifted the chance to graduate to F1 when Jacques Villeneuve was dropped by BMW Sauber. Toro Rosso then snapped him up and fourth place at the Chinese GP showed his promise.

MARK WEBBER

Mark shone like never before in 2009. He became a winner at last, making the most of having competitive equipment for the first time, and also revealed himself as one of F1's toughest racers. This year is his greatest opportunity for a title shot.

Imagine the first thought that went through this gritty Australian's mind as he fell to earth after his bicycle collided with a car during a charity triathlon at the end of 2008. Fear, of course, as he'd broken a leg. But frustration too as he knew that he had a very special season ahead of him, one that might just have yielded the biggest honour of all: the F1 world title.

He's made of doughty stuff and fought back, ignoring pain as he built up his strength to race again. Not conducting much testing hurt Mark's early-season chances as he played catch-up in getting used to the all-new car and 2009 regulations, but he was fit enough to chase team-mate Sebastian Vettel home in second place at the season's third round, the Chinese GP. He might still have been in pain, but there were points to be collected.

The record books show that Mark scored his first win at the Nurburgring mid-season and his second at Interlagos in the penultimate round. However, had it not

Mark became a winner at last in 2009 and will start this year without a broken leg...

been for a run of four grands prix in late summer in which he failed to score as much as a single point, Mark could easily have been challenging Button for the drivers'

championship title at season's end.

This year, armed with another class-of-the-field chassis from Adrian Newey, Mark will have every hope that he can not only keep the lid on the mercurial Vettel, especially in qualifying, but on Button, Hamilton and Alonso too, and so take a serious tilt at becoming Australia's first world champion since Alan Jones did the honours for Williams 30 years ago.

TRACK NOTES

Nationality:	AUSTRALIAN
Born:	27 AUGUST, 1976,
	QUEANBEYAN, AUSTRALIA
Website:	www.markwebber.com
Teams:	MINARDI 2002, JAGUAR 2003-2004,
	WILLIAMS 2005-2006, RED BULL RACING 2007-10

CAREER RECORD

First Grand Prix:	2002 AUSTRALIAN GP
Grand Prix starts:	139
Grand Prix wins:	2
	2009 German GP, Brazilian GP
Poles:	1
Fastest laps:	6
Points:	169.5
Honours:	2001 FORMULA 3000 RUNNER-UP,
	1998 FIA GT RUNNER-UP, 1996 BRITISH
	FORMULA FORD RUNNER-UP & FORMULA FORD
	FESTIVAL WINNER

A VERY PHYSICAL APPROACH

People used to laud Michael Schumacher for his fitness, but Mark has always been someone able to match him. His attitude to his racing is also hard-nosed, as he has achieved so much despite having precious little backing since coming over to Europe from Australia to win the Formula Ford Festival in 1996. Winning races in British F3 backed this up. But then Mark had to take the pragmatic approach and shelve his single-seater dreams to race for Mercedes in sportscars in 1999. A flip at Le Mans would have scared others, but two competitive years of F3000 showed that Mark still had the fire and his F1 break came in 2002, with points coming on his debut, which was no small feat in a Minardi. Two years with Jaguar were frustrating, with his speed plain to see, but top results less so. It was much the same in the following two years with Williams, but there was always the feeling that results would come if Mark got the right equipment.

McLAREN

McLaren was left in disarray with an uncompetitive car at the start of 2009, but clawed its way back to the front. Expect this year's challenger to be setting the pace from the opening round and for its drivers to be going for gold at every race.

Hamilton was a winner in 2009, but he'll be going for a second title.

Observing McLaren's form at the end of 2008, as Lewis Hamilton wrapped up the honours, there was no reason to fear that the team wouldn't be operating at the front in 2009. Sure, there was a comprehensive set of new technical regulations, but McLaren is like a brains trust, so this wasn't expected to trip the team up. But it did.

What happened between the team discovering at the first pre-season test that it was 3s per lap off the pace and the middle of the season was remarkable as the engineering side led by Paddy Lowe countered not just introducing a double diffuser but also a lack of downforce. Their pace of development was

remarkable as they hauled the car from way off the pace to setting it by season's end. That said, the gap between the front of the grid and the rear was far closer than ever before, so each small gain produced a clear advance up the order.

What makes their climb back to the front all the more remarkable is that it was achieved at a time of turmoil at the top of the team, as Ron Dennis's planned handing over of the reins to Martin Whitmarsh was brought forward by "Liegate", the debacle that was triggered by an innocuous event behind the safety car at the Australian GP, but also led to the departure of long-time team

KEY MOMENTS & KEY PEOPLE

TEAM HISTORY

Bruce McLaren was a driver with great engineering expertise and he followed Cooper team-mate Jack Brabham in starting his own team. That was in 1966 and it began winning in 1968, but Bruce was killed in 1970. The team kept going and Emerson Fittipaldi was its first world champion in 1974. James Hunt repeated the feat in 1976. But it was after Ron Dennis took over that it shone, with Alain Prost and Ayrton Senna giving it its glory years.

MARTIN WHITMARSH

The relationship between F1 and the aerospace industry bloomed in the 1980s, and Martin's move from British Aerospace to become head of operations at McLaren in 1989 was a pace-setting appointment. The way he settled in showed how his skill set translated and Martin became managing director in 1997. With Ron Dennis looking for a successor, Martin took on more duties and became chief operating officer of the McLaren Group in 2005 then was eventually handed the reins early last year.

manager Davey Ryan, and left Hamilton deeply embarrassed.

For 2010, there is no major shaking up of the regulations. Of course, the cars will differ in having to accommodate a larger fuel tank. The smaller front tyres will also affect air flow around the front of the car, and race tactics will differ as the cars have to be made to work with a full load of fuel, but these seem minor changes in comparison to last year's.

There will be no KERS used in 2010, and so one of McLaren's perceived advantages will have been denied them. Then again, the team's work on KERS undoubtedly required considerable effort from the engineers and its extra weight meant a restricted ability to put ballast where they wanted.

There was talk at the end of last season that Mercedes-Benz wanted to back out of its involvement after 15 years together, by selling its 40% share in the team and then sinking the money into buying 75% of Brawn GP instead. However, Mercedes Motorsport vice-president Norbert Haug moved quickly to deny a withdrawal, saying Mercedes' commitment to the team remained long-term. Whether that will continue beyond the end of their contract that stretches until the end of 2011 remains to be seen.

Hamilton will again lead McLaren's attack, and he will be raring to go after the disappointments at the start of last year. He will be stronger for the experience and, in many insiders' eyes, he drove better than ever in 2009.

It was mooted that Heikki Kovalainen would be ejected from the second seat due to lack of performance, with fellow Finn Kimi Raikkonen being welcomed back in his place. However, there was a stumbling block: money. Raikkonen wanted lots of it, even though he kept on saying that the only thing that would keep him in F1 was a winning car, and his return to McLaren after his spell at Ferrari was his most likely way to get one of these.

However, reigning World Champion Jenson Button elected to cross over, keen to be in what he considers will be a winning car for the defence of his world title. It's going to be a hugely interesting partnership with new team-mate Hamilton.

FOR THE RECORD

Country of origin:	England
Team base:	Woking, England
Telephone:	(44) 01483 728211
Website:	www.mclaren.com
Active in Formula One:	From 1966
Grands Prix contested:	666
Wins:	164
Pole positions:	145
Fastest laps:	137

2009 DRIVERS & RESULTS

Driver	Nationality	Races	Wins	Pts	Pos
Lewis Hamilton	British	17	2	49	5th
Heikki Kovalainen	Finnish	17	0	22	12th

THE TEAM

Team principal:	Martin Whitmarsh
Managing director:	Jonathan Neale
Engineering director:	Paddy Lowe
Design & development director:	Neil Oatley
Head of aerodynamics:	Simon Lacey
Head of vehicle engineering:	Mark Williams
Chief engineer:	Tim Goss
Team manager:	David Redding
Test driver:	tba
Chassis:	McLaren MP4-25
Engine:	Mercedes V8
Tyres:	Bridgestone

Martin Whitmarsh could well be finding reasons to smile in 2010.

JENSON BUTTON

Jenson made it two British World Champions in a row last year, but his was a ride fraught with emotion as the wheels came off the Brawn wagon midseason and he had to fight down the order to keep going. Now he's back for more, with McLaren...

Many people said to Jenson at the end of last season that it doesn't matter how you won a world title, as it's forever. In other words, it's something that no one can ever take away from you and the fact that it turned out to be such a close battle before he delivered that cracking drive in Brazil will be forgotten. He will be, whatever follows, Jenson Button, 2009 World Champion.

Jenson would obviously have preferred to have continued his early-season dominance when he won six of the opening seven races, as it would have caused him less angst. It might also not have confused some newspaper writers who failed to take into account that his Brawn BGP 001 was no longer the car to have as spring turned to summer. However, he'll have been toughened up by the process, as he admitted when the title was finally won.

Jenson's title win was exceedingly popular with the fans, though, as they recognised that his talent deserved to be rewarded, especially after years of not having the

Jenson's move to McLaren is to secure a winning car and, possibly, another title.

equipment to do the job following flashes of brilliance in his maiden year with Williams in 2000 when only 20 and then again in 2004 when he was racing for BAR.

Entering 2010, without the destabilization of having his team pull out of F1, Jenson will be praying that his smooth driving style will come into its own as drivers have to learn to live with the banning of refuelling which will force teams to consider different tactics.

TRACK NOTES

Nationality:	BRITISH
Born:	19 JANUARY, 1980, FROME, ENGLAND
Website:	www.jensonbutton.com
Teams:	WILLIAMS 2000, BENETTON/RENAULT 2001-2002, BAR/HONDA 2003-2008, BRAWN 2009

CAREER RECORD

First Grand Prix:	2000 AUSTRALIAN GP
Grand Prix starts:	171
Grand Prix wins:	7
	2006 Hungarian GP, 2009 Australian GP, Malaysian GP, Bahrain GP, Spanish GP, Monaco GP, Turkish GP
Poles:	7
Fastest laps:	2
Points:	327
Honours:	2009 FORMULA ONE WORLD CHAMPION, 1999 MACAU FORMULA THREE RUNNER-UP, 1998 FORMULA FORD FESTIVAL WINNER, BRITISH FORMULA FORD CHAMPION & McLAREN AUTOSPORT BRDC YOUNG DRIVER, 1997 EUROPEAN SUPER A KART CHAMPION,

YOUTHFUL PROMISE FINALLY FULFILLED

Jenson was one of those drivers that racing fans were aware of before he started in cars, as he kept on winning karting titles. He made an instant impact, winning the British Formula Ford title. Jenson starred in F3 the following year, 1999, and was considering whether to go back for a second season, to improve on ranking third overall, or to step up to F3000, that he was invited to test for the Prost F1 team. Then, having just turned 20, was offered a ride for 2000. He didn't disappoint, showing extra strong form at the end of the year at Suzuka, a real drivers' circuit. However, moving to Benetton wasn't a dream, as its cars weren't competitive, and it took until 2006, when he was racing for Honda, to score his first win, in Hungary. The team then took a wrong turn and, after two rotten campaigns, quit, leaving Jenson's career at the crossroads, saved only by Ross Brawn taking the reins. The rest, as they say, is history.

LEWIS HAMILTON

Lewis ended the year fifth overall, but he probably drove better than ever before as he wrestled his initially dire McLaren towards the pace which added not only to his experience, but also to his desire to win, so expect some fireworks in 2010.

Out of adversity comes opportunity, or so said Benjamin Franklin, and there were times in 2009 when the then reigning World Champion would have wished that he wasn't having to work his way through such difficult times. In the long run, though, it will have done him and everyone at McLaren a huge amount of good as they achieved a remarkable turnaround.

For 2010, Lewis will expect to have a car that's on the pace, indeed setting the pace, from the first round. In fact, he'll have had every reason to be confident that the strong form shown at last year's final round in Abu Dhabi will have been built upon.

This year will be different without KERS to assist in attack and defence now that it has been outlawed. Then again, the McLaren MP4-25 will be able to run with its weight where it wants it, which was always a problem for the cars running KERS, as they didn't have any "spare" weight to position as ballast.

Lewis will want to be back at the front of the field full-time this year and will be wary that Sebastian Vettel might take some

Lewis had his worst season in 2009, but grew in stature. Expect more wins in 2010.

quelling if the Red Bull is as effective as its predecessor.

Perhaps the biggest challenge will come from within the team, though, if McLaren's new signing Jenson Button responds to what the team has to offer and offers a serious challenge to his compatriot.

TRACK NOTES

Nationality:	BRITISH
Born: 7 JANUARY 1985, STEVENAGE, ENGLAND	
Website:	www.lewishamilton.com
Teams:	McLAREN 2007-2010

CAREER RECORD

First Grand Prix:	2007 AUSTRALIAN GP
Grand Prix starts:	52
Wins:	11
2007 Canadian GP, United States GP, Hungarian GP, Japanese GP, 2008 Australian GP, Monaco GP, British GP, German GP, Chinese GP, 2009 Hungarian GP, Singapore GP	
Pole positions:	20
Fastest laps:	3
Points:	305
Honours:	2008 FORMULA ONE WORLD CHAMPION, 2006 GP2 CHAMPION, 2005 EUROPEAN FORMULA THREE CHAMPION, 2003 BRITISH FORMULA RENAULT CHAMPION, 2000 WORLD KART CUP CHAMPION & EUROPEAN FORMULA A KARTING CHAMPION, 1999 ITALIAN INTERCONTINENTAL A KARTING CHAMPION, 1996 McLAREN MERCEDES CHAMPION OF THE FUTURE, 1995 BRITISH CADET KARTING CHAMPION

WITH A LITTLE HELP FROM HIS FRIENDS

There are three keys to Lewis's rise to the top: his natural speed, the support and drive of his father Anthony and then the mentoring by McLaren. Combine those three, and you had a surefire winner. He collected his first title, the British Cadet Kart title at the age of 10 in 1995. Three years later, he was on McLaren's books and rewarded them in 2000 by becoming World Kart Champion. Lewis's move to cars was in Formula Renault in 2002 and he was British champion the following year. Adding the European F3 title in 2005, again at his second attempt, emphasized his ability, but winning the GP2 crown as a rookie in 2006 showed that he was ready for F1. He then came within a point of being the first rookie World Champion, scoring his first win in Canada mid-season and then adding three more before being pipped by Ferrari's Kimi Raikkonen. However, he made amends by a similar margin in 2008, edging out Ferrari's Felipe Massa.

FERRARI

Ferrari was caught on the hop at the start of 2009 by other teams' interpretations of the new regulations. Like McLaren, it fought back, but the key to its passage back to the top is likely to be Fernando Alonso's arrival to accompany Felipe Massa.

Felipe Massa is back for a new season and also a new challenge.

Whatever happens in Formula 1, whether it expands or contracts, Ferrari will always be the most famous team and the most widely supported too. Just look at the incredible new Yas Marina circuit in Abu Dhabi that so dazzled the F1 regulars when it made its debut last November. Does it have a theme park called McLaren World? No, it's called Ferrari World. Their road cars are the cars of choice for the oil-rich, as ever Ferrari's prancing horse emblem the one most sought after by the world's newly monied. It's the marque of aspiration and F1 plays a considerable part in that.

To this end, fourth overall is not the most disastrous result in the world. But, by Ferrari's standards, this performance in 2009 was weak, so you can be sure that considerable effort was expended from the middle of last year to make sure that such a ranking isn't repeated.

Certainly, there are no technical rule changes for 2010, just procedural ones, but there might be concern that Ferrari was not able to respond as efficiently as arch-rivals McLaren to being caught without a double-deck diffuser at the start of last year. Although Kimi Raikkonen won at the Belgian GP, their form in the final round in Abu Dhabi was weak, whereas Lewis Hamilton put his McLaren on pole there.

Still, the 2010 Ferrari will

at least have been designed with the right ingredients and not have to be reshaped as a compromise, so it ought to be far superior to its predecessor.

Talking only of McLaren as a rival is out of date, as Red Bull Racing will surely be right at the front again, possibly as the pace-setters if its design chief Adrian Newey has his way again. Mercedes (Brawn GP last year) may have stepped up a notch too for 2010, as they must to counter the inevitably higher standard of their rivals.

This is where Fernando Alonso needs to be brought into the equation, for many feel that if Ferrari produces a car that isn't quite a match for the very best, his ability will mask the shortfall and he'll put himself right into the mix. If, on the other hand, technical director Aldo Costa has guided his design team to produce the best car

out there, then the likes of Lewis Hamilton, Sebastian Vettel and Mark Webber might only see the Spaniard's dust, which would certainly set the church bells ringing in Maranello again...

We know that Felipe Massa is quick too. Or should that say was quick too. How the Brazilian performs on his return remains to be seen, but it could be a strange environment for him as he was very much the favoured driver at Ferrari before his head injury last summer, the driver with whom the team socialised while Raikkonen went his own way. Alonso likes a team around him too, but he doesn't always fit in if there's a popular driver already there, like Hamilton at McLaren in 2007, for example...

So, team principal Stefano Domenicali could have a very lively situation on his hands controlling the drivers expectations. However, he is a far

more personable individual than his predecessor, the autocratic Jean Todt who worshipped Michael Schumacher but was down on Rubens Barrichello. Fortunately for Massa, he wasn't too down on him. Then again, Massa was being managed by Todt's son Nicolas at the time.

With its healthy budget, two great drivers who are hungry for victories and team management tightened up after a year of personnel changes as well as a car that is sure to be better considered, be very surprised if Ferrari doesn't come bouncing back in 2010.

FOR THE RECORD

Country of origin:	Italy
Team base:	Maranello, Italy
Telephone:	(39) 536 949111
Website:	www.ferrariworld.com
Active in Formula One:	From 1950
Grands Prix contested:	793
Wins:	210
Pole positions:	203
Fastest laps:	217

2009 DRIVERS & RESULTS

Driver	Nationality	Races	Wins	Pts	Pos
Luca Badoer	?	2	0	0	n/a
Giancarlo Fisichella	?	6	0	8	15th*
Felipe Massa	?	9	0	22	11th
Kimi Raikkonen	?	17	1	48	6th

* Points scored with Force India

THE TEAM

President:	Luca di Montezemolo
Team principal:	Stefano Domenicali
Technical director:	Aldo Costa
Team manager:	Chris Dyer
Engine director:	Luca Marmorini
Sporting manager:	Massimo Rivola
Chief designer:	Nikolas Tombazis
Chief aerodynamicist:	John Iley
Chief engineer:	Rob Smedley
Test driver:	Giancarlo Fisichella
Chassis:	Ferrari Fxxx
Engine:	Ferrari V8
Tyres:	Bridgestone

Stefano Domenicali will be looking forward to a less troubled year.

FELIPE MASSA

If the 2008 season was painful in missing out on the F1 title to Lewis Hamilton by a single point, then 2009 hurt Felipe even more. However, he has bounced back from the head injury he suffered in Hungary and is raring to go again for Ferrari.

This will be a very revealing season for Felipe Massa as he was establishing himself as the lead driver at Ferrari last year after his near miss in 2008. He'd come back stronger after that disappointment and reacted better than his team-mate Kimi Raikkonen to the fact that the Ferrari was one of the teams that failed to guess the new rules right and thus didn't have a double-deck diffuser on their F60. The team was in disarray, but Felipe fought on when Kimi appeared to lose interest.

He finished a strong fourth, with fastest lap, at Monaco and progress was being made. But then came the spring bouncing up into his helmet in qualifying in Hungary. It could have been the end, but improved helmet technology saved him and he was able to bounce back from his injuries to have a run out at Ferrari's test circuit last October. As everything felt right, Felipe was given the green light for a full return in 2010.

The main problem this year will probably come from within. Not from the team, as

Felipe has driven as much as possible over the winter to prepare for his racing return.

Felipe is their favoured son, having been so much more on their wavelength than Raikkonen. No, the problem within might well depend on how he finds Fernando

Alonso, a driver who may well be seen as their "next Michael Schumacher", as the only driver brilliant enough to take the world's most famous team back to win after win and, hopefully, title after title. If the Spaniard swings the focus onto his side of the garage, Felipe might suffer.

TRACK NOTES

Nationality:	BRAZILIAN
Born:	25 APRIL 1981, SAO PAULO, BRAZIL
Website:	WWW.FELIPEMASSA.COM
Teams:	SAUBER 2002 & 2004-05, FERRARI 2006-10

CAREER RECORD

First Grand Prix:	2002 AUSTRALIAN GP
Grand Prix starts:	115
Grand Prix wins:	11
	2006 Turkish GP, Brazilian GP, 2007 Bahrain GP, Spanish GP, Turkish GP, 2008 Bahrain GP, Turkish GP, French GP, European GP, Belgian P, Brazilian GP
Poles:	15
Fastest laps:	12
Points:	320
Honours:	2008 FORMULA ONE RUNNER-UP, 2001 EUROPEAN FORMULA 3000 CHAMPION, 2000 EUROPEAN & ITALIAN FORMULA RENAULT CHAMPION, 1999 BRAZILIAN FORMULA CHEVROLET CHAMPION

HE CAUGHT F1 BY SURPRISE

Motor racing used to be simple to understand. There were three rungs to the single-seater ladder before reaching F1. There was Formula Ford, F3 then F2. Now, there are numerous single-seater categories, which is how the F1 world found itself unaware of who Felipe was when Sauber took a chance on him for 2002. Indeed, he'd had one year in Europe in a junior category then stepped up to more powerful F3000 cars, but in a non-mainstream series. However, Sauber was in a mood to experiment with youth after its success in unearthing Kimi Raikkonen the year before and gave him a test. Felipe was fast but scrappy in his rookie season, but found finesse when he spent 2003 testing for Ferrari and was brought back from Sauber to race for Ferrari in 2006, scoring his first win that year, in Turkey. That he was matching, even outpacing Schumacher that year, boosted his reputation and he's been a Ferrari man ever since.

FERNANDO ALONSO

The thought of Fernando as a Ferrari driver will strike fear into the hearts of his rivals, as he has shone in a less than competitive Renault in recent years and is sure to become the team's lead weapon. It could be a marriage made in heaven.

Only the greatest drivers can come away with their talents appreciated all the more after a year spent driving a car that is off the pace. Fernando is one such driver and, even in finishing ninth in 2009, with his best result third place in Singapore, he was always talked of as someone who would surely deliver in a competitive car. That his two team-mates, Nelson Piquet Jr then Romain Grosjean, failed to score even a point reinforced the point.

So, it's new year, new team for the double World Champion, as he joins Ferrari in a multi-year deal that will leave him a wealthy man and probably with another title to his name.

The big question, for many, is whether Ferrari will provide him with the best car out there, or whether it will at least be good enough for him to drag it to the front.

Add to that the question about how well Fernando will settle in at Maranello. Certainly, the team is very excited about his arrival and feels that he will give his all, which was something they hadn't always felt was the case with his predecessor: Kimi Raikkonen.

Tempering that is the fact that he didn't

Ferrari fans have very good reason to be excited about Fernando's signing for 2010.

settle in when he joined McLaren as World Champion for 2007 and fell out so publicly with the team, so it's not a foregone conclusion that all will be sweetness and light.

In all probability, Fernando will have

learned from that and so this transition will be smooth as he attempts to prove that he can settle at a team other than Renault.

TRACK NOTES

Nationality:	SPANISH
Born:	29 JULY, 1981, OVIEDO, SPAIN
Website:	www.fernandoalonso.com
Teams:	MINARDI 2001, RENAULT 2003-2006, McLAREN 2007, RENAULT 2008-2009, FERRARI 2010

CAREER RECORD

First Grand Prix:	2001 AUSTRALIAN GP
Grand Prix starts:	140
Grand Prix wins:	21
	(2003 Hungarian GP, 2005 Malaysian GP, Bahrain GP, San Marino GP, European GP, French GP, German GP, Chinese GP, 2006 Bahrain GP, Australian GP, Spanish GP, Monaco GP, British GP, Canadian GP, Japanese GP, 2007 Malaysian GP, Monaco GP, European GP, Italian GP, 2008 Singapore GP, Japanese GP)
Poles:	17
Fastest laps:	13
Points:	667
Honours:	2005 & 2006 FORMULA ONE WORLD CHAMPION, 1999 FORMULA NISSAN CHAMPION, 1997 ITALIAN & SPANISH KART CHAMPION, 1996 WORLD & SPANISH KART CHAMPION, 1995 & 1994 SPANISH JUNIOR KART CHAMPION

CAREER HISTORY

No World Champion is going to be a fool behind the wheel, but not all blazed a trail all the way to F1. Fernando was a trailblazer from the moment he sat in a kart. At 15, he was the World Kart Champion and added further titles before he was old enough for car racing in 1999. He did so into the Euro Open by Nissan series, and was a dominant champion. F3000 was next and he rose to the challenge, coming on strong to score an imperious win at Spa. That was enough proof of his ability and Fernando was snapped up by Flavio Briatore and placed in F1 with Minardi for 2001. Test driver for Renault in 2002, he became a winner in 2003 when he joined Renault's race team and went on to win the 2005 and 2006 titles before spending a troubled year at McLaren in which he came close to making it three titles in a row. He then rejoined Renault for 2008.

WILLIAMS

There is a feeling of a new start at Williams, with two new drivers, a new engine supplier and a new partner. If the team can produce a car that works on high-speed circuits too, then this once great team will climb back to where many feels it belongs.

Will the change from Toyota power to Cosworth make a big difference?

Williams has been in the doldrums for too long. Despite winning the constructors' championship nine times, behind only Ferrari, the last of these titles came in 1997 and its most recent serious bid for glory was seven years ago when it pipped McLaren to rank second overall, just 14 points down on Ferrari.

Since then, there hasn't been a lot to cheer for Williams fans. Nico Rosberg promised much last year, albeit mainly in practice rather than in qualifying or the races, but the car was never the one to have, so he was only racing in hope of glory rather than expectation.

Kazuki Nakajima had flashes of speed, but failed to score even once. So, this is why Frank Williams and Patrick Head will be excited to have a proven winner and the hottest up-and-coming star from the junior ranks at the wheel of their FW32s for the season ahead.

For 2010, the recharged Rubens Barrichello will lead the attack, fresh from rediscovering his winning ways with Brawn GP. Despite being the most experienced driver in F1 history, Rubens will have learned some lessons last year and is sure to have an improved focus on what it takes to win. He will also enjoy being the undisputed number one driver in the team, something he hasn't ever been in his career to date.

KEY MOMENTS & KEY PEOPLE

TEAM HISTORY
Frank Williams hit F1 in 1969, but nearly quit when Piers Courage died in 1970. It was hand-to-mouth until he formed Williams Grand Prix Engineering with Patrick Head in 1977. They started winning in 1979, and claimed both titles in 1980, with Alan Jones its first champion. Nigel Mansell remains a Williams great, winning the 1992 title after being pipped in 1986. Keke Rosberg (1982), Nelson Piquet (1987), Alain Prost (1993), Damon Hill (1996) and Jacques Villeneuve (1997) are its others.

SAM MICHAEL
Having been involved with Formula Holden while studying mechanical engineering, Sam joined Lotus to work on data acquisition. For 1994, he moved to Jordan and within two years was head of R&D. He engineered Ralf Schumacher and Heinz-Harald Frentzen during his winning streak in 1999. However, becoming chief operations engineer at Williams was Sam's next step and he was promoted to be technical director in 2004.

In support, Williams has a superstar in the making in Nico Hulkenberg. He first showed his pace when he burst on the A1GP scene and cleaned up for Germany in 2006/2007, then dominated the European F3 scene in 2008 and was that rare thing, a rookie champion in GP2 last year, by a good margin too. The 22-year-old also has the advantage of knowing the team as well, having been on their books since 2008.

If Williams is taking a gamble this year, it's in its choice of engine, with Cosworth replacing Toyota. This famous engine builder is only just returning to F1 after three years away and has the added difficulty of supplying five of the teams. However, rev limitations have made the engines closer to being equal than ever before, so perhaps this won't prove such a problem.

What makes this partnership appealing is that Williams and Cosworth have a good history together, with the first two of the team's constructors' titles having been won together.

Looking back at last year, in a year when F1 was closer and more competitive than ever before, it has to be asked whether Williams could have done better. In fact, especially so as Williams had been one of only three teams to guess the new regulations correctly and start the season with a double-deck diffuser. Rosberg's fastest lap in the opening round in Australia hinted at the big time, but perhaps it was typical that Nakajima blew his chance that day. Then Rosberg led in the second round, in Malaysia, until the rains came. And, with that, the team failed to deliver when its chance was greatest.

The truth is that the other teams caught up or, in McLaren's case, overhauled it. Rosberg was a consistent scorer, usually between fourth and sixth by flagfall, but failed to make the podium even once, although but for a slip-up leaving the pits in Singapore, he would have been second there.

Yet, the relative decline was made plain at the final round in Abu Dhabi when Rosberg couldn't even make the points despite having no problems.

For technical director Sam Michael, this will be a telling season, but with new investment from GT racer Toto Wolff, a great deal more is going to be expected of the team.

FOR THE RECORD

Country of origin:	England
Team base:	Grove, England
Telephone:	(44) 01235 777700
Website:	www.attwilliams.com
Active in Formula One:	From 1972
Grands Prix contested:	585
Wins:	113
Pole positions:	125
Fastest laps:	130

2009 DRIVERS & RESULTS

Driver	Nationality	Races	Wins	Pts	Pos
Kazuki Nakajima	Japanese	17	0	0	n/a
Nico Rosberg	German	17	0	34.5	7th

THE TEAM

Chairman: Team principal:	Sir Frank Williams
Director of engineering:	Patrick Head
Chief executive officer:	Adam Parr
Technical director:	Sam Michael
Chief operating officer:	Alex Burns
Chief designer:	Ed Wood
Head of aerodynamics:	Jon Tomlinson
Senior systems engineer:	John Russell
Chief operations engineer:	Rod Nelson
Team manager:	Tim Newton
Test driver:	tba
Chassis:	Williams FW32
Engine:	Cosworth V8
Tyres:	Bridgestone

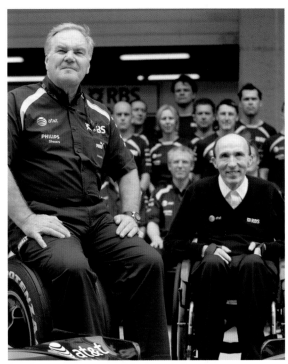

Patrick Head and Frank Williams still love the competition of F1.

RUBENS BARRICHELLO

Formula One's most experienced driver looked to be on the scrapheap when Honda quit F1, but his form with the team that replaced it, Brawn GP, showed why he has plenty to offer Williams in 2010 as he clearly rediscovered his love of winning.

This season is a new beginning for Rubens. He is, for the first time in his career, leading a team. He will be expected to show maturity and leadership as well as speed. And he will be doing it in an environment new to him at Williams. It's a good thing that he arrives with his tail up after a strong year with Brawn, as this is a team that doesn't treat its drivers with kid gloves. It wants results. But, Rubens knows that. What he must do is keep his emotions in check and deliver the maximum the machinery will afford him. Whether that will be wins remains to be seen.

However you look at it, 2009 was an extraordinary year. He was 36 and out of a drive. But he never gave up hope and convinced Brawn GP to keep him on as the team metamorphosed from Honda, rather than taking rookie driver Bruno Senna.

Then, with team-mate Jenson Button winning everything in sight in the opening races, he was left reeling. People asked how come Button had found the winning

Rubens had a rollercoaster year, but came out smiling, reinvigorated for racing again.

touch and he hadn't. Then Rubens showed his emotional side, with some outbursts of temper. But, after some serious discussions with boss Ross Brawn, Rubens knuckled down and started to shine. True, the car had changed to become more suited to his style of driving, getting heat into its tyres more effectively as he chucked it around. But his serious application and total joy at winning again was plain for all to see.

TRACK NOTES

Nationality:	BRAZILIAN
Born:	23 MAY, 1972, SAO PAULO, BRAZIL
Website:	www.barrichello.com.br
Teams:	JORDAN 1993-1996,
	STEWART 1997-1999, FERRARI 2000-2005,
	HONDA RACING 2006-2008, BRAWN 2009,
	WILLIAMS 2010

CAREER RECORD

First Grand Prix:	1993 SOUTH AFRICAN GP
Grand Prix starts:	287
Grand Prix wins:	11
	2000 German GP, 2002 European GP,
	Hungarian GP, Italian GP, US GP, 2003 British GP,
	Japanese GP, 2004 Italian GP, Chinese GP,
	2009 European GP, Italian GP
Poles:	14
Fastest laps:	17
Points:	607
Honours:	2002 FORMULA ONE RUNNER-UP,
	1991 BRITISH FORMULA THREE CHAMPION,
	1990 EUROPEAN FORMULA OPEL CHAMPION,
	1988 BRAZILIAN KART CHAMPION

QUICK RISE, LONG STAY

Rubens was a driver always destined for the top, and it was clear to those who watched him as he raced to the Brazilian karting title in 1988. So clear, in fact, that a group of businessmen bought in on the action and offered to finance his progress, for a future return of course. His first year of racing in Europe, 1990, yielded the Formula Opel title, and he followed this up by beating David Coulthard to the British F3 crown in 1991. Third overall in Formula 3000 in 1992, he was an F1 racer by the age of 20, running second on only his third outing for Jordan, in the wet at Donington Park. A spell at Stewart followed Jordan, but again he found himself with a car that could finish no higher than second. Winning did follow, after a move to Ferrari in 2000, but being runner-up to Michael Schumacher in 2004 was Rubens' best result before joining Honda in 2006. Rubens has since taken the record for the most grand prix starts.

NICO HULKENBERG

Here is a driver who truly deserves to be in F1. There are some who arrive courtesy of a wedge of sponsorship money, but this tall German is one who is here solely by dint of the startling success he has achieved in every category he has contested.

It's not always the best drivers who win championship titles. However, a driver who collects titles year in, year out, is clearly something special. Nico is one such driver.

He is managed by Willi Weber, longtime manager of Michael Schumacher, and he's a man who clearly knows a talent when he sees one. So, when he describes Nico as an "unbelievable talent", people really should take heed. One glance at Nico's career record is all it takes to see why he is clearly a driver of the highest calibre.

With almost every single-seater formula beneath F1 being one-make, with drivers racing rivals driving the same chassis, it's hard for a driver to find much of an advantage, but Nico has the ability to do that. Some of his drives in A1GP were of staggering dominance, especially in the rain. In GP2 as well, his rivals generally knew that they would be going for second place and only the series' reversal of the grid for the second of its two races, with the winner of the first race starting eighth

Nico is one of the most highly-rated talents to hit the F1 scene for many a season.

and vice versa, keeping Nico from adding to his five wins last year.

Sir Frank Williams is one person who needed no further persuasion and he snapped Nico up to perform test driving

duties back at the end of 2007 and certainly wasn't disappointed with what he saw. If testing hadn't been curtailed through the season, Nico would be starting 2010 with even more of a bang.

However, if he can learn from his new team-mate Rubens Barrichello's experience and ally this with his natural speed, then he could be a revelation to those who don't look below F1.

TRACK NOTES

Nationality:	GERMAN
Born:	19 AUGUST 1987,
	EMMERICH AM RHEIN, GERMANY
Website:	www.nico-huelkenberg.com
Teams:	WILLIAMS 2010

CAREER RECORD	
First Grand Prix:	2010 BAHRAIN GP
Grand Prix starts:	0
Grand Prix wins:	0
Poles:	0
Fastest laps:	0
Points:	0
Honours:	2009 GP2 CHAMPION,
	2008 EUROPEAN F3 CHAMPION,
	2007 MASTERS F3 WINNER, 2006/07 A1GP
	CHAMPION, 2005 GERMAN FORMULA BMW
	CHAMPION, 2003 GERMAN KART CHAMPION,
	2002 GERMAN JUNIOR KART CHAMPION

A WINNER ALL THE WAY

Nico started in karting at the age of 10 and was a star from the outset, rounding out with national titles in 2002 and 2003. As soon as he was old enough to go car racing in 2005, he started winning in that. German Formula BMW champion in 2005, he then shone in his maiden year of F3, even with a less-than-fancied Ligier chassis. However, a test in a more powerful A1GP car was what made people pay attention and he was all but unbeaten after being selected to drive Germany's entry. With Willi Weber managing his career, Nico lined up a season of European F3 for 2007 with the ASM squad and ranked third. Joining the crack ART team for 2008, he won that at a canter. GP2 has long been considered a two-year job, but Nico gained speed with every round in 2009 until he started winning for ART before cleaning up in 2009, winning five of the 20 rounds.

RENAULT

Renault went through the wars last autumn and took a hit for their fixing of the Singapore GP in 2008. Out went Flavio Briatore and Pat Symonds, plus several sponsors. For 2010, it's a new-look team pinning its hopes on Robert Kubica.

Renault is racing on in 2010, but the team is under new ownership.

It was very much an annus horibilis for Renault, and the biggest success that the team clocked up in 2009 was simply making it through to 2010, as all indications were for much of the season, and then even more so just after the racing came to an end in Abu Dhabi, that the doors would be closed and that it would follow Toyota out of the door marked "exit".

Last November, frustratingly for all, Renault Chief Executive Officer Carlos Ghosn could "only guarantee the announcement – about whether the team would stay or go – would be made before the end of the year."

It became clear that several parties were lining up a takeover bid and the decision as to which would partner Renault was announced on 16 December, with Gerard Lopez having beaten Prodrive's David Richards in the race to take over 75% of the team's Enstone facility, but not its engine manufacturing base at Viry-Chatillon.

Lopez heads Genii Capital, a Luxembourg-based investment company that also has sporting interests through the Gravity driver management agency.

Renault has been in and out of F1 since it turned up with the first turbocharged F1 car in 1977. If the marque hasn't been involved by entering a team, as it did from 1977 to 1985 and then again from 2002, it has been very much part of F1 by

KEY MOMENTS & KEY PEOPLE

TEAM HISTORY
This is a team that has had two lives. The French manufacturer joined the circus in 1977, introducing the first turbocharged F1 car. Results were slow to follow, but Jean-Pierre Jabouille gave the marque its first win in 1979 before Alain Prost just missed out on the 1983 title. Renault quit at the end of 1985 and returned in 2000. However, when it did, it merely took over the team that had been running as Benetton and Toleman before that. Fernando Alonso won the 2005 and 2006 titles for Renault before moving on.

BOB BELL
Belfast-born Bob moved into racing with McLaren in 1982 and became head of R&D before taking a new angle in 1990 to head up its land speed record project. This was still-born and Bob worked on other McLaren projects from 1995 until joining Benetton as senior aerodynamicist in 1997. After a spell at Jordan, Bob returned to Benetton (now Renault) in 2001 as deputy technical director, rising to technical director and then, of course, to team principal last year.

supplying engines to other teams, as it did with notable success to Williams (winning titles in 1992, 1993, 1996 and 1997) and Benetton (1995). Indeed, even with the Renault team ending up ranked eighth of the 10 teams last year, its engines powered Red Bull Racing to second overall, producing six wins. The works team, despite Renault's double World Champion Fernando Alonso's best efforts, reached the podium only once, with a third place finish in Singapore.

Having ranked fourth in 2008, with Alonso winning twice – even if one of these wins was perhaps handed to him by Nelson Piquet Jr's crash in the Singapore GP – this was quite a fall from grace. Some have pointed fingers at the fact that the team cut back on its design staff for 2009 to fit in with the then restrictive rules in wind tunnel useage and perhaps paid the price for cutting back more than was eventually required.

Clearly, its R29 wasn't the most competitive car, largely due to not having an effective front wing. Alonso wrestled it around as fast as he could, but it was clearly a struggle and any good grid position was due to running with a light fuel load rather than any new-found competitiveness.

Piquet Jr was far less effective and he knew the writing was on the wall and started accusing team chief Flavio Briatore of being his "executioner" rather than supporting him as his manager. Whatever his complaints, the outcome was "Crashgate", as he produced evidence that the FIA leapt upon to charge the team for what it said was race-fixing in Singapore in 2008.

The outcome rocked the team as both Briatore and executive director of engineering Pat Symonds left the team in the fall-out, with the team also being given a suspended sentence. So,

technical director Bob Bell took over as team principal for the remaining grands prix of the season. For 2010, though the team will be guided by new team principal Eric Boullier, stepping up from GP2, with Bell returning to his previous role.

No driver announcements were made when Genii Capital took over,

but Robert Kubica was expected to honour his signing for the team before the change of ownership. He'll be a focused team leader. A list of possible number twos was mooted, including Nick Heidfeld, Bertrand Baguette, Gravity-contracted Ho-Pin Tung, 1997 World Champion Jacques Villeneuve or even Romain Grosjean staying on.

FOR THE RECORD

Country of origin:	England
Team base:	Enstone, England
Telephone:	(44) 01608 678000
Website:	www.renaultf1.com
Active in Formula One:	From 1977-85 then from 2002
Grands Prix contested:	263*
Wins:	35
Pole positions:	50
Fastest laps:	29

* Note that these figures don't include the 238 races that the team ran as Benetton

2009 DRIVERS & RESULTS

Driver	Nationality	Races	Wins	Pts	Pos
Fernando Alonso	Spanish	17	0	26	9th
Romain Grosjean	French/Swiss	7	0	0	n/a
Nelson Piquet Jr	Brazilian	10	0	0	n/a

THE TEAM

Owner:	Gerard Lopez
Managing director:	Jean-Francois Caubet
Team principal:	Eric Boullier
Technical director:	Bob Bell
Deputy managing director, engine:	Rob White
Deputy managing director, support operations:	Laurent Chedorge
Chief designer:	Tim Densham
Operations director:	John Mardle
Sporting director:	Steve Nielsen
Test driver:	tba
Chassis:	Renault R30
Engine:	Renault V8
Tyres:	Bridgestone

The F1 paddock will be far less entertaining without Flavio Briatore.

ROBERT KUBICA*

He is the driver with perhaps the most to prove in 2010 after a weak season last year as his team floundered. Having signed on the dotted line to lead Renault's attack, he must be hoping that this team can bounce back to its former level.

We all know that Formula 1 can be a volatile environment. Take last year, with the established team order truly turned on its head by a raft of new technical rules.

That was nothing, though, as to the F1 driver merry-go-round being given the biggest push it has had in years. Robert was one of the early ones to sign a contract for 2010, with Renault. But then, much to his concern, the French manufacturer stated talking of quitting the sport.

This was unsettling, to say the least and, at the time of the announcement that Genii Capital had taken the main stakeholding in the team, he was not mentioned. Indeed, the drivers for 2010 were not named at all. And Robert was still being talked of as the driver for the second seat at Mercedes GP should Michael Schumacher not make his racing return with them.

A year before, fresh from scoring his maiden win in the Canadian GP, Robert had looked forward to the 2009 campaign with

Robert became frustrated at BMW Sauber and will expect an improvement this year.

BMW Sauber, but hopes of more wins and even a title shot were soon dashed. The car simply wasn't competitive. By mid-season, he had just one point-scoring drive to his name, a seventh place in Turkey.

And then news broke that BMW was going to pull out of F1. Fortunately, with a Renault deal seemingly in his pocket, he shone with second in Brazil to restore his confidence for the close-season.

* Leading candidate at time of going to press at the very end of 2009.

TRACK NOTES

Nationality:	POLISH
Born:	7 DECEMBER 1984, KRACOW, POLAND
Website:	www.kubica.pl
Teams:	2006-2009 BMW SAUBER,
	2010 RENAULT

CAREER RECORD	
First Grand Prix:	2006 HUNGARIAN GP
Grand Prix starts:	57
Grand Prix wins:	1
	2008 Canadian GP
Poles:	1
Fastest laps:	0
Points:	137
Honours:	2005 WORLD SERIES BY
	RENAULT CHAMPION, 1999 GERMAN &
	ITALIAN KART CHAMPION & MONACO
	KART CUP WINNER, 1998 ITALIAN KART
	CHAMPION & MONACO KART CUP WINNER,
	1997 POLISH KART CHAMPION

RENAULT SUPPORT FROM EARLY ON

Robert's determination to succeed is clear from the fact that he left his native Poland to pursue his dreams when he was 13 and won karting titles in Italy from 1998. It paid off, as he became well known there and was signed to race in Italian Formula Renault as soon as he was old enough, in 2001. Renault noticed Robert's ability and put him on to their driver development books as he completed his first full season as runner-up to Jose Maria Lopez. Formula 3 beckoned for 2003, but he suffered a broken arm after a road accident in which someone else was driving. Robert missed much of the season, so it was only in 2005 that his career got back on track as he won the World Series by Renault and this convinced BMW Sauber to sign him as its F1 test driver in 2006. Robert then was given his race debut as a replacement for Jacques Villeneuve, finishing third at Monza on only his third outing. He improved on that by winning the Canadian GP in 2008 and ranked fourth overall at year's end.

BERTRAND BAGUETTE*

Renault had a wide choice of drivers for its second seat for 2010, with even its lead driver selection delayed by uncertainty over its new ownership. As 2009 came to a close, this talented Belgian was looking to be the man most likely to land the ride.

The change of team ownership altered the scene and appeared to put a spanner in the works, with Nick Heidfeld, Christian Klien and even Jacques Villeneuve being mentioned for this ride, plus Gravity's Jerome d'Ambrosio and Ho-Pin Tung.

From Bertrand's point-of-view, this would be his big break, as it would save him from having to prove his craft in GP2 – as his predecessor as World Series champion, Giedo van der Garde, had to do and struggled before shining in the second half of his 2009 GP2 campaign. It's a formula in which drivers can get stuck and see their F1 hopes dwindle then disappear.

Renault would be delighted if he made the cut too, to add greater credibility to World Series by Renault.

The F1 drivers market was more confused than in living memory at the end of 2009 as this book closed for press, with the new teams adding opportunity for aspiring drivers to have a crack at F1 that would otherwise have been denied

Bertrand will be seeking to gain as much F1 knowledge as he can from the team.

to most of them. Then, with teams such as Renault changing ownership, there was further scope for a young driver to gain a place with one of the established teams,

suddenly promoting drivers associated with a manufacturer such as Renault up the list of likely drivers.

Add to this the fact that Renault's long-signed lead driver Robert Kubica had an escape clause in his contract – as the team had changed hands – and was eyeing the second seat at Mercedes should Michael Schumacher not take it, and the driver market was incredibly fluid, making it extremely hard for any team with vacancies to balance their driver line-ups for 2010.

* Leading candidate at time of going to press at the start of 2010.

TRACK NOTES

Nationality:	BELGIAN
Born:	23 FEBRUARY 1986, VERVIERS, BELGIUM
Website:	www.bertrand-baguette.com
Teams:	2010 RENAULT

CAREER RECORD

First Grand Prix:	2010 BAHRAIN GP
Grand Prix starts:	0
Grand Prix wins:	0
Poles:	0
Fastest laps:	0
Points:	0
Honours:	2009 WORLD SERIES BY RENAULT CHAMPION, 2003 BELGIAN ICA KART CHAMPION

THREE YEARS THEN GLORY

Bertrand started kart racing at the age of 14 and did well, winning the Belgian ICA championship three years later. Car racing was next, and he advanced to Belgium's unique Formula Renault 1600 class, finishing third at his first attempt. This was enough to merit graduation to Formula Renault in 2005. He ranked seventh and improved to fourth in 2006. Looking for more power to play with, he joined KTR to compete in World Series by Renault in 2007 and showed promise with third place at Donington Park then peaked with second in the final round at Barcelona, but didn't finish enough to rank higher than 17th. Staying on in 2008, this time with Draco, he climbed to seventh overall, winning at Spa-Francorchamps, also making a few Superleague Formula outings. However, it all came right in his third year in World Series by Renault as he won five times to lift the title, then rounded out the year with an F1 test for Renault as his prize.

FORCE INDIA F1

When Giancarlo Fisichella put Force India on pole at Spa-Francorchamps last year, it was a shock, but this was more the case of a team getting back to where it once was, when it was Jordan. Vijay Mallya's billions may buy more success in the year ahead.

F1 fans may well become accustomed to Force India scoring points.

Vijay Mallya is an exceedingly wealthy individual with a considerable love of motor racing. However, that alone hasn't been enough for his team – the team that started life as Jordan in 1991 – to set the world of F1 on fire since he invested in taking it over at the end of 2007. There was the highlight of Giancarlo Fisichella claiming pole position for the Belgian GP last autumn, with the Italian veteran coming within a second of exceeding that in the race the following day as he led early on then pushed Kimi Raikkonen's Ferrari to the finish, crossing the finish line second. Amazingly, this was Force India's first ever helping of points, and it was so close to being a victory.

Adrian Sutil displayed flashes of speed, too, as you would expect from a driver known to be quick in a car powered by Mercedes' V8, a unit acknowledged to be the pick of the pack. Sadly, Sutil was also involved in more than his fair share of collisions, and rotated out of sixth place in the wet Chinese GP early in the year.

However, the greatest success of the 2009 season was actually landing the Mercedes engines in the first place and its power was seen time and again in speed trap figures at almost every circuit, as the VJM02 was nothing if not slippery in a straight line, thus its strong

KEY MOMENTS & KEY PEOPLE

TEAM HISTORY
Few teams have had as many changes of name. It started life in 1991 as Jordan, formed out of Eddie Jordan's F3000 team. It was a challenger immediately but didn't win until 1998 when Damon Hill led a one-two in Belgium. Heinz-Harald Frentzen gave it more wins in 1999, leaving the team ranked third. For 2005, the team was renamed Midland F1 after a change of ownership and became Spyker for 2007, before it became Force India for 2008.

VIJAY MALLYA
One of the movers and shakers of the burgeoning Indian economy, Vijay is a racer at heart, showing that he isn't in F1 simply to put his companies' names on the sides of his team's cars. He raced single-seaters in India in the 1980s, but it was his business career that really took him forward, as head of the UB Group. This led to him promoting its Kingfisher beer brand on the Benetton F1 team in 1996, but he wanted more so bought the Spyker team and renamed it as Force India for 2008.

showings at Spa then Monza when Force India collected pole position and second place at the former then fourth and fastest lap at the latter.

Just before the end of last season, chief operating officer Simon Roberts was replaced by former Honda F1 front man Otmar Szafnauer, with Roberts returning to McLaren after his year "on loan" from McLaren Applied Technologies which supplied Force India with transmissions to accompany the Mercedes engines.

The key to this year, under technical director James Key, is to rediscover its strongest form, which seemed to ebb away in the closing races when neither Sutil nor Vitantonio Liuzzi, who had stepped up to replace Fisichella after he'd jumped ship to Ferrari as the second replacement for the injured Felipe Massa managed to finish in the top 10 places in the final four grands prix.

Although Sutil still has unfinished business at Force India, he was showing his ambition by touting around for a ride with another team for this season, but Liuzzi was keen simply to get his hands on a regular drive for 2010 and so was more amenable to the team's overtures.

If there is a blot on the horizon after a season of notable improvement, it's that the finances didn't appear to be as healthy as they ought, with a standoff over payment for their grand prix motorhome. Then, just after the season ended, there was some sparring with the incoming Lotus team, with Force India claiming that there were a number of similarities between the front wing on the 2010 Lotus wind tunnel model and the 2009 Force India, pointing out that Lotus's technical chief Mike Gascoyne used to work for the team and so did Aerolab, when it ran the

team's wind tunnel.

In the future, this team might realise one of its initial ambitions, which is to field an Indian driver. This was once thought to be former Jordan racer Narain Karthikeyan, then long-time GP2 challenger Karun Chandhok. However, perhaps the most likely is Neel Jani, a Swiss driver with an Indian father, and one of the stars of the A1GP series over the past four years. He has F1 experience too, having been Toro Rosso's reserve driver in 2006.

FOR THE RECORD

Country of origin:	England
Team base:	Silverstone, England
Telephone:	(44) 01327 850800
Website:	www.forceindiaf1.com
Active in Formula One:	From 1991 (as Jordan then Midland in 2006 then Spyker in 2007)
Grands Prix contested:	320
Wins:	4
Pole positions:	3
Fastest laps:	3

2009 DRIVERS & RESULTS

Driver	Nationality	Races	Wins	Pts	Pos
Giancarlo Fisichella	Italian	12	0	8	15th
Vitantonio Liuzzi	Italian	5	0	0	n/a
Adrian Sutil	German	17	0	5	17th

THE TEAM

Team owner:	Vijay Mallya
Co-owner:	Luciano Secchi
Team director:	Bob Fernley
Chief operating officer:	Otmar Szafnauer
Director of business affairs:	Ian Phillips
Technical director:	James Key
Design director:	Mark Smith
Design project leader:	Akio Haga
Team manager:	Andy Stevenson
Chief engineer:	Dominic Harlow
Test driver:	tba
Chassis:	Force India VJM03
Engine:	Mercedes V8
Tyres:	Bridgestone

Vijay Mallya is a racer and is increasingly going to demand results.

ADRIAN SUTIL

Now is the time that Adrian must match his obvious speed with some circumspection, as he was starting to gain something of a reputation last year, which is not what you want in your third year of F1 when you should be settled.

There were times last year when it seemed extraordinary how fast the Force Indias were travelling. Sadly for the team, this was largely in practice, and their table-topping form tended to be through the speed trap rather than around an entire lap. Yet, there was firm progress through the season as the team developed its car and Adrian came oh so close to grabbing pole position at the Italian GP. He came away with fourth place in the race and fastest lap in what turned out to be his only points-scoring drive of the year, helped in no small measure by the car's preference for low-downforce circuits.

There were other chances for points, most notably the Chinese GP where he was heading for sixth until crashing with six laps to go.

If Force India can start 2010 as well as they finished last year, then Adrian will find himself fighting at the sharp end of the field and, perhaps, this will be the year when he knits together a perfect

Adrian showed good speed, but will be looking to have fewer clashes during 2010.

performance, racing from start to finish without tangling with a rival.

It was interesting to see Adrian's reaction at the Brazilian GP as a livid

Jarno Trulli remonstrated with him after their clash eliminated both from the race when the Italian veteran tried to pass him for third place. He was firm, sure of his convictions and so displayed the mindset of a driver who feels he's now part of the establishment. How this will unfold is anyone's guess, but he's a bright individual and must string it all together and nail down points-scoring drives on a regular basis and prove that, if the car is good enough, then so is he.

TRACK NOTES

Nationality:	GERMAN
Born:	11 JANUARY 1983, GRAFELFING, GERMANY
Website:	www.adriansutil.com
Teams:	SPYKER/FORCE INDIA 2007-2010

CAREER RECORD	
First Grand Prix:	2007 AUSTRALIAN GP
Grand Prix starts:	52
Grand Prix wins:	0
	(best result: fourth, 2009 Italian GP)
Poles:	0
Fastest laps:	1
Points:	6
Honours:	2006 JAPANESE FORMULA THREE CHAMPION, 2005 EUROPEAN FORMULA THREE RUNNER-UP, 2002 SWISS FORMULA FORD CHAMPION

HE PUSHED HAMILTON IN F3

Mike Hailwood was a skilled trumpet player, and Elio de Angelis wonderful on the piano, but few of today's drivers have a musical talent as their childhoods have been dedicated to working their way through the kart racing formulae. Adrian was performing on the piano from an early age, but his head was turned when he tried a kart and he swapped potential careers. In karts, he played catch-up, then won the Swiss Formula Ford title in his first year in cars. After gaining experience in Formula BMW in 2003, he tried F3 in 2004, and he really started to make a name for himself in the European series. In 2005, his team-mate was Lewis Hamilton and he ended the year runner-up to him. After racing for Germany in A1GP, Adrian became the reserve driver for Spyker and took over a race seat for 2007, famously losing his first points when Kimi Raikkonen knocked him out of fourth place at Monaco in 2008.

VITANTONIO LIUZZI

Some drivers get a chance to shine, others simply hit Formula One with the wrong team at the wrong time. However, with Force India on the rise through 2009, late-season substitute Vitantonio will be going all-out to make it work in 2010.

Vitantonio has had an unusual racing career in which momentum has been lost at vital moments and he has now pulled off that hardest of feats, getting back to F1 after losing your drive. Being yesterday's man is always difficult when there is a vacancy in F1, as the habit is for team chiefs to look to fill the ride with the hottest up-and-coming rookie, usually at the expense of someone who has slid to the sidelines.

So, although Tonio won't wish a repeat of Felipe Massa's head injury from last year, it was this that gave him the chance to get his foot back in the door once Giancarlo Fisichella moved from Force India to Ferrari to stand in for Massa.

There should have been a fairytale to go with this return – back for the first time since he raced for Scuderia Toro Rosso in 2007 – as Vitantonio has been heading for points until gearbox failure.

Looking ahead to a full campaign, Vitantonio knows that he has a quick team-mate in Adrian Sutil, and that will give him

Vitantonio will be relishing the chance to get his teeth back into F1 across a season.

extra incentive to really go for it in qualifying, which he acknowledged was a weak point in the five grands prix he entered in 2009.

Having been on the sidelines as a test driver, especially last year when F1 testing was reduced to nothing during the season, was something that Tonio found painful. So much so that he headed off to race in A1GP to satisfy his competitive instincts. So, with a full season lined up, expect him to grasp this opportunity with both hands. Expect points.

TRACK NOTES

Nationality:	ITALIAN
Born:	6 APRIL, 1981, LOCOROTONDO, ITALY
Website:	www.liuzzi.com
Teams:	RED BULL 2005, SCUDERIA TORO ROSSO 2006-2007, FORCE INDIA 2009-2010

CAREER RECORD

First Grand Prix:	2005 SAN MARINO GP
Grand Prix starts:	44
Grand Prix wins:	0
	(best result: sixth, 2007 Chinese GP)
Poles:	0
Fastest laps:	0
Points:	5
Honours:	2004 FORMULA 3000 CHAMPION, 2001 WORLD KART CHAMPION, 2000 WORLD KART CUP RUNNER-UP, 1999 EUROPEAN FORMULA SUPER A KART CHAMPION, 1997 ITALIAN FORMULA A KART RUNNER-UP, 1996 ITALIAN JICA KART CHAMPION, 1995 WORLD KART RUNNER-UP, 1994 ITALIAN KART RUNNER-UP, 1993 ITALIAN KART CHAMPION

THE KING OF KARTING

Anyone who kept an eye on international kart racing would tell you that Vitantonio was worth watching, as he'd dominated the Italian series, then done the same on a European level. He made a good impression in Formula Renault in 2001, but also claimed the world kart title. His form wasn't as strong as expected in F3 in 2002, but backer Red Bull promoted him to F3000, ranking fourth. Racing for Arden in 2004, he was dominant after winning six of the first seven races. Vitantonio got his F1 break in 2005 with Red Bull Racing, sharing the ride with Christian Klien. A move to Scuderia Toro Rosso in 2006 produced his first point, at Indianapolis, and he improved on that with sixth place in China in 2007 after suffering the frustration of crashing out of fourth place in Canada on debris trapped under his car from Robert Kubica's monumental accident. But then he missed out on a possible Williams drive for 2008 and agreed to test for Force India.

TORO ROSSO

This is the year that Toro Rosso has to stand on its own two feet and no longer use cars designed for Red Bull. This is the year, too, when last year's rookies Sebastien Buemi and Jaime Alguersuari will have to make use of the experience gained in 2009.

Toro Rosso's cars will be easier to differentiate from Red Bulls in 2010.

Through last season, it took an eagle-eyed fan to be able to tell a Red Bull from a Toro Rosso at 30 paces. Their body shape was all but identical, and their liveries similarly dark blue with a red, charging bull emblazoned on their flanks. Yes, the nose of the Toro Rosso was gold rather than yellow, but it took concentration to discern between the two teams.

Not in the grands prix, though, as the Red Bulls were invariably racing around at the front, challenging for wins. However, the Toro Rossos really made progress as the season came to its conclusion, especially with Sebastien Buemi getting into the final qualifying session for the

10 fastest cars and racing into the points in the final rounds in Brazil and Abu Dhabi.

This year, Scuderia Toro Rosso's greatest advantage has been stripped away, as it has had to design and build its own chassis, whereas the team has previously been given a dispensation to use a lightly adapted Red Bull chassis, something that was a considerable advantage last year as the Adrian Newey-designed RB5 was perhaps the chassis of the season.

Now, with its design facilities built up at its base in Faenza, the new chassis, the STR5, will come from there rather than Red Bull Technologies' Milton

KEY MOMENTS & KEY PEOPLE

TEAM HISTORY

This team ran for 21 years as Minardi, a team that had graduated from F2 to F1 in 1985. It struggled for a budget, but Pierluigi Martini qualified on the front row at Phoenix in 1990. Paul Stoddart bought the team for 2001 and Mark Webber raced to fifth in Australia in 2002, but money became ever more of a problem. Red Bull bought it for 2006 and the peak came at the 2008 Italian GP, when Sebastien Vettel raced from pole to victory.

FRANZ TOST

Franz was a racing driver before he turned to team management, starting in Formula Ford – he was Austrian champion in 1983 – and reaching F3. He then became the director of the Walter Lechner Racing School in his native Austria. In 1989, he ran the Eufra F3 team and continued in F3 before joining Weber Management in 1995. From there, he joined Williams BMW in 2000, as race track operations manager. When Red Bull money financed the purchase of Minardi, for 2006, Franz was brought in as team principal.

Keynes base. The new chassis will again be Ferrari-powered, which was its chief point of differentiation from last year's Renault-powered Red Bull.

Some of the design team still exists from when the team was Minardi before it was taken over by Dietrich Mateschitz's Red Bull billions, and they will do much of the detail work under technical chief Giorgio Ascanelli.

Team principal Franz Tost has elected to keep on last year's rookie duo - certainly the youngest ever F1 pairing - of Buemi and Jaime Alguersuari for 2010, and will look for evidence of solid improvement as they start to revisit circuits they have now experienced. Both come with a good pedigree, so there is no reason why they shouldn't make a step forward in the season ahead

However, it must be noted that

Tost and team owner Mateschitz aren't inclined to wait forever for strong, consistent form, as was shown last year when they fired Sebastien Bourdais for failing to provide the team with the progress and chassis set-up guidance it had hoped for from a driver of his reputation and experience. Alguersuari was the beneficiary of the French driver's dismissal and he is certainly aware that the occasional accident he had last year, such as in the Japanese GP, will not be tolerated this time around.

Whether this new-found experience can be matched with a chassis that is as relatively capable as it was in 2009 remains to be seen, but one feels that, whatever the teams' respective liveries and body shapes, the Red Bull racers will still be the ones at the front,

with the Toro Rossos coming along somewhere in their wake.

Two years ago, Sebastian Vettel gave Scuderia Toro Rosso its day of days when he won the Italian GP from pole position in streaming wet conditions. Perhaps such heady heights will never be reached again, but one senses that this is a team determined to establish itself in

the midfield and then build from there, clearly hoping that its two young drivers live up to the team's expectations and match Vettel's historic feat at Monza 2008. They, in turn, know that strong form might earn them promotion to Red Bull Racing, as it did for Vettel, so the incentive to achieve is most certainly there to shoot at.

FOR THE RECORD

Country of origin:	Italy
Team base:	Faenza, Italy
Telephone:	(39) 546 696111
Website:	www.scuderiatororosso.com
Active in Formula One:	From 1985 (as Minardi until 2006)
Grands Prix contested:	393
Wins:	1
Pole positions:	1
Fastest laps:	0

2009 DRIVERS & RESULTS

Driver	Nationality	Races	Wins	Pts	Pos
Jaime Alguersuari	Spanish	8	0	0	n/a
Sebastien Bourdais	French	9	0	2	19th
Sebastien Buemi	Swiss	17	0	6	16th

THE TEAM

Team owner:	Dietrich Mateschitz
Team principal:	Franz Tost
Technical director:	Giorgio Ascanelli
Team manager:	Gianfranco Fantuzzi
Chief engineer:	Laurent Mekies
Technical co-ordinator:	Sandro Parrini
Logistics manager:	Domenico Sangiorgi
Senior test engineer:	Gianvito Amico
Test driver:	tba
Chassis:	Toro Rosso STR5
Engine:	Ferrari V8
Tyres:	Bridgestone

Franz Tost will be hoping his drivers progress in the season ahead.

SEBASTIEN BUEMI

Sebastien did extremely well in his maiden season of Formula 1 last year, with Scuderia Toro Rosso, scoring on his debut and then three more times. Back for more in 2010, expect further progress from this increasingly confident and competent Swiss driver.

Formula 1 is a funny old game. Perhaps because it's the pinnacle of motor sport, it's insular in many ways, ignoring much of what happens beneath it, bothering to consider intruders only on arrival, seldom before.

This 21-year-old Swiss driver is a case in point, with F1's insiders ready to be scornful of anyone who hadn't at the very least finished in the top couple of places in the GP2 feeder series.

By season's end, though, there was near universal respect for what Sebastien had achieved, to the extent that people were no longer surprised when he qualified in the top 10. Indeed, at the Abu Dhabi finale, he did better than that and not only finishing fourth fastest in the third practice session but then setting the second fastest lap of the race en route to eighth place.

For this year, Sebastien will again be armed with an Adrian Newey-designed car, which can only be a huge benefit. It will be Ferrari-powered, unlike the Red Bulls, and will be fielded by Toro Rosso - the team that was

This is the year for Sebastien to cement the ever-improving form he showed last season.

once Minardi and so still struggles to attract the very best staff to work at its Italian headquarters - and not Red Bull Racing.

However, Franz Tost and the gang are getting better each year and Sebastien will certainly go into this year's campaign with a spring in his step, the tracks all committed to his memory banks and the confidence to attack that little bit harder than before. With Ferrari sure to be back on the attack again after its weak 2009 season, points will be harder to come by, but don't count this young driver out.

POWERED BY RED BULL

Racing drivers' careers in the 21st century can be a bit like an iceberg if you don't keep your eye on the international karting scene, as they can have a decade of kart racing before they hit cars. Then, as in Sebastien's case, they vault from Formula BMW to F1 in the blink of an eye. The signs were there that he was good - certainly good enough for Red Bull to snap him up as one of its developing drivers - when he came second in German Formula BMW in his maiden season. He was then runner-up in the European F3 series behind Sebastien Grosjean at his second attempt in 2007, also having a few outings in the A1GP series for Switzerland. He ran a GP2 programme in tandem, showing speed but little in the way of results, but this was useful experience as he ranked sixth in GP2 in 2008, when still only 19. This, though, was enough for graduation to F1 with sponsor Red Bull's junior team, Scuderia Toro Rosso.

JAIME ALGUERSUARI*

There was uproar when this teenager was promoted to F1 by Toro Rosso midway through 2009 as the testing ban meant that he had only ever done straightline testing. Yet, despite this lack of F1 experience, Jaime didn't disgrace himself.

Red Bull's considerable young driver sponsorship programme helped Jaime to climb motorsport's ladder, having been backed by them since the age of 16. Their support has been rewarded and so, in turn, was he as the energy drink company's patronage landed him a testing role with Red Bull Racing to run alongside his campaign in the World Series by Renault. This turned to career gold as he was thus lined up to replace Sebastien Bourdais when the French driver was sacked by Red Bull's second team, Scuderia Toro Rosso, for a lack of results. The trouble was, F1's in-season testing ban meant that his F1 experience consisted of just straightline testing. That his F1 debut was going to be at a circuit that was incredibly twisty, the Hungaroring, led to uproar from the established drivers, who were all convinced that he would get in their way and probably cause an accident.

That Jaime didn't blot his copybook earned him credit. That he finished the

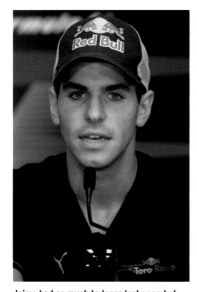

Jaime had so much to learn last year, but will be stronger this year, now that he's 20.

Hungarian GP was a further accolade, but it's safe to say that F1's testing rules were given further thought after that, with dispensations mooted for young drivers.

Jaime's lack of experience was revealed at that most unforgiving of circuits, Suzuka, and at 130R at that, but he stepped away from the wreckage of that and is sure to carry considerable benefit from the eight grands prix he contested, but will learn a huge amount more over the close season, when testing is allowed, when he can focus on the art of driving an F1 car away from the glare and pressure of a grand prix meeting.

* Leading candidate at time of going to press at the very end of 2009.

TRACK NOTES

Nationality:	SPANISH
Born:	23 MARCH, 1990, BARCELONA, SPAIN
Website:	www.jalguersuari.com
Teams:	TORO ROSSO 2009-10

CAREER RECORD	
First Grand Prix:	2009 HUNGARIAN GP
Grand Prix starts:	8
Grand Prix wins:	0
Poles:	0
Fastest laps:	0
Points:	0
Honours:	2008 BRITISH F3 CHAMPION,
	2007 ITALIAN FORMULA RENAULT RUNNER-UP,
	2006 ITALIAN FORMULA RENAULT WINTER
	SERIES CHAMPION

TWICE AS MANY WHEELS AS HIS FATHER

The son of a motorcycle racer, also Jaime but known as "Tortajada", Jaime was always destined for a life in motorised competition, but chose four wheels instead of two. Jaime Snr organises the World Series by Renault, so the family connection is strong. Jaime moved from karting to cars when he was just 15, racing in the Italian Formula Junior series in 2005. He tried the Formula Renault Euroseries at the end of that year and raced on in that through 2006 and 2007, ranking fifth at his second attempt and runner-up in the Italian series. However, 2008 was his year of years as he did something extremely rare: he won the British F3 series as a rookie, which was made all the more impressive as he was racing on circuits that he didn't know. He duly graduated with Carlin Motorsport to the World Series by Renault for 2009 and raced strongly in these more powerful cars until getting the call mid-season to add F1 to his programme.

CAMPOS META F1

Spain's hopes of its first ever grand prix team, headed by former racer Adrian Campos look great, but a problem raising the budget has made its entry precarious.

Adrian Campos (right) is plainly delighted at Bruno Senna's signing.

If it hadn't been for Fernando Alonso's considerable success in F1, which led to vastly increased crowds in his home country and Spain hosting two grands prix every year since 2008, there would be no Campos Meta F1 team. Alonso won world titles in 2005 and 2006 and now Spain has its very own grand prix team for the first time. The country's long tradtion includes having hosted a grand prix on and off since 1951 and non-championship grands prix in the 1930s. It may be the start of something big as Campos and the Epsilon Euskadi team that tried but failed to get one of the three coveted F1 entries offered last June are at the vanguard of the country's attempts to establish a motor sport industry.

Headed by former F1 racer Adrian Campos, who has long run teams in the junior single-seater categories, this new team joined forces with Meta Image, a sports marketing company that established itself as a leading player through handling the careers of Spain's leading tennis players Rafael Nadal and Arantxa Sanchez Vicario plus five-time Tour de France winner Miguel Indurain. It's headed by Enrique Rodriguez de Castro, and he has brought more than his Meta brand to the team name as he is also going to be the team's chief executive officer.

Although the team's offices

KEY MOMENTS & KEY PEOPLE

TEAM HISTORY
Established in 1998, Campos Racing guided Marc Gene to the Open Fortuna by Nissan title. It then gave Fernando Alonso his break, and he won the same title in 1999. After that, GP2 was the team's focus, winning the teams' title in 2008 thanks to the efforts of Lucas di Grassi and Vitaly Petrov before selling his stake to Alejandro Agag, who renamed it Barwa Addax, to enable him to concentrate on his move to F1, albeit continuing to run a team in Spanish F3.

ADRIAN CAMPOS
Spanish champion in radio-controlled car racing, Adrian moved on to car racing and finished third in German F3 in 1985. After just a few F3000 races, his family wealth bought him an F1 seat for 1987 with Minardi, but one and a half seasons produced just two finishes, the better of which was a 14th place. He was replaced by Pierluigi Martini after failing to qualify for three races in a row, then competed in touring cars, becoming Spanish champion in 1994, and sports cars before setting up his own team.

are in Madrid, it's a fractured programme as the technical centre is near Valencia, from where Campos Racing has run its Formula 3 team.

The third part of the puzzle is that the chassis will be built in Parma, Italy, at the headquarters of leading racing constructor Dallara. Work started on the design of the car last May and the workforce dedicated to it doubled after Campos Meta F1 landed its place for 2010.

With Dallara's reputation forged on building cars for single-make formulae, like F3, it's often forgotten that Gianpaolo Dallara was first involved in F1 in 1970 when he designed the short-lived de Tomaso entry entered by Frank Williams for Piers Courage. His next crack

at F1 was from 1988 to 1992, building cars for Scuderia Italia, with both Andrea de Cesaris and JJ Lehto achieving third place finishes. He later designed the car for Honda's aborted F1 project in 1998. The company continued to grow and grow outside F1 and it's got all the tools at its disposal to produce a sensible car with which the new team can cut it teeth.

The plan for the future, however, is to build the cars at its base in Spain, with a deal being lined up for them to be Ferrari-powered from 2011.

Like the other new entries, Campos Meta's cars will be powered by Cosworth V8s which will certainly give spectators an accurate yardstick for judging which one of these teams is

making the best entry into the sport's top category.

Many thought that Campos was launching a Spanish team, but he said from early on that it was also to represent South America. So it was no surprise when he plucked a driver from that continent as his first signing, albeit a Portuguese rather than Spanish-speaking one in the late Ayrton Senna's nephew Bruno, thus bringing one of F1's most

revered names back into F1.

It was expected that McLaren test driver Pedro de la Rosa would be brought back into the racing arena to add his considerable experience. However, with the talk that the team was even seeking a new shareholder, it also wanted someone who would bring a sizeable budget, so it came down to a choice between de la Rosa, Vitaly Petrov, Pastor Maldonado and Nelson Piquet Jr.

FOR THE RECORD

Country of origin:	Spain
Team base:	Alzira, Spain
Telephone:	(34) 915 613 561
Website:	www.camposmeta.com
Active in Formula One:	From 2010
Grands Prix contested:	0
Wins:	0
Pole positions:	0
Fastest laps:	0

2009 DRIVERS & RESULTS

Driver	Nationality	Races	Wins	Pts	Pos
Not applicable					

THE TEAM

Team principal:	Adrian Campos
Team president:	Jose Ramon Carabante
Chief executive officer:	Enrique Rodriguez de Castro
Technical director:	Daniele Audetto
Team manager:	tba
Chief designer:	tba
Chief aerodynamicist:	tba
Chief engineer:	Toni Cuquerella
Test driver:	tba
Chassis:	Campos Dallara
Engine:	Cosworth V8
Tyres:	Bridgestone

Boss Adrian Campos brings a racer's eye to the team.

PEDRO DE LA ROSA*

The teams new to F1 in 2010 required money, facilities and quick drivers, too. Yet, in order to advance, they needed an experienced head as well, someone who has been there, done that. Campos Meta wanted him, so did Sauber and Team US F1.

The biggest block to this erudite Spaniard landing one of the seats for this new Spanish team is money. Or the lack of it. Campos certainly wants Pedro's excellence as a development driver and the benefit that his pairing would be for rookie Bruno Senna as the team finds its feet. However, the need for finance suggests that a paying driver such as Pastor Maldonado or Vitaly Petrov would take precedence.

In fact, as it's a full time drive – his first since competing for Jaguar Racing in 2002 – this campaign will be Pedro's third crack at F1, as his first spell with Arrows and Jaguar from 1999 to 2002 was followed by outings for McLaren in 2005 and 2006 before he returned to his test and development role for the Woking team.

It had been thought likely that he would join Spain's new team, Campos Meta F1, but a lack of sponsorship meant that he was edged aside to make way for a driver with bulging pockets as Adrian Campos chased the well-financed Pastor

Pedro's considerable testing experience will be very useful in developing the car.

Maldonado and Vitaly Petrov for the number two seat. But then Meta's Enrique Rodriguez de Castro said mid-December that Pedro was still very much on the new

team's radar as they rated his experience so highly. That he is Spanish as well was certainly not an impediment...

So, with his 30s coming to a close next February, this is likely to be Pedro's final foray into F1, a chance to race again as a reward for all the years that he has spent pounding around circuits testing.

* Leading candidate at time of going to press at the start of 2010

TRACK NOTES

Nationality:	SPANISH
Born:	24 FEBRUARY 1971, BARCELONA, SPAIN
Website:	www.pedrodelarosa.com
Teams:	ARROWS 1999-2000, JAGUAR 2001-2002, MCLAREN 2005-2006, CAMPOS META 2010

CAREER RECORD	
First Grand Prix:	1999 AUSTRALIAN GP
Grand Prix starts:	71
Grand Prix wins:	0
	best result: second, 2006 Hungarian GP
Poles:	0
Fastest laps:	1
Points:	29
Honours:	1997 FORMULA NIPPON CHAMPION & JAPANESE GT CHAMPION, 1996 JAPANESE F3 CHAMPION, 1992 BRITISH & EUROPEAN FORMULA RENAULT CHAMPION, 1990 SPANISH FORMULA FORD CHAMPION

SAVED BY A STINT IN JAPAN

Motor racing was still the poor relation to motorbike racing in Spain when Pedro won the Spanish Formula Ford title. However, he was sponsored to have a crack at British Formula Renault in 1991. Pedro was British and European champion in 1992. British F3 was next, but the choice of a Renault engine hurt his chances and it took a move to Japan to revive Pedro's reputation as he won the Japanese F3 title. For 1996, he moved up to Formula Nippon and won that title in 1997, also landing the Japanese GT crown. Pedro landed a test ride with Jordan that turned into a race seat with Arrows for 1999. Points were hard to come by with Arrows then Jaguar and so Pedro became test driver for McLaren in 2003, a post he has held ever since, brightened by standing-in for the race team when Juan Pablo Montoya was injured in 2005 and after the Colombian quit midway through 2006, claiming second in Hungary in 2006.

BRUNO SENNA

The incredibly strong desire for having racing dynasties in Formula One has struck again and the late, great Ayrton Senna's nephew Bruno has been picked by the new Campos Meta 1 team, and now it's up to him to show that he has talent to match.

So, having come oh so close to landing a drive last year with the team that became Brawn GP, before losing out to Rubens Barrichello, Bruno is now part of the gang. He has made it to F1.

The question that everyone will be asking "is how good is he?". With an uncle as illustrious as three-time World Champion Ayrton Senna, considered to be perhaps the greatest driver ever, that's hardly surprising. Fortunately, Bruno has been used to that sort of examination since he started racing cars six years ago. This was made all the more intense for Bruno as he'd not raced karts because of family opposition after his uncle's death in 1994, so he started at a massive disadvantage to all of his rivals who'd spent their childhoods pounding around kart circuits, week in, week out.

Better still, by driving for one of F1's batch of new teams, the pressure on Bruno will be reduced, as few reckon that these teams will make up anything but

Bruno is bright, charming and a sponsor's dream. He's also a very quick pedaller.

the back of the grid in their first year.

Fans will also be aware that Bruno has been away from single-seaters since racing to the runner-up spot in the 2008

GP2 series in which he won at both Monaco and Silverstone and may need a little time to play himself back in after spending last year racing sportscars.

However, Bruno is an unusually bright individual and has some good advisors around him, to say nothing of his more experienced team-mate Pedro de la Rosa, so expect him to look, listen and learn through his first F1 campaign.

Don't expect points straight away, or even at all, in this first year. Don't expect Bruno to be Ayrton Senna II. But do expect solid improvement as the year progresses. And do expect even more interest in F1 in Brazil, as the name lives on.

A LATE-STARTER IN SINGLE-SEATERS

Bruno would have loved to race karts, but he was prevented from doing so by his family after his uncle Ayrton's death in the San Marino GP when Bruno was 12. It took until he was 22, in 2004, before his mother Viviane relented and let him go car racing. He tried a few rounds of the British Formula BMW series and used that experience of British tracks when he came back the following year to step up to F3. Impressively, he twice finished second. Then in 2006, he won the first three races before ending up third overall. Stepping up to GP2 in 2007, he won on only his third outing, at Barcelona, but slid to eighth overall. His 2008 campaign with iSport International was better, and Bruno won twice but had to settle for being runner-up behind Giorgio Pantano. With no F1 ride for 2009, Bruno considered touring cars and the DTM, but raced sportscars for the ORECA team in the Le Mans Series to keep his hand in.

TRACK NOTES

Nationality:	BRAZILIAN
Born:	15 APRIL 1982, SAO PAULO, BRAZIL
Website:	www.brunosenna.com.br
Teams:	CAMPOS META 2010

CAREER RECORD

First Grand Prix:	2010 BAHRAIN GP
Grand Prix starts:	0
Grand Prix wins:	0
Poles:	0
Fastest laps:	0
Points:	0
Honours:	2008 GP2 RUNNER-UP

LOTUS F1 RACING

One of F1's famous names, Lotus, is back, but don't look too deep to find a link. Think instead of a team that will eventually be based in Malaysia, home of the Proton car company that owns the Lotus name. Mike Gascoyne will create its pedigree.

The 2010 Lotus challenger shown in initial wind tunnel testing.

Whether long-time fans like the concept of the Lotus name, or any other famous F1 name, being resurrected is a matter for debate. Look beyond this, though, and the new Lotus, or Lotus F1 Racing to give it its full name, is an interesting team.

First off, it is starting life in Norfolk, Lotus's old stamping ground. Secondly, this is just the first step before the team will set itself up in the land of its finance: Malaysia, at Sepang. That is some way off and this project that was propelled into action by former Lotus employees Steve Kenchington and Nino Judge with Johnny Herbert as a team ambassador has grown and grown since

they first broached the idea as Litespeed when the FIA started talking of budget-capping and other incentives for more teams to come to the party.

Few thought that there was sufficient pedigree in this former F3 team to land one of the coveted places for new teams, especially with the likes of Lola and Prodrive in the mix. But, a place they got, with the Lotus name and backing from both the Malaysian government and a consortium of Malaysian businesses, and then the team started to show its hand, with head of Air Asia Tony Fernandes heading the project and long-time F1 technical chief Mike Gascoyne leading its technical side.

KEY MOMENTS & KEY PEOPLE

TEAM HISTORY

One could talk here about the illustrious history of Lotus, the marque that shaped F1 through the 1960s. But there is no connection between the Lotus that won 79 grands prix and drivers' titles for Jim Clark, Graham Hill, Emerson Fittipaldi and Mario Andretti and this team save for the fact that both hail from Norfolk. Its closest racing connection is with Litespeed, a Norfolk-based F3 team set up by Lotus engineers Nino Judge and Steve Kenchington.

MIKE GASCOYNE

A Cambridge engineering graduate, Mike had his first taste of F1 with McLaren in 1989 as an aerodynamicist. He has been on the move ever since, gaining experience at Tyrrell and Sauber before returning to Tyrrell. He achieved great success with Jordan in 1999 then joined Benetton in 2001 before taking up the challenge of Toyota as its technical director in 2004. After a spell with Spyker and the team it morphed into, Force India, he became involved with the Lotus F1 Team bid from its outset.

There is good motorsport pedigree in the parent company, the Lotus Group, builders of road-going sports cars – and its director of motorsport is Claudio Berro, formerly press supremo of Ferrari then Maserati and most recently operations director of the Middle Eastern-based Speedcar series. He reports to Dany Bahar, also formerly of Ferrari and now chief executive officer of the Lotus Group.

Keen to include Malaysians in the management structure of this Malaysian-financed team, Riad Asmat, 38, was appointed last autumn as chief executive officer, bringing management experience from being a general manager at Proton.

So, what of the nuts and bolts of this second edition of Lotus in F1? We all know that Gascoyne can mastermind a competitive car, but the headquarters in Hingham aren't yet the equal of say McLaren's at Woking, and they never will be due to the plans to relocate to Sepang. Instead, Lotus has hooked up with wind tunnel specialist Aerolab and joined forces with its parent company Fondtech to help with the design of the new Lotus. However, this caused a stink, as the Jean-Claude Migeot-led Aerolab company had previously worked with Toyota, Renault and Force India at its Sant'Agata Bolognese base, and Force India felt convinced that the first photographs of the Lotus bore more than a passing resemblance to its own car and so took the matter to court.

Gascoyne pushed hard for Jarno Trulli to bring his speed and considerable experience to lead the team's driving force, having worked with him at Jordan and Toyota.

There was talk of Malaysian driver Fairuz Fauzy – with family links to Proton – filling the second seat, but Gascoyne reckoned that it was better to have him as test and reserve driver for 2010, to give him the experience to step up in 2011. And this left the way clear for Heikki Kovalainen to bring his experience from McLaren.

Although money is tight for all these new teams, the aim is first of all to beat the other new teams and build from there.

Gascoyne reckoned that Lotus started three months after their rivals but is typically bullish that they won't be last.

In the long-term, just as Team US F1 wants to be to America, so Lotus F1 Racing wants to be to Malaysia, with a car designed by Malaysians, engineered by Malaysians and driven by Malaysians. Former F1 racer Alex Yoong will head its Asian driver search programme.

FOR THE RECORD

Country of origin:	England
Team base:	Hingham, England
Telephone:	(44) 01953 851411
Website:	www.lotusf1racing.my
Active in Formula One:	From 2010*
Grands Prix contested:	0
Wins:	0
Pole positions:	0
Fastest laps:	0

* THIS TEAM HAS NOTHING TO DO WITH THE LOTUS TEAM THAT RAN FROM 1958-1994

2009 DRIVERS & RESULTS

Driver	Nationality	Races	Wins	Pts	Pos
Not applicable					

THE TEAM

Team principal:	Tony Fernandes
Chief executive officer:	Riad Asmat
Chief technical officer:	Mike Gascoyne
Chief operating officer:	Keith Saunt
Team manager:	tba
Chief designer:	tba
Chief aerodynamicist:	tba
Chief engineer:	tba
Test driver:	Fairuz Fauzy
Chassis:	Lotus
Engine:	Cosworth V8
Tyres:	Bridgestone

Technical chief Mike Gascoyne will drive this new team forward.

JARNO TRULLI

It's all-change for this veteran Italian racer for 2010 as he swaps his Toyota overalls for Lotus ones and attempts to resurrect his F1 career with strong race performances to match his trademark scintillating flying laps in qualifying.

Fans of this enigmatic Italian spent much of last autumn, what would become of Jarno as Toyota kept hesitating over whether it was going to keep him on for a sixth season, then withdrew altogether.

After that, Jarno had a NASCAR test last November for Michael Waltrip Racing, allegedly "just for fun", along with former F1 racer Mika Salo, with both supported by their former employer Toyota.

Yet, thankfully, Jarno still had several irons in F1's fire and was finally announced as the lead driver for Lotus F1 Racing in the run-up to Christmas.

This will reunite Jarno with Mike Gascoyne, with whom he worked at both Jordan then Renault and he will surely enjoy more support than he apeared to be getting from the management at Toyota, even though he qualified on pole position for last year's Bahrain GP and peaked with second place at the Japanese GP.

Jarno will probably also enjoy the more

Jarno will relish the new challenge and also working with Mike Gascoyne again.

"pure" racing nature of Tony Fernandes' new team after the management-heavy nature of Toyota, where the automotive manufacturer ensured that that team operated less like a racing team than their rivals.

So, there's no move to NASCAR for Jarno for now, but an opportunity to gain satisfaction from propelling a new team from the back of the grid towards the midfield. He may be further from the front than in 2009, but he might enjoy it more.

TRACK NOTES

Nationality:	ITALIAN
Born:	13 JULY 1974, PESCARA, ITALY
Website:	www.jarnotrulli.com
Teams:	MINARDI 1997
	PROST 1997-1999, JORDAN 2000-2001, RENAULT
	2002-2004, TOYOTA 2005-2009, LOTUS 2010

CAREER RECORD

First Grand Prix:	1997 AUSTRALIAN GP
Grand Prix starts:	219
Grand Prix wins:	1
	2004 Monaco GP
Poles:	4
Fastest laps:	1
Points:	246.5
Honours:	1996 GERMAN FORMULA THREE
	CHAMPION, 1995 ITALIAN KARTING
	CHAMPION, 1994 EUROPEAN & NORTH
	AMERICAN KARTING CHAMPION,
	1991 WORLD KARTING CHAMPION

MADE FOR FORMULA ONE

One of a handful of former World Kart Champions now competing in F1, Jarno didn't take long to vault through the junior car racing formulae. Not long at all. He was snapped up by Flavio Briatore and propelled straight into F3 midway through 1995, and he was an instant hit in the German F3 Championship, winning races before the year was out ahead of the far more experienced Ralf Schumacher. He stayed on for a full season in 1996 and claimed the German title ahead of the likes of Nick Heidfeld. At this point, Jarno said that he was ready for F1 after one and a half years of car racing and so didn't need to bother himself with Formula 3000. So it proved when he joined Minardi for 1997, with Jarno really showing his ability when he swapped midseason to Prost after Olivier Panis was injured and immediately led the Austrian GP. Sadly, his ability has seldom been matched with a competitive car and it seems inconceivable that he has won only once and is better known for qualifying laps.

HEIKKI KOVALAINEN

The step from McLaren to Lotus F1 Racing is going to be a big one, demanding a new perspective for 2010, but Heikki is an adaptable sort of character and will grab this career redemption with both of his hands and do his utmost to make it work.

In his heart of hearts, Heikki knows that he would have loved to have stayed on at McLaren. He loved the team and the team loved him, but the results just didn't come his way last year. Even Lewis Hamilton struggled in the first half of the year, and he knew that he hadn't done quite enough to stay on for a third campaign with the team from Woking.

With McLaren expected to start this year with a car that could be the class of the field and, if not, certainly a car with race-winning potential, that must have been hard, knowing that you were going to have to step down a rung or two to remain in F1.

Enter a raft of new teams, all offering hope, before chosing Lotus F1 Racing. Heikki will certainly bring a positive attitude as well as the knowledge of how to win a grand prix. He will also bring experience of working with a well-funded and meticulous enterprise that will no doubt assist Lotus F1 Racing as it starts to establish its future base at Sepang.

On the racing front, though, Heikki

Heikki will bring welcome big team experience from McLaren to little Lotus.

will have to be patient, as technical chief Mike Gascoyne has pointed out that Lotus started its new car after the other incoming teams and there will be a lot of catching up to be done.

Heikki acknowledged at the driver announcement shortly before Christmas that there would be tough times at the beginning, but he has seen how ambitious team principal Tony Fernandes is and knows how tenacious Gascoyne is, so he is changing teams with his eyes open. His ready smile will be a valuable asset until this new team truly finds it feet.

TRACK NOTES

Nationality:	FINNISH
Born:	19 OCTOBER 1981, SUOMUSSALMI, FINLAND
Website:	www.heikkikovalainen.net?
Teams:	RENAULT 2007, MCLAREN 2008-2009, LOTUS 2010

CAREER RECORD	
First Grand Prix:	2007 AUSTRALIAN GP
Grand Prix starts:	52
Grand Prix wins:	1
	2008 Hungarian GP
Poles:	1
Fastest laps:	2
Points:	105
Honours:	2005 GP2 RUNNER-UP, 2004 FORMULA NISSAN WORLD SERIES CHAMPION, 2004 CHAMPION OF CHAMPIONS AT RACE OF CHAMPIONS, 2000 NORDIC KARTING CHAMPION

HE COULD HAVE BEEN A RALLY DRIVER

Having been born far from Finland's few cities in the south, Heikki was brought up on its western coast, in rally country. Near Suomussalmi, it's all gravel roads, forests and lakes. Yet, success in karting took his competition career towards car racing and he raced in British Formula Renault when he was 19 in 2001. He impressed, and came on strong as the year progressed. Having ranked fourth, he stepped up to F3 in 2002 and was third in the British series, then finished second in the Macau F3 GP. So he stepped up to World Series by Nissan in 2003 and was runner-up behind Franck Montagny before winning the title in 2004. Second to Nico Rosberg in GP2 in 2005, Heikki also tested for the Renault F1 team and it was with them that he made his F1 debut in 2007. On the podium at the Japanese GP, he then joined McLaren for 2008 and won the Hungarian GP.

SAUBER

When the other teams refused to admit a 14th team for 2010, it looked as though Peter Sauber's hopes of reviving his team following BMW's withdrawal would come to nothing. Then Toyota backed out as well, freeing the way for this Swiss team's return.

Sauber's days with BMW are now over and the future is uncertain.

Formula 1 is a fickle sport and thanks to budget-capping plus a worldwide decline in car sales, a team that had been subsumed by a manufacturer – BMW – is back running in its own right for the first time in five years. This team is Sauber and its founder Peter Sauber is back at the helm, having been reduced to a sidelined role during BMW's four-year reign.

For several months, it appeared that the team had been bought by Qadbak, a Swiss and Middle Eastern investment company that backed the Notts County Football Club in England. However, that came to naught and so it will continue at Hinwil in Switzerland, as it has been

even during the years after BMW took it over, but with a desperate need for a financial partner.

Although BMW announced that it was pulling out at the end of 2009 during last season, it had at least already financed some of the development of this year's car, so development of the chassis ought to be more accomplished and advanced than those from the quartet of all-new teams.

Furthermore, Sauber's engine choice – Ferrari – means that its V8 engines ought to be strong ones, most likely stronger than those from the Cosworth that the all-new teams will be using. Better still, Sauber has used Ferrari engines before – from

KEY MOMENTS & KEY PEOPLE

TEAM HISTORY
First there was Sauber the sports car builder in the 1970s. Then Sauber the works Mercedes partner in sports cars, winning at Le Mans in 1989. Then a mooted F1 bid together, but Mercedes pulled out and Sauber went into F1 on its own in 1993. The team was midfield and often anonymous, but its fortunes were transformed when it was taken over by BMW for 2006. The first win came in Canada in 2008, but no more, then BMW said it was pulling out at the end of 2009.

PETER SAUBER
Peter started competing in hillclimbs, sharing a VW Beetle. He built his own sports car in 1970 and progressed to ever higher levels of sports car racing, with Herbert Muller winning the 1976 Interserie title in a Sauber. After a couple of strong showings at Le Mans, Sauber built F3 cars for 1979 and one of his drivers, Max Welti, later became his racing manager and helped to convince Mercedes to fit its engines in their sports cars in 1985, leading to sports car and later his own F1 team, starting in 1993.

1997 to 2005, after which BMW took the team over – and it was mooted last autumn that part of their deal for using them again was that Ferrari reserve driver Giancarlo Fisichella would fill one of the team's race seats. Of course, Fisichella has a connection with Sauber too, having raced for the team in 2004 and racking up a healthy tally of 22 points, almost twice as many as team-mate Felipe Massa scored that year.

Hopefully, Nick Heidfeld, the team's most loyal servant will be the team's lead driver through having driven for Sauber or BMW Sauber for seven of the past nine years. At this stage in his career, with few other seats available even with the teams likely to be fighting over mid grid positions, he was left with few options when BMW announced that it would be pulling out and

it's only fair that such an unsung driver hasn't been left out in the cold. Indeed, had he gone for intermediate tyres rather than full wets when conditions were changing almost by the lap in the wet-dry Malaysian GP, he might have finally come away with his first grand prix win. However, second it was, and it was only late in the season that the team's cars were able to challenge for points on a regular basis. In itself, this was unusual, as Sauber and more recently BMW Sauber have tended to start the season well and then gone backwards.

Kamui Kobayashi impressed hugely in his two outings for Toyota at the end of 2009 and he will surely keep whoever signs as the team's lead driver on their toes once he has settled in. Mario Theissen, team principal during BMW's spell of ownership of the

team was obviously torn when BMW announced that it wanted to pull out. He wanted to stay on, but his confidence will have been dented by the team's decline in form, as they tumbled down the order from a very competitive third overall in 2008, when they weren't far off Ferrari and McLaren at the top of the constructors' points table. Last year, they fell to sixth and had been eighth with just two grands prix to go before

vaulting past Renault and Willams when Robert Kubica finished a surprise second in Brazil then Heidfeld came home fifth in the Abu Dhabi finale.

So, providing Sauber can attract some backing and the team makes good use of the leftovers of BMW's considerable investment, perhaps the team can mimic the success of a team that was left in a similar position 12 months earlier: Brawn GP.

FOR THE RECORD

Country of origin:	Switzerland
Team base:	Hinwil, Switzerland
Telephone:	(41) 44 937 9000
Website:	www.sauber-f1.com
Active in Formula One:	From 1993 (as Sauber)
Grands Prix contested:	287
Wins:	1
Pole positions:	1
Fastest laps:	2

2009 DRIVERS & RESULTS

Driver	Nationality	Races	Wins	Pts	Pos
Nick Heidfeld	German	17	0	19	13th
Robert Kubica	Polish	17	0	17	14th

THE TEAM

Team owner:	Peter Sauber
Team principal:	tba
Technical co-ordinator:	Willy Rampf
Head of powertrain:	Mrkus Duesmann
Chief designer:	Christoph Zimmermann
Head of aerodynamics:	Willem Toet
Team manager:	Beat Zehnder
Test driver:	tba
Chassis:	Sauber
Engine:	Ferrari V8
Tyres:	Bridgestone

Team owner Peter Sauber had to wait to be allowed back in for 2010.

NICK HEIDFELD*

After spending last autumn chasing the second seat at Mercedes GP, Nick's options appeared to have dwindled and some said that Sauber didn't want him back, as it considered Pedro de la Rosa and Giancarlo Fisichella, but Nick could still stay on.

Nick seems to have been around Formula 1 for a very long time and to have become one of the old guard almost without anyone noticing.

Indeed, Nick is a driver that people overlook. He's quick, everyone knows that, but he's not spectacular. Last year was expected to be the one in which he slipped down the order, having been outpaced by his BMW Sauber team-mate, the rising star Robert Kubica. However, they were both saddled with less than competitive cars and it was, surprise, surprise, Nick who came out ahead on points at the end of the season, albeit ranking 13th overall to the Pole's 14th.

The reason for this is that Nick is the sort of driver to make the best of a bad situation. He will plug away, seldom complain and simply drive. Then, when his planets are in alignment or whatever it is by which some people swear, he delivers. One such occasion was the Malaysian GP when

Nick has always been seen as a safe pair of hands, as his style is far from obtrusive.

right hit in true monsoon style. Had he been bold enough to opt for intermediate tyres at his pitstop, rather than a set of full wets, he could have claimed the first grand prix win that has been eluding him since his F1 debut in 2000.

When BMW pulled out of F1 late last year, Nick looked as though his time in F1 was up. Then, when Sauber was readmitted, the door swung open again for F1's silent man.

* Leading candidate at time of going to press at the start of 2010.

TRACK NOTES

Nationality:	GERMAN
Born:	10 MAY 1977, MOENCHENGLADBACH
Website:	www.nickheidfeld.de
Teams:	2000 PROST, 2001-2003 SAUBER, 2004 JORDAN, 2005 WILLIAMS, 2006-2009 BMW SAUBER, 2010 SAUBER

CAREER RECORD	
First Grand Prix:	2000 AUSTRALIAN GP
Grand Prix starts:	169
Grand Prix wins:	0 (best result: second - 2009 MALAYSIAN GP, 2008 AUSTRALIAN GP, CANADIAN, BELGIAN GPs, 2007 CANADIAN GP, 2005 MONACO, EUROPEAN GPs)
Poles:	1
Fastest laps:	2
Points:	219
Honours:	1999 F3000 CHAMPION, 1998 F3000 RUNNER-UP, 1997 GERMAN F3 CHAMPION, 1994 GERMAN FF1600 CHAMPION

A FEW TWISTS AND TURNS

It comes as no surprise that almost every Formula 1 driver that has reached the top has done so by succeeding in the junior categories. Actually, not all did, as some simply bought their way in. Nick, however, was a driver who collected trophies aplenty along the way, normally taking two bites at each cherry and delivering in the second year. This was the case in German Formula Ford, and then again in German F3, having been restricted to third place in his maiden season in 1996 by champion Jarno Trulli. Pipped by Juan Pablo Montoya to the F3000 crown in 1998, Nick made certain in 1999, scoring almost twice as many points as the runner-up. Having already shown great pace in tests for McLaren, he made it to F1 with the Prost team, before a three-year stint with Sauber established him as a safe pair of hands. F1 is a fast-moving game, though, and Nick was soon eclipsed. Despite a year spent at Jordan then another at Williams before rejoining Sauber, Nick has effectively been a one-team man.

KAMUI KOBAYASHI

Jenson Button fans wouldn't have had a clue who Kamui was before last year's Brazilian GP, but they did after it, as he kept the World Champion elect behind him. With further speed in Abu Dhabi and a tidy amount of backing, he's back for more.

Life can change in all manner of ways, but it's safe to say that Kamui's has swung like a pendulum in the past six months.

First off, he was considering what his future might hold after a second disappointing season in GP2 when he was given a lifeline by the Toyota F1 team, for whom he had been an occasional test driver since 2007. Timo Glock had injured himself at Suzuka and he was needed to step up and drive in practice there.

Secondly, Glock hadn't recovered, or was perhaps kept on one side for the final two grands prix, giving him the chance to make his F1 break in Brazil and follow it up in Abu Dhabi. He took the chance with both hands, showed that he could run as fast as Button, or at least stay in front of him, in Brazil and then picked up points for sixth place in the season closer.

With these drives, he put himself into contention for a full-time ride with Toyota for 2010, but the team was expected to pull

Kamui is fast and will look to build on his two unflappable F1 outings in the year ahead.

out of F1 and it duly did just that.

If it hadn't been for the Toyota call-up, Kamui was facing up to a difficult decision: whether to call time on his racing career and go back to work in his father's sushi restaurant as they had run out of money to back him, or whether to hang on.

So, with his reputation enhanced, Kamui needed to keep his momentum going and it was announced just before Christmas that he'd joined Sauber. With Peter Sauber's reputation for developing young talent, this could be a great learning year for Kamui.

TRACK NOTES

Nationality:	JAPANESE
Born:	13 SEPTEMBER 1986, HYOGO, JAPAN
Website:	www.kamui-kobayashi.com
Teams:	TOYOTA 2009, SAUBER 2010

CAREER RECORD

First Grand Prix:	2009 BRAZILIAN GP
Grand Prix starts:	2
Grand Prix wins:	0
	(best result: sixth, 2009 Abu Dhabi GP)
Poles:	0
Fastest laps:	0
Points:	3
Honours:	2008 GP2 ASIA CHAMPION, 2005 EUROPEAN & ITALIAN FORMULA RENAULT CHAMPION, 2003 JAPANESE FORMULA TOYOTA RUNNER-UP, 2001 ALL-JAPAN ICA KART CHAMPION, 2000 SUZUKA KART CHAMPION

JAPAN'S EURO STAR

The record of Japanese drivers winning championship titles in Europe is a short one, so when Kamui built on his karting skills to win the European and Italian Formula Renault titles at his second attempt, in 2004, people started to watch his progress. Kamui advanced to Formula 3 in 2006 and finished the campaign as the highest-ranked rookie, in eighth overall for the ASM team, with his season reaching a crescendo by qualifying on pole for the year-ending Macau GP. He then advanced to fourth overall in 2007, again with ASM, finishing behind only his team-mate Romain Grosjean, Sebastien Buemi and Nico Hulkenberg after winning at Magny-Cours. GP2 beckoned and Kamui dipped his toe in the water by ranking sixth in the GP2 Asia series, winning at Sepang and Sakhir, and then endured an erratic season in Europe with DAMS as he failed to build on his reverse-grid win in the second race, at Barcelona, leaving him 16th overall. He then won the second GP2 Asia series after taking wins in Dubai and Sakhir.

TEAM US F1

F1 needs America more than America needs F1, but this new team is hoping to change all that, with the eventual aim of winning with American drivers and engineers.

Design work was carried out at US F1's North Carolina headquarters.

Everyone in F1 is enthusiastic about Team US F1, as its very presence on the grid at grands prix will give greater exposure in the US market to their own sponsors. Exposure that is to the largest economy in the world and one that has never had a particular interest in F1.

To understand why F1 has had an increasingly difficult time to break into the American market, one needs to understand why even American single-seater racing, topped by Indycars, struggles for TV airtime. In a word, it's because NASCAR stock car series hog the airwaves.

Team US F1 founders know that only an American driver winning races in an America car designed, engineered and run by Americans from a base in the US of A will convince them to watch racing that many NASCAR say is for "cheese and wine party" sort of people.

However, with considerable ambition, Ken Anderson and Peter Windsor launched the Team US F1 project to do just this, and it gained considerable momentum when Chad Hurley, founder of YouTube, signed up to sponsor their efforts.

Basing itself in Charlotte, North Carolina shows great patriotism, rather than taking the easier route of setting up shop in Europe along with all of the other teams. But, this is

KEY MOMENTS & KEY PEOPLE

TEAM HISTORY
As this team has been created from scratch, it's worth considering what went before in terms of American F1 teams. There was Scarab, Eagle, Parnelli and Penske, with Eagle and Penske winning once apiece. That was all a long time ago, with the last of these wins coming in 1976. Peter Windsor has considerable F1 background since the 1970s, as a journalist, then sponsorship manager at Williams then general manager at Ferrari, before working in TV.

KEN ANDERSON
Ken is an engineer with the broadest of backgrounds. He was drawn from motocross to cars by Rick Mears, who got him to design shock absorbers for his Indycar. Through him, Ken joined Penske in 1984, also doing suspension work for Williams in a contra-deal. He joined Ligier in 1988, as tech director, later joining Onyx. When this folded, he returned to Indycars, with Chip Ganassi Racing, also setting up G-Force with Ganassi, with cars from here winning the Indy 500. Ken worked in NASCAR until setting up US F1.

in the heart of NASCAR country and Team US F1 will share some of the facilities and expertise of the nearby Haas/CNC NASCAR team for which Anderson was technical director.

For the course of the European season, the team will base itself at the new MotorLand Aragon circuit in Spain, though design and manufacturing work will continue to be based at Charlotte. One of the advantages of the Tilke-designed circuit is that it may well be selected as an F1 testing venue.

The long-term aim is to have a pair of American drivers, but for the first season it was always going to be that a driver with experience would be in one car, simply to hurry the team through gaining the experience on which it will need to build for future campaigns. With no American drivers fitting this

bill, the joint team principals had to look elsewhere.

Pedro de la Rosa became a favourite for this ride after Alex Wurz declined it, starting a race with Campos Meta to sign him, with Jacques Villeneuve as an outside shot.

Then Jose Maria Lopez hove into view with a budget and became the only driver being mentioned before we closed for press before Christmas.

Of the Americans US F1 wanted to run in its second car, Jonathan Summerton seemed to move to the front of the queue ahead of Graham Rahal, JR Hildebrand Jr and John Edwards for 2011 and beyond.

For the future, and perhaps as the quickest way to get NASCAR fans to take a look at F1, NASCAR racer Kyle Busch has been linked with a drive with the team for 2011, which

would take F1 to a new audience if the millions of NASCAR fans turned their attention to F1.

Anderson had told the press in June at the British GP that the team planned to have its car testing by November, but rumours of a lack of progress abounded last year as summer turned to winter, and the team's website wasn't even up and running by that date and Windsor had to refute

claims that the team's crash-testing programme hadn't been started and even that the team was up for sale. Perhaps more realistically, the team's maiden test was pushed back to Febuary in Alabama, and everyone involved had their fingers crossed that all would proceed according to their plans, as the very concept of Team US F1 is one that is essential for the future growth of F1.

FOR THE RECORD

Country of origin:	USA
Team base:	Charlotte, USA
Telephone:	tba
Website:	www.usgpe.com
Active in Formula One:	From 2010
Grands Prix contested:	0
Wins:	0
Pole positions:	0
Fastest laps:	0

2009 DRIVERS & RESULTS

Driver	Nationality	Races	Wins	Pts	Pos
Not applicable					

THE TEAM

President, chief executive officer & team principal:	Ken Anderson
Sporting director:	Peter Windsor
Technical director:	tba
Team manager:	John Anderson
Chief designer:	tba
Chief aerodynamicist:	tba
Chief engineer:	tba
European supplier liaison:	Bernard Ferguson
Test driver:	tba
Chassis:	US F1
Engine:	Cosworth V8
Tyres:	Bridgestone

Ken Anderson and Peter Windsor have great ambitions for Team US F1.

JONATHAN SUMMERTON*

One US F1 seat may be filled with an experienced driver or someone with a budget, like James Rossiter, but the driver around whom it really wants to build its future is Jonathan, an American with a good knowledge of the European racing scene.

When Team US F1 was instigated, it was thought that it would start with a driver with considerable Formula 1 experience and run a young American rookie alongside him to learn the ropes then gear up and take over as the team number one and gun for the world title if ever the team produced machinery capable of challenging the best the established teams had on offer.

The target was to be 100% successful and 100% American. But then, with the global economy as it was, these plans became diluted and it looked as though this would be to the detriment of Jonathan's hopes as drivers with big budgets were sought ahead of him. Still, a role as the team's test driver would be a good foot in the door.

What this 21-year-old Floridian can bring to the party, apart from his sunny disposition, is obvious speed, with a great grounding in the European racing scene - not something that all up-and-coming Americans seek out - and knowledge of the Asian circuits through

Jonathan has raced against many of his potential F1 rivals before, in Europe.

racing in A1GP. Indeed, his one win for A1 Team USA in that came at Shanghai.

And so, he had earned the respect of Team

US F1's sporting director Peter Windsor, even before he headed back to the USA in 2008 and spent that season and last showing his form against the best home-grown talent in Formula Atlantic and the Indy Light series.

At the time of going to press, Jonathan is very much an outside shot at landing a ride, as financial clout could be considered ahead of talent. If investor Chad Hurley can be convinced to give him a shot, it could be one of the key steps to this patriotic team achieving its ambitious goal.

* Leading candidate at time of going to press at the start of 2010.

HEADING ABROAD TO CHASE F1 DREAM

Jonathan advanced from karts to cars in late 2003, racing in Skip Barber's Southern Region series. He then stepped up to Formula BMW and won a scholarship to race in Formula BMW USA and finished third in that. Showing a cosmopolitan approach to his racing, and with F1 as his target, he headed to Europe in 2005, aged just 17, to race in the German Formula BMW series, ranking ninth as he learned the tracks, and Nico Hulkenberg and Sebastien Buemi shared the spoils. Stepping up to F3 in 2006, Jonathan ranked ninth in the Euro series, coming on strong as the season advanced but being pipped for the rookie title by Kamui Kobayashi. He also stepped up to the more powerful A1GP formula, representing the United States and he won a race at Shanghai in early 2008, setting up his season back in the USA in which he ranked third in Formula Atlantic. In 2009, he scored the same number of points as the Formula Atlantic champion John Edwards, but lost out on countback.

TRACK NOTES

Nationality:	AMERICAN
Born:	21 APRIL 1988, KISSIMMEE, USA
Website:	www.formulajon.com
Teams:	2010 TEAM US F1

CAREER RECORD

First Grand Prix:	2010 BAHRAIN GP
Grand Prix starts:	0
Grand Prix wins:	0
Poles:	0
Fastest laps:	0
Points:	0
Honours:	2009 FORMULA ATLANTIC RUNNER-UP, 2003 FLORIDA ROTAX JUNIOR KART WINTER CHAMPION

JOSE MARIA LOPEZ*

Argentina, the country that sprung the little-known Esteban Tuero on F1 in 1998, has done it again, with Jose Maria Lopez being plucked from the Argentinian touring car scene to restore his single-seater career in the very top category.

If you don't know what an Argentinian TC2000 car looks like, visit Jose Maria's website. The racing is great, very competitive, and he's won the title for the past two seasons, but Formula 1 it ain't. It's light years away, which makes his decision to take a shot at F1 all the more extraordinary.

Bringing a healthy budget from his native Argentina has to be the prime reason why Jose Maria has been selected by Team US F1's Ken Anderson and Peter Windsor, as unfortunately his track record in single-seaters is patchy at best.

Yes, he was a champion in Italian Formula Renault in 2001 and then stepped up the power range and won the Formula Renault V6 title in 2003, but that was a poorly supported series and so isn't as big an achievement as it might seem.

You need to examine Jose Maria's record in GP2 - one rung down from F1 - to be able to gauge how quick he might be. He raced for one of the top teams, DAMS, in 2005 and yet his top result was a win in

Jose Maria has plenty to prove to silence his critics as he returns to single-seaters.

the reverse-grid second race at Barcelona as he ranked ninth overall after an erratic campaign. Moving across to Super Nova for 2006, Jose Maria ended the year one place lower overall, 10th, although there were

flashes of speed, but still a lack of results that suggested an F1 future.

However, his F1 aspirations were plain all the way back in 2004 when money from a sponsor bought him a test run with Minardi, with another outing following in 2006, this time for Renault as he was part of Renault's Driver Development programme.

So, while American F1 fans hoped for at least one American driver at US F1, Jose Maria was tipped to fill the other.

* Leading candidate at time of going to press at the very end of 2009.

TRACK NOTES

Nationality:	ARGENTINIAN
Born:	26 APRIL 1983, RIO TERCERO, ARGENTINA
Website:	www.pechitolopez.com.ar
Teams:	US F1 2010

CAREER RECORD	
First Grand Prix:	2010 BAHRAIN GP
Grand Prix starts:	0
Grand Prix wins:	0
Poles:	0
Fastest laps:	0
Points:	0
Honours:	2008 & 2009 ARGENTINIAN TC2000 CHAMPION, 2003 FORMULA RENAULT V6 CHAMPION, 2002 ITALIAN FORMULA RENAULT CHAMPION

TAKING AN UNUSUAL COURSE

After the obligatory childhood spent karting, Jose Maria, or "Pechito" as he likes to be called, headed for Europe in 2001 and competed in the European Formula Renault Championship. He did well in 2002, ranking fourth in Europe, one pleace ahead of a certain Lewis Hamilton, and winning the Italian series. Stepping up to the more powerful Formula Renault V6 series and winning the title looks better than it was, as it was poorly supported. F3000 came next in 2004 and Jose Maria ranked sixth in that. F3000 was then replaced as F1's feeder formula by GP2 for 2005 and he ranked ninth then 10th in his two seasons at this level. Then, with his budget exhausted, he went home to Argentina and raced in the TC2000 touring car series, showing good speed. Fifth in 2007, he was champion in 2008 and then again last year for the works Honda team.

VIRGIN RACING

Here is the team set up to carry Virgin's banner in F1 after its toe in the water with Brawn last year. Formed from Manor Motorsport and Wirth Research, the team is built on good, solid people, but will need time to gain experience and so hit its potential.

Virgin's Richard Branson had his first taste of F1 last year with Brawn.

Manor Motorsport started the ball rolling when it applied to step up from the lower formulae as one of F1's new teams for 2010, attracted by a proposed budget cap. Its entry would be called Manor GP. Yet, before last year was out, Manor had to stand back from the limelight as Richard Branson's Virgin Group had bought the naming rights, thus Virgin Racing.

Although known and widely respected throughout the ranks of junior single-seater racing, Manor Motorsport wasn't considered a team likely to attempt joining the World Championship, especially with the more highly rated Lola and Prodrive concerns in the mix, even when a stringent £40m budget cap was mooted to bring the affordability of entering F1 down into the reach of many more teams in these straightened economic times. However, Manor went ahead and made its bid to join the sport's biggest stage, got the wobbles when this price cap was scrapped shortly thereafter, yet, after teaming up with Wirth Research to beef up its technical side, here it is ready to go. Better still, it has backing from the mighty Virgin Group to boot after it decided that continuing with Brawn GP would be too expensive for 2010.

Nick Wirth has considerable F1 experience from being an

KEY MOMENTS & KEY PEOPLE

TEAM HISTORY
Manor has considerable pedigree in the junior categories, driven all along by Formula Ford racer John Booth. When he noticed that he was old enough to be his rivals' fathers, he stepped back to run teams. That was in 1990 and his Sheffield-based team ran cars in Formula Renault, later helping the likes of Kimi Raikkonen and Lewis Hamilton on their way to greater things. F3 was added to Manor's portfolio in 1999, immediately taking the British title. Its focus has been on the European series in recent years.

JOHN BOOTH
This proud Yorkshireman – Manor's badge is the white rose – started his racing in Formula Ford at 24 in 1978, having already become Europe's youngest known qualified pilot at 17. A meat trader by profession, he was known as "Butcher" Booth to differentiate him from a rival with the same name. He advanced to F3, but reverted to Formula Ford for the rest of the 1980s, focusing on the northern-based championships, and keeping all the rising stars honest.

aerodynamicist for March after graduating and then being recruited by Max Mosley to head the Simtek Research company. This became all his own when Mosley became FIA President and entered an F1 team for 1994. Financial troubles forced it to close part way through 1995. Next stop was a spell as Benetton's chief designer and Wirth has most recently run the Acura Le Mans Prototype programme in the USA.

Virgin Racing will have its commercial offices in London, but the team will be run from Manor's long-time base at Dinnington outside Sheffield, but this is far short of matching the technical facilities of the established F1 teams, so the design and development work on the cars will be carried out from Wirth Research's base in Bicester, some 100 miles away.

One first that Manor will be introducing is that its 2010 car will be designed using only CFD (computer fluid dynamics) rather than spending time in a wind tunnel. In fact, as the new team doesn't possess a wind tunnel, that has a certain logic, although many feel that it looks like someone trying to traverse a tightrope without the back-up of a safety net. It might work, but on the other hand…

Critics state that CFD simply won't be fast enough at simulating the myriad factors for many of the thousands of variables of ride height, roll, yaw and other factors.

Wirth calls it "development in the digital domain" and made much use of his "driver in the loop" simulator to virtually test the car before any parts were produced. He's not doing this blind, though, having used the approach to design race-winning Acura sports cars for the American Le Mans Series.

The car – the Cosworth-powered Virgin VR-01 – wasn't due to hit the tracks until February, so everyone was hoping that Wirth was correct in his assumptions.

As with almost all other teams, driver choice was unusually delayed, but former Toyota driver Timo Glock was picked to lead the attack, with Brazilian racer Lucas di Grassi winning the race to compete alongside him after four years of being a frontrunner in GP2.

Lloyds Development Capital has been attracted by Richard Branson's push into F1 and has invested millions in the team. That said, Branson reckons that Virgin Racing will be operating with the smallest budget of any of the teams on the grid.

FOR THE RECORD

Country of origin:	England
Team base:	Dinnington, England
Telephone:	(44) 01909 560331
Website:	www.manorgp.com
Active in Formula One:	From 2010
Grands Prix contested:	0
Wins:	0
Pole positions:	0
Fastest laps:	0

2009 DRIVERS & RESULTS

Driver	Nationality	Races	Wins	Pts	Pos
Not applicable					

THE TEAM

Team principal & CEO:	Alex Tai
Non-executive chairman:	Etienne de Villiers
Sporting director:	John Booth
Technical director:	Nick Wirth
Director of racing:	Graeme Lowden
Team manager:	Dave O'Neill
Test drivers:	Alvaro Parente & Luiz Razia
Chassis:	Virgin VR-01
Engine:	Cosworth V8
Tyres:	Bridgestone

John Booth brings years of team management skills with him to F1.

TIMO GLOCK

Timo will be having a new start in 2010, leading Virgin Racing's attack, and he will be hoping not only for a competitive car but also for strong race management, as his best chance last year, at Sepang, was wasted with less than inspired tactics.

This rock steady German is going to enjoy his F1 this year with the new Virgin Racing team, because the atmosphere is going to be rather different to the difficult one that existed at the Toyota team before it quit last November.

The challenge will be very different, as he will be looking to help this new team advance up the order rather than racing for a team that had great facilities and money aplenty but an inability to give him a car that was consistent.

Timo is a no-nonsense, get-on-with-it sort of racer. He's not flash. He's not controversial. And he's not more interested in his image. He simply gets on with it.

With Toyota's continued participation, a topic that was debated through last year until the announcement was made that it wasn't carrying on, other teams made their desire to run Timo known, with Renault at the front of the queue in front of several of the new teams, but Virgin Racing won the race to sign him for the season ahead.

Timo will find his new environment refreshing and is sure to give his all to help it progress.

Timo ended last year 10th overall, as he had in 2008, but he could reasonably have expected to have finished higher judging by the strong form shown by Toyota early in the season as the team started off with a double diffuser and reaped the advantages. Or, frankly, didn't reap the advantages, even when he and team-mate Jarno Trulli shared the front row in Sepang.

A gashed leg and cracked vertebra suffered in Japan meant that he was made to miss that race and the final two grands prix as well, handily giving an opportunity for Kamui Kobayashi that just might have encouraged Toyota to remain in F1.

TRACK NOTES

Nationality:	GERMAN
Born:	18 MARCH, 1982, LINDENFELS, GERMANY
Website:	www.timo-glock.de
Teams:	JORDAN 2004, TOYOTA 2008-2009, VIRGIN RACING 2010

CAREER RECORD	
First Grand Prix:	2004 CANADIAN GP
Grand Prix starts:	37
Grand Prix wins:	0
(best result: second, 2008 Hungarian GP, 2009 Singapore GP)	
Poles:	0
Fastest laps:	1
Points:	51
Honours:	2007 GP2 CHAMPION, 2001 GERMAN FORMULA BMW CHAMPION, 2000 GERMAN FORMULA BMW JUNIOR CHAMPION

A STRUGGLE REWARDED

It's a truism that you don't get many second chances in sport, and F1 is especially so, but Timo bucked that trend. He had had a textbook ascent through the junior formulae, winning the BMW Formula Junior Cup at his first attempt in 2000, then adding the Formula BMW title the following year. He was competitive in F3 in Gemany and on the European scene before replacing Giorgio Pantano at Jordan midway through 2004, finishing seventh first time out in Canada. But he lost his F1 ride and many thought that would be that as he headed off to race Indycars. Although he ended the season as top rookie and had come very close to winning a round, he was anxious to make it back to F1. Timo raced in GP2 in 2006, but was fourth as Lewis Hamilton became champion. With one last roll of the dice, he raced in GP2 again in 2007 and won the title, regaining his place in F1 with Toyota for 2008, impressing with second place in Hungary.

LUCAS DI GRASSI

Standing at the entrance to Formula 1 can be a nerve-wracking business, but the creation of new teams for 2010 has provided this 25-year-old with his chance to join the big time after fully four years on the final rung of the ladder to the top.

There has been a list of fast, capable drivers who never managed to take that final step into F1 if you look back over the records of F2, its successor F3000 or the current secondary formulae: GP2. Many a driver has been ready to become a grand prix driver, only to find that there were no openings in F1, no teams with a drive to spare.

Lucas was looking very much as though he was going to be the latest in the long line of those who fell just short. Then, to his relief, the target was made larger with the arrival of four new teams.

Already favoured by Renault, for whom he was a test driver in 2008, Lucas was talked of increasingly as the driver bound for the second seat at Virgin Racing. It took until 10 days before Christmas, though, before his drive was finally announced, and his previous connection with Manor Motorsport, which will be responsible for running Virgin Racing's cars surely played a part in the Brazilian landing the ride.

He knows the Manor crew well already, having raced for its F3 team in 2005,

Lucas has finally been given his F1 break and he comes with F1 testing experience.

finishing third overall in the Euro F3 series behind Lewis Hamilton and Adrian Sutil but ahead of Sebastian Vettel. They also won the Macau F3 GP together. So, there is a mutual admiration and the fact that

he will know many of his crew so well is good news, for he, team-mate Timo Glock and the team are all going to have to pull together to help the team to find its feet.

The 2010 season will not be one for prima donna behaviour, for keeping set-up information from a team-mate. This will be all hands to the pumps, but importantly Lucas finally has his foot in the door.

TRACK NOTES

Nationality:	BRAZILIAN
Born:	11 AUGUST 1984, SAO PAULO, BRAZIL
Website:	www.lucasdigrassi.com.br
Teams:	2010 VIRGIN RACING

CAREER RECORD	
First Grand Prix:	2010 BAHRAIN GP
Grand Prix starts:	0
Grand Prix wins:	0
Poles:	0
Fastest laps:	0
Points:	0
Honours:	2007 GP2 RUNNER-UP, 2005 MACAU F3 GP WINNER, 2003 SOUTH AMERICAN F3 RUNNER-UP, 2002 BRAZILIAN FORMULA RENAULT RUNNER-UP, 2000 PAN-AMERICAN KART CHAMPION, 1999 SOUTH AMERICAN KART CHAMPION, 1998 BRAZILIAN KART CHAMPION, 1997 SAO PAULO KART CHAMPION

TRY, TRY AND TRY AGAIN

Very much the shining light of the South American karting scene, Lucas started kart racing at 13, copying his father Vito who used to race. His success was notable as he rose from Sao Paulo champion to Pan-American champion in three years. After showing talent in Formula Renault then Formula Three in Brazil, Lucas headed for Europe in 2004, racing in British F3. Scoring two wins proved he was good, and he then ranked third in Euro F3 in 2005, also winning the Macau street race. Next up was GP2 and Lucas struggled with Durango in 2006, but was runner-up with ART in 2007, behind Timo Glock. He then started 2008 as a Renault F1 test driver, but joined GP2 after three rounds and was still able to rank third overall as Giorgio Pantano became champion, and he was third again last year behind Nico Hulkenberg and Vitaly Petrov, winning once, at Istanbul.

TALKING POINT: TECHNICAL CHANGES FOR 2010

The banning of refuelling at pitstops is most likely to be the most mind-focusing change, but narrower front tyres, a higher minimum weight and the decision by the teams to drop KERS will certainly also make a difference to the way teams plan their race strategies.

There are pros and cons to the dropping of refuelling for the season ahead. Gone will be the risk of a flash fuel fire during the pit stop, with all of its associated dangers. That's good. However, it will also remove one of the factors that has always supplied pit stops with that element of lottery, as a team attempting to hurry its refuelling could trip itself up by not engaging the fuel nozzle at the first time of asking, or fail to get it off fully, to the frustration of the driver who would thus have pressed like crazy on the track for no good as the driver he was trying to hunt down would thus be handed back those precious seconds and all would have been for nothing.

The difference on track will be harder to spot, as all cars will be carrying all but identical amounts of fuel at the start of the race, rather than some starting light and going for an early refuelling stop, a tactic that was used most notably by Renault and BMW Sauber when they threw everything into qualifying well by running a fuel-light car.

This year, race strategies will be shaped more by how hard teams want their drivers to push their tyres, as that will dictate how soon they will stop, and how often. Running at a lower speed will make the tyres last longer, but leave a driver exposed to being passed by a driver who is going more hell-for-leather at that point in the grand prix.

To accommodate the extra fuel required to run a grand prix distance, fuel tanks will have to be enlarged by about 75%, and this will involve considerable work in the packaging of the car. Externally, it will make little difference other than a broader hump behind the driver's shoulders, but under the skin it will, with both the length of the gearbox casing and the wheelbase likely area that will require change to make space, with the associated effects on weight distribution.

If only life was as "simple" as that for the design teams who, largely, spent much of last year getting up to speed with double diffusers and a comprehensive sweep of technical regulation changes.

This year's mixture will be made even less predictable by the cars being made to run on front tyres that are 15% narrower than before. While this will reduce the grip offered, it will also improve the aerodynamics of the cars, making them cut through the air more cleanly and allow more air to reach the radiators, which will help with engine cooling. As ever, what a designer gains on the one hand, he loses with the other, or vice versa.

KERS wasn't to everyone's liking in 2009 but, for the teams that pushed ahead with it, it was a real boost. Well, who wouldn't want an extra 80bhp to use in attack or defence? It wasn't fair for those that didn't have it, but it added another twist on the blast to the first corner and, let's face it, life isn't always fair.

Cars will also have to run to a minimum weight 15kg higher than in 2009.

As we all saw last year, rule changes shake up Formula 1's order, and that's never a bad thing. The drivers will also have to adapt their style to get the best out of the new-look cars and really think about how hard to push their cars at different points in the grand prix. The tactics will be intriguing to watch and, hopefully, the race order will see-saw to and fro as they do so.

Busy pit stops like this are now confined to history, as refuelling has been banned.

2009   2010

FUEL LOAD:
Carrying up to 180kg of fuel – previously around 60kg – will change weight distribution dramatically

Engine & gearbox:
Moved further back to accommodate larger fuel tank

Fuel tank:
Bigger, higher – capacity increased from 80 litres to 250 litres

Wheelbase:
Extended

Weight:
Minimum 620kg (up from 605kg) to allow for increased size

QUALIFYING:
Slowest eight cars removed after each qualifying session.
Final qualifying using low-fuel configuration

Refuelling during race now banned. Pit stops will continue for tyre changes – now expected to take under four seconds

Two dry-weather compounds
Unless wet, drivers must use both.
Soft compound has green stripe

TYRES:
Front wheel width down from 270mm to 245mm, reducing grip

Balance will shift from rear to front as fuel level drops

Wheel fairings banned

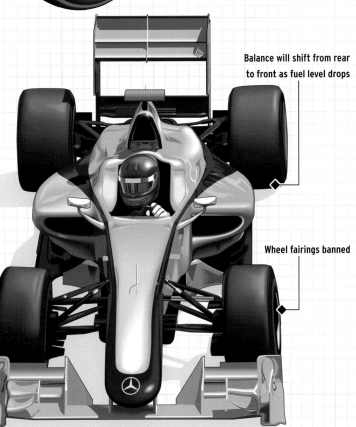

Smaller front wheel requires changes to front wing aerodynamics

TALKING POINT:
THE RETURN OF COSWORTH

Cosworth built Formula One's most successful engine, the DFV, in 1967, and remained a mainstay until the manufacturers arrived in bulk and started letting other teams use their engines, leading to Cosworth's withdrawal after 2006. Now, with new teams joining in, it's back, in force.

What do the following teams Formula 1 teams – Campos Meta F1, Lotus F1 Team, Virgin Racing and Team US F1 – have in common? At first glance, not much as they draw their inspiration from Spain, Malaysia, England and the USA, but they will all be racing with the same engine. It comes from Cosworth, a classic British engineering company, bringing it back into the spotlight after three years away from the sport's top stage.

The reason that Cosworth is able to come back and take on the giant motor manufacturers such as Mercedes and Renault again is because of the budget cap that was implemented for this year, with Cosworth's new V8 the most affordable F1 engine of all. With a three-year deal with each team, Cosworth will have the stability that was conspicuous by its absence before it dropped out of F1 at the end of 2006.

Cosworth is a pure engineering firm with a wide range of activities spread across aerospace and defence. However, when Mike Costin and Keith Duckworth got together in 1959, combined their surnames and came up with Cosworth as the name for their company, their focus was building competition engines and they were an instant hit.

Always allied with Ford, they received an inspired piece of investment from the blue oval when they convinced Ford's competitions chief Walter Hayes to pay £100,000 for Ford's name to be on its double-four-valve (DFV) F1 engine. This was in 1967 and the rewards were immediate when Lotus gave the V8 engine its debut in the Dutch GP and Graham Hill started on pole, then Jim Clark raced off to win as he pleased. Three more wins for Lotus-DFVs followed before the year was out, with its horsepower advantage and the fact that the engine could be used as a stressed member of the chassis, so that the rear suspension could be bolted straight onto it, offered a serious weight saving. Small wonder that two other teams lined up to use DFVs for 1968 and that that number turned to four teams, the top four teams, in 1969.

Cosworth even built its own F1 car, in 1969, when experimenting with four-wheel drive, but it never raced as its designer Robin Herd moved on to form March and Duckworth decided to focus entirely on racing engines.

Hill became World Champion in 1968 after Clark was killed, then Cosworth's DFV powered Jackie Stewart to three titles in five years, interspersed with Jochen Rindt and Emerson Fittipaldi using DFVs to be champions for Lotus. DFV power then took Fittipaldi to another title in 1974, for McLaren, the same team that helped James Hunt to the 1976 crown. Mario Andretti (Lotus), Alan Jones (Williams), Nelson Piquet (Brabham) and Keke

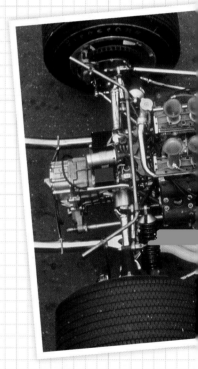

Rosberg (Williams) were also DFV-motivated as they raced to the world titles in 1978, 1980, 1981 and 1982 respectively.

Then, with turbocharged engines proving the way to go, Michele Alboreto guided the engine to its final win in the 1983 Detroit GP, bringing the tally for the DFV and its derivatives to a record-breaking 155 victories.

Scuderia Toro Rosso and Williams were the

Left: The Cosworth name is back in F1, its engines powering Williams and all four of the new teams.

Right: Michele Alboreto heads for Cosworth's most recent win, for Tyrrell in Detroit in 1983.

Below right : Williams last had Cosworth power in 2006.

Below: Cosworth made its debut with Lotus in 1967. This is Graham Hill.

last teams that Cosworth supplied before it withdrew to focus on other elements of its portfolio. However, the opening up of F1 for 2010 left the way clear for a way back in, with former Jordan and Jaguar marketing leader Mark Gallagher returning to F1 late last year to head its F1 Business Unit after heading

Ireland's title-winning A1GP team.

Gallagher will have a battle on his hands to turn these new teams into winners. Not just because they are new, but also because the Cosworth V8 is thought to be likely to struggle for fuel efficiency, which will be

important as refuelling has been banned.

However, it has another card to play, in that it is becoming reunited with Williams, which will obviously be its flaghip team as it lays down its marker in F1 again.

KNOW THE TRACKS 2010

The World Championship just keeps on adding new venues to its roster, with South Korea the latest addition as Formula One continues the shifting of its balance away from Europe towards the east. Old friends are welcomed back as well, with the Circuit Gilles Villeneuve back with the return of the Canadian Grand Prix. With Donington Park's bid to host a grand prix for a second time having failed, it left Silverstone as the home of the British GP, to considerable delight from the teams.

For many years, decades even, there was precious little change to the World Championship calendar. It was predominantly European-centred with a handful of races in North America, South Africa, Japan and Australia to provide a cosmopolitan air.

This is no longer the case, as the European races now number just eight of the 19 events, albeit with the Turkish GP being just across the River Bosporus in Asia Minor, with its inclusion still bringing the total of 'European' races to fewer than half.

Such is the change among the non-European grands prix that the Middle East now has two grands prix, Asia has five, with traditional grands prix in Australia and Brazil completing the 19 set for 2010. It's hard to know what earlier British World Champions Mike Hawthorn, Jim Clark, Graham Hill or James Hunt might have made of this.

You can certainly imagine that these racing greats would also have been bamboozled by the races in Abu Dhabi and Singapore as well, with their day-night and night time format that not only adds variety but caters for the needs of the predominant European-based television viewing audience.

Not all races have been put back, though, as the Malaysian GP has reversed last year's move back towards late afternoon, by sliding forward an hour to avoid the farcical events of last April when a tropical storm at Sepang stopped play and there wasn't sufficient daylight to start again when the rain eased.

The nose of the campaign has been altered, with Australia losing its position as the season opener. Bahrain couldn't be more different and will certainly lack the intimate, gossipy feel of Melbourne, but it carries the considerable advantage of running its race at a time when Europe is awake, albeit with its grandstands traditionally less than full.

The tally of 19 grands prix means that there are a lot to fit in, thus Australia's race being followed a week later by Malaysia's, with China's a fortnight later before the first of the European races, in Spain.

As in the past two years, this is the first of two races in Spain, largely thanks to the boom in popularity of F1 in the country since Fernando Alonso's recent world titles. That he will be racing for Ferrari fits with F1's image even better. Seven weeks after Barcelona's go, the European GP will be held again around the port area in Valencia, albeit this time a couple of months earlier than before in an attempt to avoid the tarmac-melting heat there in high summer.

Like Valencia, the race at Istanbul Park in Turkey is also kept away from the hottest months, while its position on an island in the St Laurence River in Quebec keeps the Canadian GP relatively cool, although it's a circuit that takes its toll on the cars come what may as so much of its lap is spent with the engines running at maximum revs. Then, of course, there are concrete walls enclosing almost all of its lap, making any little slip a big one...

After that, the races move to northern Europe, although Hungary in August is seldom less than very hot and humid.

After much debate, the British GP remains at Silverstone after a year or so of waiting to see whether Donington Park could come up with the finance to reinvent itself and take over the hosting rights.

South Korea has been striving for years to take its place in the World Championship and now it will, with a stunning new circuit built on the coast in the south-west of the county. As it's unlikely to finish being built until July, the teams will travel there with a considerable degree of guesswork on set-up.

Offered a year off to catch its breath after the Lewis Hamilton/Felipe Massa title shoot-out in 2008, the Brazilian GP at Interlagos was due to host the season-closer again, but its battered facilities will in fact be visited before Abu Dhabi's Yas Marina circuit as in 2009.

All in all, the Formula One World Championship has a diverse range of track types, day racing, night racing, cool venues, hot venues and the scope for another season of ebbs and flows in form as teams have to learn to accept that some venues will favour their cars and drivers, and others will not.

BAHRAIN

The first of two grands prix in the Gulf, Bahrain's circuit was made to look bland by Abu Dhabi's, but it provides some great corners and a challenge for drivers to attack.

Whether slotted into the F1 calendar at the start of the season or near the end, it's still a shock when the teams turn up in Bahrain, as the conditions seem so alien. The race facilities are tip-top, but there's no escaping the fact that the circuit is surrounded by dusty, rocky desert. Cosmopolitan Monaco or verdant Spa-Francorchamps it most certainly is not.

Yet, for Formula One's seventh visit, the circuit comes as less of a shock as teams know precisely what to expect.

The circuit has a good flow to it, as well as an exciting start and finish to the lap.

Turn 1 is a trademark of circuit designer Hermann Tilke, as it's approached down a long straight into a corner that doubles back onto itself. Overtaking is welcomed here and is more than likely.

Get out of shape, though, and a driver will lose places at Turn 2 that follows almost immediately or at least fall into the clutches of a chasing driver who will then try to slipstream past on the long run up to the hairpin at Turn 4.

The downhill esses through Turns 5 to 7 are spectacular, but in many ways the best is saved for the end of the lap, with Turn 14, a tight right-hander onto the start/finish straight just right for some late-braking or at least for getting into position to make a move past the pits.

INSIDE TRACK

BAHRAIN GRAND PRIX

Date:	**14 March**
Circuit name:	**Bahrain International Circuit**
Circuit length:	**3.366 miles/5.417km**
Number of laps:	**57**
Telephone:	**00 973 406222**
Website:	**www.bahraingp.com.bh**

PREVIOUS WINNERS

2004	**Michael Schumacher**	FERRARI
2005	**Fernando Alonso**	RENAULT
2006	**Fernando Alonso**	RENAULT
2007	**Felipe Massa**	FERRARI
2008	**Felipe Massa**	FERRARI
2009	**Jenson Button**	BRAWN

Formula One and Bahrain: Arab drivers have yet to make a splash on the racing scene, but 22-year-old Hamad Al Fardan is the highest ranked, having raced in British and German Formula Three then contested the GP2 Asia series before dominating Formula Renault V6 Asia last year. Salman Al Khalifa, who raced in F3, seems to have fallen by the wayside, showing the lack of strength in depth, which isn't surprising with so little racing at home.

Trickiest corner: Turn 12 wins the prize, not just because it's a fifth gear sweeper taken at over 150mph, but because drivers can never discount that it will feel different from the previous lap, since dust is a perennial problem as it blows in from the surrounding desert.

Do you remember when?: F1 came to Bahrain for the first time in 2004 and fittingly, since it's the most famous team to people new to racing, Ferrari dominated, with Michael Schumacher leading Rubens Barrichello home for a one-two, with Jenson Button advancing to third for BAR.

Who designed it?: Hermann Tilke, whose decision to split the circuit so that the area around the pit and paddock is "oasis" with heavily-watered grass verges, and the rest as desert helps add some character.

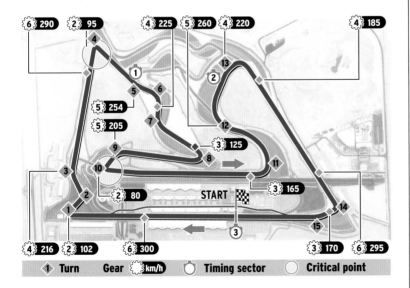

Turn ◆   **Gear**   **km/h**   **Timing sector** ○   **Critical point** ○

2009 POLE TIME: TRULLI (TOYOTA), 1M33.431S, 129.696MPH/208.725KPH
2009 WINNER'S AVERAGE SPEED: 125.179MPH/201.456KPH 2009

FASTEST LAP: TRULLI (TOYOTA), 1M34.556S, 128.033MPH/206.049KPH
LAP RECORD: M SCHUMACHER (FERRARI), 1M30.252S, 134.260MPH/216.061KPH, 2004

MELBOURNE

Traditionally the home of the first round, it will feel odd to be hosting the second, but it will still provide sunshine and spectacular racing on this stop-start circuit around a lake.

From time to time, there is talk of Melbourne giving up hosting the Australian Grand Prix, usually down to the cost of hosting it. Arch-rival Sydney suggests that it will take over, but its Eastern Creek raceway is out of town and would need considerable development. The beauty of Melbourne's Albert Park is that it is right in the city, with the towers of the central business district providing a distinctive backdrop.

The teams and drivers like racing in Melbourne, and that's not just because the hotels are both close by and excellent, and the choice of restaurants wide, but because it's a good track with first-rate facilities. Furthermore, the crowd is always a good size, on all three days, providing a real atmosphere to their activities.

The track does have a flow to it as it runs clockwise around the lake, but this is frequently broken by chicanes and 90-degree corners. The first two corners are effectively an esse, thankfully with a large gravel trap to catch the cars that get it wrong at the start. Hemmed in by concrete barriers, the track feels narrow until it reaches Turn 6 and then runs across open landscape along the far side of the lake.

It's fast, but with a few blind corner entries before drivers have to brake hard for Turn 13 before everything becomes a bit right-left-right for the rest of the lap.

INSIDE TRACK

AUSTRALIAN GRAND PRIX

Date:	**28 March**
Circuit name:	**Albert Park**
Circuit length:	**3.295 miles/5.3km**
Number of laps:	**58**
Telephone:	**00 61 3 92587100**
Website:	**www.grandprix.com.au**

PREVIOUS WINNERS

2000	**Michael Schumacher** FERRARI
2001	**Michael Schumacher** FERRARI
2002	**Michael Schumacher** FERRARI
2003	**David Coulthard** McLAREN
2004	**Michael Schumacher** FERRARI
2005	**Giancarlo Fisichella** RENAULT
2006	**Fernando Alonso** RENAULT
2007	**Kimi Raikkonen** FERRARI
2008	**Lewis Hamilton** McLAREN
2009	**Jenson Button** BRAWN

Formula One and Australia: Australia has hosted grands prix at only two circuits, in Adelaide and Melbourne, and it had to wait until 1985 for the first of those, which is a surprise, as Jack Brabham put the country on the map back in 1959 when he won the first of his three drivers' titles. Alan Jones also had his winning days behind him when the country took its World Championship bow. Adelaide's street circuit gave way to Melbourne's Albert Park in 1996, where the race has remained ever since.

Trickiest corner: Turn 1 never fails to provide action on lap 1, but Turn 3 is better for overtaking throughout the race.

Do you remember when?: Martin Brundle was still a driver in 1996 and gave his future colleagues a chance to get excited. This on lap 1 when he rolled his Jordan over the pack at Turn 3 after colliding with David Coulthard's McLaren. Crashing back to earth, he scrambled out and was able to take the restart in the spare car, only to go out after clashing with Pedro Diniz's Ligier. It was to be his final season.

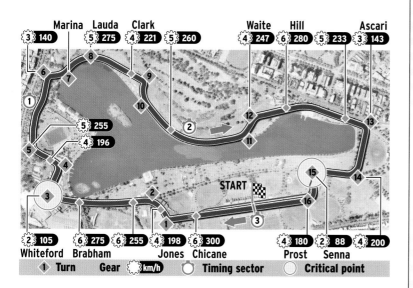

Marina	Lauda	Clark		Waite	Hill		Ascari
3 140	5 275	4 221	5 260	4 247	6 280	5 233	3 143

5 255
4 196

START

Whiteford	Brabham		Jones	Chicane		Prost	Senna	
2 105	6 275	6 255	4 198	6 300		4 180	2 88	4 200

1 Turn   Gear   km/h   ○ Timing sector   ○ Critical point

2009 POLE TIME: BUTTON (BRAWN), 1M26.202S, 137.607MPH/221/457KPH
2009 WINNER'S AVERAGE SPEED: 121.649MPH/195.775KPH

2009 FASTEST LAP: ROSBERG (WILLIAMS), 1M27.706S, 135.252MPH/217.667KPH
LAP RECORD: **M SCHUMACHER (FERRARI), 1M24.125S, 141.016MPH/226.933KPH, 2004**

SEPANG

It's always hot and very humid in Malaysia, with rain a constant threat, but the greatest feature of the Sepang circuit is that it remains one of the best for racing.

Last year revealed that pushing the Malaysian GP start time back by two hours to fit in better with the European TV audience had its drawbacks, as light ran out before play could resume after the race had to be stopped because of a tropical downpour that left drivers aquaplaning off the circuit. This year, the start time has been shifted again, being moved forward by an hour, to 16:00.

With the race being held at the same time of year, there remains the danger of one of the tropical storms that tend to arrive in the late afternoon, but at least there will be one more hour's worth of light with which to play.

Rain or no rain, the circuit is a gem, with perhaps the best flow of any circuit bar Istanbul Park. It's also made for overtaking, with the long straights into the tight first and last corners tailor-made for having a go at getting past the car ahead.

In between, there are some amazingly challenging sections, notably the stretch from Turn 4 to Turn 8 and then from Turn 11 down to Turn 14, where a good driver really can make a difference.

Corner exit speeds from the corners onto the two long straights are of paramount importance, both to help a driver make an overtaking bid or, equally, to defend against one.

INSIDE TRACK

MALAYSIAN GRAND PRIX

Date:	**4 April**
Circuit name:	**Sepang Circuit**
Circuit length:	**3.444 miles/5.542km**
Number of laps:	**56**
Telephone:	**00 60 3 85262000**
Website:	**www.malaysiangp.com.my**

PREVIOUS WINNERS

2000	**Michael Schumacher** FERRARI
2001	**Michael Schumacher** FERRARI
2002	**Ralf Schumacher** WILLIAMS
2003	**Kimi Raikkonen** McLAREN
2004	**Michael Schumacher** FERRARI
2005	**Fernando Alonso** RENAULT
2006	**Giancarlo Fisichella** RENAULT
2007	**Fernando Alonso** McLAREN
2008	**Kimi Raikkonen** FERRARI
2009	**Jenson Button** BRAWN

Formula One and Malaysia: There has been racing in Malaysia since the 1960s, largely at Shah Alam, as well as on temporary street circuits. But, its round of the World Endurance Championship for sportscars in 1985 apart, the country truly moved onto the international stage when Sepang hosted a grand prix for the first time in 1999. Only Alex Yoong has reached F1, with Minardi, but Malaysian ownership of the revamped Lotus team should change all that.

Trickiest corner: Turn 12 sorts the men from the boys. This fifth gear left-hander is a 155mph kink, approached slightly downhill then flattening. Off the racing line, it's very dusty and catches more than a few out.

Do you remember when?: The first Malaysian GP, the penultimate race of 1999, still stands out for the way that Ferrari used Michael Schumacher – returning from a broken leg – to help Eddie Irvine escape to victory, holding off McLaren's points leader Mika Hakkinen. The Ferraris were then found to have oversized bargeboards, but allowed to keep their results.

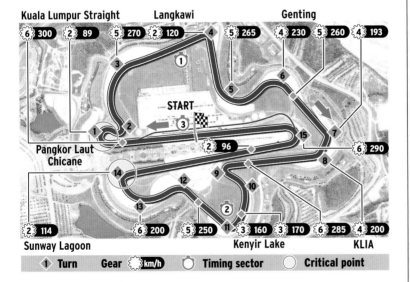

2009 POLE TIME: **BUTTON (BRAWN)**, 1M35.181S, 130.261MPH/209.636KPH
2009 WINNER'S AVERAGE SPEED: 115.407MPH/185.730KPH 2009

FASTEST LAP: **BUTTON (BRAWN)**, 1M36.461S, 128.303MPH/206.484KPH
LAP RECORD: **MONTOYA (WILLIAMS)**, 1M34.223S, 131.595MPH/211.772KPH, 2004

SHANGHAI

Stunning in its concept, yet flawed in its execution might describe some of China's myriad building projects, but the main flaw at this ultra-modern circuit is that it's too big.

At 3.39 miles, its lap length is only just over average for a grand prix circuit, but it's the circuit infrastructure that is oversized, with grandstands for 200,000 spectators, which is way in excess of the number that come.

Quite simply, ticket prices remain too high to attract the man in the street and so the entire section of grandstands at the complex of corners (Turns 11 to 13) that feed the cars onto the back straight is covered with sponsors' banners to mask the fact that they are deserted. It was a case of building for a trend that hasn't caught on.

The grandstands opposite the pits are unbelievably tall, yet look normal until you get a reference for scale and realize that they are as tall as many downtown blocks of flats. Sit at the top and a fan will have a view over much of the circuit, as it's all flat bar the Turn 1-3 complex.

Built on reclaimed marshland, with sunken piles of polystyrene offering stability, the circuit is an engineering masterpiece. Stretches of the circuit challenge the drivers too, most notably the mirror-image sets of corners at Turns 1-3 and Turns 11-13, the first coming off the start/finish straight, the second feeding onto the extremely long back straight. An ability to brake as late as possible for Turn 14 at the far end of this also gives drivers an advantage if they're trying to overtake.

INSIDE TRACK

CHINESE GRAND PRIX

Date:	**18 April**
Circuit name:	**Shanghai International Circuit**
Circuit length:	**3.390 miles/5.450km**
Number of laps:	**57**
Telephone:	**00 86 2162520000**
Website:	**www.f1china.com.cn**

PREVIOUS WINNERS

2004	**Rubens Barrichello**	FERRARI
2005	**Fernando Alonso**	RENAULT
2006	**Michael Schumacher**	FERRARI
2007	**Kimi Raikkonen**	FERRARI
2008	**Lewis Hamilton**	McLAREN
2009	**Sebastian Vettel**	RED BULL

Formula One and China: Chinese progress in almost all sports on the Olympic spectrum demonstrates how important the country's overlords rate winning on the world stage to be. Yet their drivers are taking longer to scale the heights, with not one having reached F1. Yet, it's just five and a half years since the country's first grand prix and so patience should be allowed as Ho-Pin Tung and Congfu Cheng continue their ascent through the international formulae.

Trickiest corner: Turn 3 is really difficult, as the track drops as soon as it starts turning to the left out of Turn 2, with a driver who has been too tight through Turn 2 losing speed, but those who had gone too wide unable to get onto the right line to exit with as much momentum as possible.

Do you remember when?: Michael Schumacher didn't always get things right, and one of his most inexplicable errors came in the 2005 Chinese GP. He had taken Christijan Albers off on his recognition lap, then had to start his Ferrari from the pit lane and bowed out by spinning off when the field was running behind the safety car.

Who designed it?: Hermann Tilke shaped this one in the marshland surrounding Shanghai in his trademark style with a long straight into a tight opening corner, with room to pass.

Turn ◆	Gear ✿	🔘 km/h	⏱ Timing sector	○ Critical point

2009 POLE TIME: VETTEL (RED BULL),
1M36.184S, 126.773MPH/204.021KPH
2009 WINNER'S AVERAGE SPEED:
96.611MPH/155.480KPH 2009

FASTEST LAP: BARRICHELLO (BRAWN),
1M52.592S, 108.298MPH/174.289KPH
LAP RECORD: M SCHUMACHER (FERRARI),
1M32.238S, 132.202MPH/212.759KPH, 2004

BARCELONA

The Circuit de Catalunya is excellent, but it is not an excellent racing circuit, with the fans in the grandstands all too often disappointed by a lack of overtaking action.

What's the main difference between Barcelona's Circuit de Catalunya and Valencia's street circuit? No, it's not that one hosts the Spanish GP and the other the European GP. It's that the former is well supported and that the latter, after just two years, is facing a decline.

Also, the Circuit de Catalunya, although not well known for overtaking, does offer a chance to get up close to a car ahead down the long start/finish straight and then attempt a passing move into Turn 1, Elf.

In the days when testing wasn't so limited, the Circuit de Catalunya was a second home to the teams, as its suitability for testing made it frequently visited. The reason that it was so useful wasn't just the warm Spanish weather but its mixture of corners, with fast, medium and low-speed bends helping the engineers understand their cars' behaviour.

The run to Elf is downhill and the esse that feeds into Turn 2 on the level before the track climbs up through Turn 3 and all the way to Repsol and doubling back before climbing further to Turn 5. Then it drops, runs flat to Turn 7 then fires the car up to a crest at Campsa before dropping again to La Caixa. Hard on the brakes here, the drivers then accelerate up through Banc Sabadel and Europcar before dipping back to the start/finish line.

INSIDE TRACK

SPANISH GRAND PRIX

Date:	9 May
Circuit name:	Circuit de Catalunya
Circuit length:	2.875 miles/4.627km
Number of laps:	65
Telephone:	00 34 93 5719771
Website:	www.circuitcat.com

PREVIOUS WINNERS

2000	**Mika Hakkinen** McLAREN
2001	**Michael Schumacher** FERRARI
2002	**Michael Schumacher** FERRARI
2003	**Michael Schumacher** FERRARI
2004	**Michael Schumacher** FERRARI
2005	**Kimi Raikkonen** McLAREN
2006	**Fernando Alonso** RENAULT
2007	**Felipe Massa** FERRARI
2008	**Kimi Raikkonen** FERRARI
2009	**Jenson Button** BRAWN

Formula One and Spain: It's hard to believe now that Spain has two grands prix and a team of its own that the country was an underachiever at this level until Fernando Alonso came along. "Fon" de Portago showed promise in the 1950s, but died at the wheel. Then there was not one star in the making until Alonso. The grand prix moved around between Barcelona, Madrid and Jerez, but only found a home of any permanence when it settled on the Circuit de Catalunya in 1991.

Trickiest corner: The circuit has been modified in recent years, with the chicane put in before the final corner taking the bite out of what had been a fast corner. Since then, Campsa has been the toughest, as it's taken over a crest that takes commitment when the driver's brain is suggesting a lift off the throttle.

Do you remember when?: Alonso sent the crowd wild. It was in 2006, at his fifth attempt, and he upset the odds by taking his Michelin-shod Renault to victory over Michael Schumacher's Bridgestone-tyred Ferrari.

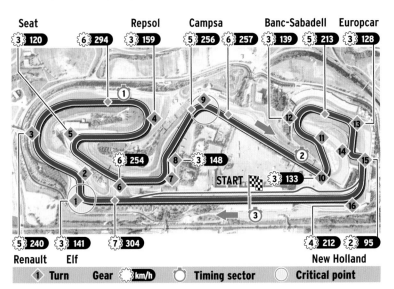

Seat — 3 120
Repsol — 6 294 / 3 159
Campsa — 5 256 / 6 257
Banc-Sabadell — 3 139 / 5 213
Europcar — 3 128

Renault — 5 240 / 3 141
Elf — 7 304
New Holland — 4 212 / 2 95

6 254 / 8 / 3 148
START / 3 133

♦ Turn   Gear   km/h   ○ Timing sector   ○ Critical point

2009 POLE TIME: **RAIKKONEN (FERRARI)**, 1M21.813S, 126.508MPH/203.595KPH
2008 WINNER'S AVERAGE SPEED: 116.454MPH/187.415KPH 2008

FASTEST LAP: **RAIKKONEN (FERRARI)**, 1M21.670S, 127.500MPH/205.192KPH
LAP RECORD: **RAIKKONEN (FERRARI)**, 1M21.670S, 127.500MPH/205.192KPH, 2008

MONACO

Monaco is antiquated and narrow, with next to no chance to overtake. The working conditions for the teams are truly appalling too, but it remains the face of Formula One.

Imagine Formula One without Monaco and it would be a blander sport by far. Everyone involved acknowledges that it's not the most exciting circuit but, to the public, it's the most glamorous, the most colourful and the one that they would most want to attend. So, it stays and so it should.

Thank goodness for this, as Formula One has been shedding its traditional circuits over the past decade and it's so important to keep this living link with the past. In Monaco's case, that means all the way back to its first grand prix in 1929.

Facilities for the teams were improved considerably a few years ago, with pit garages almost worthy of the name, whereas

before they had been closer to cupboards.

The running surface is little changed, though, and it's still a steep and narrow street circuit. Passing is hard, but hitting the barriers is not and the trickiest part of all seems to be the approach to the Nouvelle Chicane after the drivers have burst back into the daylight after speeding through the tunnel and reckon that they have a sniff of a passing move as they arrive on the harbourside, then find out that there isn't enough space...

If you want to see overtaking, your best bet is to watch the start and the massed charge to Ste Devote. After that, it's few and far between.

INSIDE TRACK

MONACO GRAND PRIX

Date:	16 May
Circuit name:	Monte Carlo Circuit
Circuit length:	2.075 miles/3.339km
Number of laps:	78
Telephone:	00 377 93152600
Website:	www.acm.mc

PREVIOUS WINNERS

2000	**David Coulthard**	McLAREN
2001	**Michael Schumacher**	FERRARI
2002	**David Coulthard**	McLAREN
2003	**Juan Pablo Montoya**	WILLIAMS
2004	**Jarno Trulli**	RENAULT
2005	**Kimi Raikkonen**	McLAREN
2006	**Fernando Alonso**	RENAULT
2007	**Fernando Alonso**	McLAREN
2008	**Lewis Hamilton**	McLAREN
2009	**Jenson Button**	BRAWN

Formula One and Monaco: Many a grand prix driver lives in Monaco, but that's for the tax breaks first and foremost, as there are certainly cheaper places to live if they just want sunshine. However, having held a grand prix for more than 80 years, it's not surprising that it has enticed some of the real Monegasques to race, with Andre Chiron the pick of the bunch, finishing third here for Maserati in 1950.

Trickiest corner: Massenet, the left-hander at the top of the hill before the cars burst into Casino Square is very narrow and its entry is blind. The fact that it's approached at 170mph in sixth outlines just how difficult it is as drivers carry as much momentum into it as possible.

Do you remember when?: One of the most extraordinary of races at Monaco came in 1968 when Johnny Servoz-Gavin burst onto the scene in a Matra. It was his first start in a pukka F1 car, after trying the race in 1967 in an F2 car. He qualified on the front row, led away and was pulling clear, until he clipped a barrier and broke a driveshaft. Graham Hill went on to win.

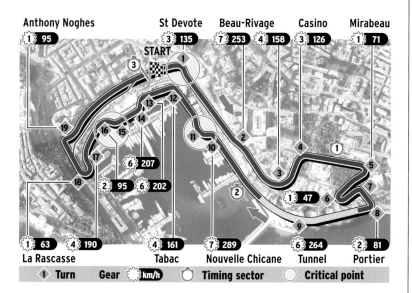

Anthony Noghes	St Devote	Beau-Rivage	Casino	Mirabeau
1 95	3 135	7 253 4 158	3 126	1 71

START

La Rascasse	Tabac	Nouvelle Chicane	Tunnel	Portier
1 63 4 190	4 161	7 289	6 264	2 81

6 207
2 95 6 202
1 47

1 Turn   Gear   km/h   ◯ Timing sector   ◯ Critical point

2009 POLE TIME: **BUTTON (BRAWN)**, 1M14.902S, 99.748MPH/160.529KPH	FASTEST LAP: **MASSA (FERRARI)**, 1M15.154S, 99.414MPH/159.991KPH
2009 WINNER'S AVERAGE SPEED: 96.415MPH/155.166KPH 2009	LAP RECORD: **M SCHUMACHER (FERRARI)**, 1M14.439S, 100.373MPH/161.527KPH, 2004

ISTANBUL

This is a magnificent circuit, a flowing strip of tarmac that stretches the drivers like few others. It's just a shame that so few fans turn up there to watch the action.

A Formula One car is spectacular enough driving flat-out in a straight line, all speed and noise. What takes it to a level higher is watching one brake hard, scrubbing off speed at an unbelievable rate. Most astonishing of all, though, is the sight of an F1 car being driven at speed through a fifth or sixth gear corner, especially if there is an immediate change of direction.

Istanbul Park is one of a handful of circuits worldwide that offers that option, with the early part of its lap replete with dipping, swerving but above all fast sequences of bends.

Better still, there's Turn 8, a triple-apex corner that really sorts the men from the boys. There can be no doubt that this is the greatest of the circuits from Hermann Tilke's design office, with its use of gradient adding to its appeal, especially out of Turn 1 as this tight left-hander mimics the first turn at Interlagos, providing an exciting start to the opening lap.

Some of the tighter corners provide excitement, too, such as Turn 10, where Sebastian Vettel tripped up on lap 1 last year and handed the lead to Jenson Button.

Then, of course, there's Turn 12 at the end of the back straight, where drivers are hard on the anchors, and there's always the scope for a dive down the inside.

INSIDE TRACK

TURKISH GRAND PRIX

Date:	**30 May**
Circuit name:	**Istanbul Park Circuit**
Circuit length:	**3.317 miles/5.338km**
Number of laps:	**58**
Telephone:	**00 90 216 418 5222**
Website:	**www.formula1-istanbul.com**

PREVIOUS WINNERS

2005	**Kimi Raikkonen** McLAREN
2006	**Felipe Massa** FERRARI
2007	**Felipe Massa** FERRARI
2008	**Felipe Massa** FERRARI
2009	**Jenson Button** BRAWN

Formula One and Turkey: Turkey is still awaiting its first F1 driver. That's not surprising, though, as Istanbul Park, which was opened only in 2005, was their first permanent circuit, thus meaning that up-and-coming drivers had nowhere to hone their craft before then. Jason Tahinci reached GP2, but his career has stalled. With the country's rugged terrain more suited to rallying, it's not surprising that most aspiring drivers have headed in that direction.

Trickiest corner: Without a shadow of a doubt, Turn 8 is the hardest of the circuit's 14 corners. Approached in sixth gear, drivers have to hook fourth and then hit the apex at not one or two but three points as it kinks ever more to the left, with exit speed critical for a lap that a driver can be proud off. It's very easy to spin here.

Do you remember when?: Kimi Raikkonen was chasing Fernando Alonso in the championship in 2005 when F1 made its first visit. He led all the way, but needed all the support he could get from his McLaren team-mate Juan Pablo Montoya in keeping Renault's Fernando Alonso at bay. But the Colombian slipped wide on the penultimate lap and Alonso slipped past.

Who designed it?: Formula One's "in-house" track designer Hermann Tilke can hold up his hand for this one, with pride.

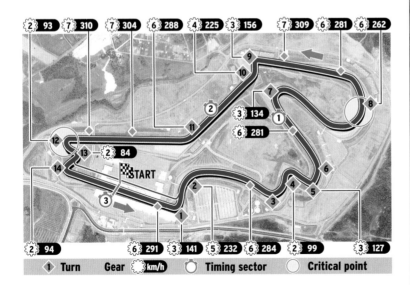

2 93	7 310	7 304	6 288	4 225	3 156	7 309	6 281	6 262	

2 84

3 134
6 281

2 94   6 291   3 141   5 232   6 284   2 99   3 127

◆ **Turn**   **Gear** ◐ **km/h**   ○ **Timing sector**   ○ **Critical point**

START

2009 POLE TIME: VETTEL (RED BULL), 1M28.316S, 135.210MPH/217.600KPH
2009 WINNER'S AVERAGE SPEED: 133.485MPH/214.824KPH 2009

FASTEST LAP: BUTTON (BRAWN), 1M27.579S, 136.342MPH/219.422KPH
LAP RECORD: MONTOYA (McLAREN), 1M24.770S, 138.096MPH/222.167KPH, 2005

MONTREAL

The grand prix teams issued a cheer last autumn when it was announced that Montreal was returning, even though it's a tough, car-breaking circuit and has walls that bite.

The reason that everyone involved loves the Canadian GP is largely down to the city of Montreal, as it's cosmopolitan and attractive, a place where they can all meet and eat away from the track, unlike when racing at circuits in the countryside.

Another reason is that it provides dramatic racing. This is largely down to the fact that there is an esse into the first corner, a hairpin for having a go at passing, and an exciting chicane to complete the lap, where even the smallest of slips can fire a car into the wall.

Built on a narrow island in the St Laurence River, the circuit seems to be more water than land, as there's a lake in its middle and the 1976 Olympic Games rowing lake right behind the paddock. In fact, so tight is the space, that everything feels cramped here but unusually personal too.

The first corner sequence, through the esse (Coin Senna) and into the Island Hairpin that follows straight after it, is always the scene of good and bad passing attempts on the opening lap. What follows, the back section, is a sequence of hard acceleration and esse-style corners through which drivers have to find a flow. Then the cars burst from the tree-lined section into the sunlight and jostle to attack into the far hairpin.

INSIDE TRACK

CANADIAN GRAND PRIX

Date:	**13 June**
Circuit name:	**Circuit Gilles Villeneuve**
Circuit length:	**2.710 miles/4.361km**
Number of laps:	**70**
Telephone:	**001 514 350 0000**
Website:	**www.grandprix.ca**

PREVIOUS WINNERS

1999	**Mika Hakkinen** McLAREN
2000	**Michael Schumacher** FERRARI
2001	**Ralf Schumacher** WILLIAMS
2002	**Michael Schumacher** FERRARI
2003	**Michael Schumacher** FERRARI
2004	**Michael Schumacher** FERRARI
2005	**Kimi Raikkonen** McLAREN
2006	**Fernando Alonso** RENAULT
2007	**Lewis Hamilton** McLAREN
2008	**Robert Kubica** BMW SAUBER

Formula One and Canada: If it wasn't for the Villeneuve family, Canada wouldn't have much to boast about. Gilles set the ball rolling in the late 1970s. He won six grands prix, but played second fiddle to Ferrari team-mate in 1979 when Jody Schekcter took the title. Son Jacques was World Champion for Williams in 1997. Before the Canadian GP came to Montreal in 1978, it was held at Mosport Park from 1967, with two years at St Jovite in the hills.

Trickiest corner: Judging by the list of people who have crashed there, the final chicane must be the toughest, as it's approached at 200mph and requires dropping to second gear and going through without catching too much kerb, as they frequently tip cars into the wall.

Do you remember when?: In 1978, Gilles Villeneuve gave his home crowd everything they could have hoped for on F1's first visit to Montreal, winning for Ferrari after Lotus stand-in Jean-Pierre Jarier led most of the race before retiring. It came as no surprise when the circuit was immediately renamed in his honour.

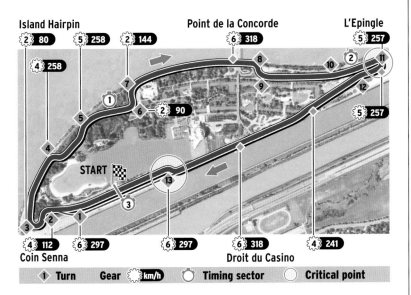

Island Hairpin — Point de la Concorde — **L'Epingle**

Coin Senna — **Droit du Casino**

◆ **Turn**   **Gear**   km/h   ○ **Timing sector**   ○ **Critical point**

2008 POLE TIME: **HAMILTON (McLAREN),**
1M17.886S, 125.260MPH/201.587KPH
2008 WINNER'S AVERAGE SPEED:
118.077MPH/190.027KPH

2008 FASTEST LAP: **RAIKKONEN (FERRARI),**
1M17.387S, 126.058MPH/202.871KPH
LAP RECORD: **BARRICHELLO (FERRARI),**
1M13.622S, 132.511MPH/213.246KPH, 2004

VALENCIA

There was talk that the Valencia street circuit had run its course as a grand prix venue after just two renditions, but it was instantly put back onto the calendar for 2010.

The reason that the sport's insiders had thought that Valencia would become a venue confined to Formula One history was that the crowds weren't strong for its inaugural grand prix in 2008 and appeared to have dwindled last year. Furthermore, the backdrop looked shabby, although improved in 2009, and worst of all, it offered no scope whatsoever for overtaking. A procession around a dull-looking circuit is no recipe for a spectacle, doing no good to anyone.

However, it lives to fight another day and being placed earlier in the calendar ought to help the fans who chose to sit in the grandstands around the dockside track, as the heat in June, although hot, is always a few degrees cooler than the 40-plus degree days endured by last year's crowds, almost all of which left them sitting in the full sun.

Built around the docks of this working port, there is no gradient change to enjoy, just a series of tightish corners interspersed with several arcing straights and, unusually, a sprint across a bridge between Turns 9 and 10. Technically difficult, it's a horror for drivers trying to overtake a slower car as there simply isn't a good place for passing and it's very dusty when they move off the racing line. The one real chance to overtake is at Turn 2 on the opening lap.

INSIDE TRACK

EUROPEAN GRAND PRIX

Date:	**27 June**
Circuit name:	**Valencia Circuit**
Circuit length:	**3.401 miles/5.474km**
Number of laps:	**57**
Telephone:	**00 34 963164007**
Website:	**www.valenciastreetcircuit.co**

PREVIOUS WINNERS

2008	**Felipe Massa** Ferrari
2009	**Rubens Barrichello** Brawn

Formula One and Europe: The European GP is an honorary title that has been passed around since it was used in 1923 as an extra title for the Italian GP at Monza, simply being added to the race's name. This all changed in 1983, when it was granted as the title for a race held at Brands Hatch in addition to that year's British GP at Silverstone. The Nurburgring, Donington Park and Jerez were also awarded the title when their countries held their grand prix at other tracks.

Trickiest corner: Turn 14 is one of many where the merest slip off the line will be punished with a trip off the line onto the dusty area beyond and, here, that means the barriers on the outside. To make matters tougher still, this one has got a blind entry.

Do you remember when?: Having hosted but two grands prix to date, there's not much to remember yet, but the 2008 grand prix was the more exciting of the two. The race belonged, almost from start to finish, to Ferrari's Felipe Massa, with Lewis Hamilton second and Robert Kubica finishing a distant third, with home driver Fernando Alonso taken out on lap 1 by Kazuki Nakajima.

Who designed it?: Hermann Tilke penned the shape, having to work with what was already there and fit it over the existing docks so that it offered a variety of corners and, for interest, crossed the harbour bridge.

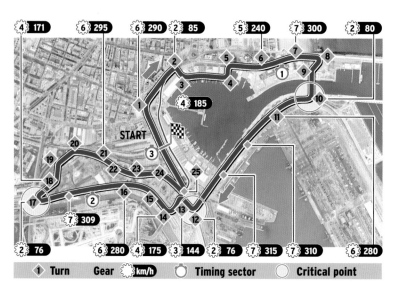

4 171	6 295	6 290	2 85	5 240	7 300	2 80

4 185

START

7 309

2 76	6 280	4 175	3 144	2 76	7 315	7 310	6 280

① Turn   Gear ❋km/h   ○ Timing sector   ○ Critical point

2009 POLE TIME: **HAMILTON (McLAREN),**
1M39.498S, 121.824MPH/196.056KPH
2009 WINNER'S AVERAGE SPEED:
120.138MPH/193.344KPH 2009

FASTEST LAP: **GLOCK (TOYOTA), 1M38.683S,**
122.837MPH/197.687KPH
LAP RECORD: **GLOCK (TOYOTA), 1M38.683S,**
122.837MPH/197.687KPH, 2009

SILVERSTONE

Silverstone had to wait on the sidelines while its nominal replacement, Donington Park, fiddled. Now, it's back to fill the gap and keep the British GP on the calendar.

Silverstone has had a tense decade as F1 boss Bernie Ecclestone has denigrated it. Perhaps this has been part of a plan to coerce the government to dip its hand into its pocket and finance a comprehensive modernization programme, perhaps not. Either way, British fans were left with the impression that he wanted to take his show anywhere else.

The trouble is, it's only governments of developing nations who care to finance their turn under the media spotlight.

When the Donington Park deal looked set only for failure due to a lack of finance, Silverstone and Ecclestone reopened negotiations, but the former wanted a new long-term deal, the latter just a one-year stop-gap. Eventually, sense prevailed, after considerable lobbying by the teams who didn't want to lose another classic venue. It's also the home race for the majority of them.

Silverstone is loved by the drivers for the challenge it offers, possessing a flow to its lay-out, with the sight of cars tackling the Becketts sweepers a joy to behold.

The track is being given a facelift for 2010, with a new pits complex located between Club and Abbey corners before a new section of circuit kinks the cars right onto an infield loop before rejoining the 2009 circuit at Priory.

At the time of writing, it hasn't been decided whether the new circuit will be used or held back for the 2011 British GP.

INSIDE TRACK

BRITISH GRAND PRIX

Date:	11 July
Circuit name:	Silverstone
Circuit length:	3.523 miles/5.670km
Number of laps:	60
Telephone:	01327 857271
Website:	www.silverstone.co.uk

PREVIOUS WINNERS

2000	**David Coulthard**	McLAREN
2001	**Mika Hakkinen**	McLAREN
2002	**Michael Schumacher**	FERRARI
2003	**Rubens Barrichello**	FERRARI
2004	**Michael Schumacher**	FERRARI
2005	**Juan Pablo Montoya**	McLAREN
2006	**Fernando Alonso**	RENAULT
2007	**Kimi Raikkonen**	FERRARI
2008	**Lewis Hamilton**	McLAREN
2009	**Sebastian Vettel**	RED BULL

Formula One and Britain: This goes back to the opening round of the inaugural World Championship in 1950, held at Silverstone. Liverpool's Aintree circuit had a spell hosting the race from 1955, before Brands Hatch took over, alternating with Silverstone, until 1986. Britain is also home to more champions than any other country, and the majority of teams.

Trickiest corner: Without a doubt, this is the Becketts esses, one of the toughest corners the drivers face all year. It's a right-left-right sequence taken in fourth where balance is all as the cars change direction very quickly.

Do you remember when?: Lewis Hamilton walked on water in 2008. He'd promised great things in 2007, then failed to deliver. But, at his second attempt, when it was wet, dry and all conditions in between, he was supreme.

Who designed it?: Silverstone hasn't come from the pen of one architect. It has been organic in its growth since cars first raced around the access roads of the ex-World War II aerodrome, with nips and tucks since.

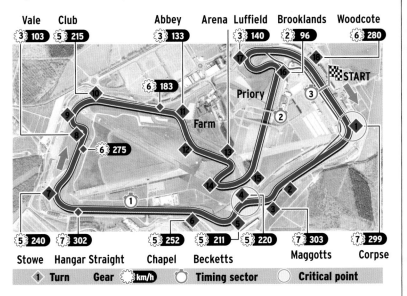

Vale	Club	Abbey	Arena	Luffield	Brooklands	Woodcote
3 103	**5** 215	**3** 133	**3** 140		**2** 96	**6** 280

START

Priory

Farm

6 183

6 275

Stowe	Hangar Straight	Chapel	Becketts	Maggotts	Corpse
5 240	**7** 302	**5** 252	**5** 211	**5** 220	**7** 303	**7** 299

◆ **Turn**   **Gear** ⚙ **km/h**   ⭘ **Timing sector**   ⭘ **Critical point**

2009 POLE TIME: **VETTEL (RED BULL)**, 1M19.509S, 144.618MPH/232.740KPH
2009 WINNER'S AVERAGE SPEED: **138.805MPH/223.385KPH**

2009 FASTEST LAP: **VETTEL (RED BULL)**, 1M20.735S, 142.442MPH/229.239KPH
LAP RECORD: **M SCHUMACHER (FERRARI)**, 1M18.739S, 146.059MPH/235.048KPH, 2004

HOCKENHEIM

Despite Michael Schumacher being followed by Sebastian Vettel as one of Formula One's main men, Germany is struggling to hold on to its grand prix, which is crazy.

Until 2006, Germany enjoyed two grands prix per year, much as Italy used to at Monza and Imola, and Spain does now with Barcelona and Valencia, to capitalize in the massive popularity of that one-man-winning-machine known as Michael Schumacher. However, since this arrangement stopped, Germany's two circuits - Hockenheim and the Nurburgring - have reached financial meltdown and have had to alternate. Going into 2009, Hockenheim was looking likely to be the first to drop its annual grand prix, as it simply couldn't afford the fees demanded to host the race.

However, after negotiation, it's still with us, ensuring a home grand prix not just for Vettel and his fellow German drivers but also for Mercedes-Benz. For one of the sport's most prominent manufacturers, the loss of a race on home turf would be unthinkable.

So, what of the circuit? Well, it is, like so many others, a shadow of its former self. Cut back in 2002 to lose the long, flat-out blasts through the forest for which it was so famous, the circuit largely runs now within the arena in front of the famously high-banked grandstands, with a far more open and high-speed loop up to the Spitzkehre hairpin before it feeds its way back to the arena again via a tight left in front of a standalone grandstand at Turn 8.

INSIDE TRACK

GERMAN GRAND PRIX

Date:	25 July
Circuit name:	Hockenheim
Circuit length:	2.842 miles/4.574km
Number of laps:	67
Telephone:	00 49 6205 95005
Website:	www.hockenheimring.de

PREVIOUS WINNERS	
1998	**Mika Hakkinen** McLAREN
1999	**Eddie Irvine** FERRARI
2000	**Rubens Barrichello** FERRARI
2001	**Ralf Schumacher** WILLIAMS
2002	**Michael Schumacher** FERRARI
2003	**Juan Pablo Montoya** WILLIAMS
2004	**Michael Schumacher** FERRARI
2005	**Fernando Alonso** RENAULT
2006	**Michael Schumacher** FERRARI
2008	**Lewis Hamilton** McLAREN

Formula One and Germany: Germany was an underachiever, with the exception of Mercedes before its withdrawal in 1955. Wolfgang von Trips was tipped to be World Champion, but died in 1961, and the wait lasted until 1994 when Michael Schumacher took the first of his seven titles. The 14-mile Nurburing Nordschleife was the home to the grand prix. Avus provided variety, but Hockenheim and the shortened Nurburgring have been the race's home ever since.

Trickiest corner: The Turn 2/3/4 complex is not only tight and twisty, as drivers drop from sixth to second, but getting the exit through fourth-gear Turn 4 is vital as it feeds onto the longest "straight" that arcs left all the way to the hairpin.

Do you remember when?: Gerhard Berger had a torrid 1997, missing three races with sinus problems. But he came back at Hockenheim and stuck his Benetton on pole, set fastest lap and won, having announced that he would be quitting at the end of the year, One of his replacements, Giancarlo Fisichella, pushed him hardest before retiring his Jordan.

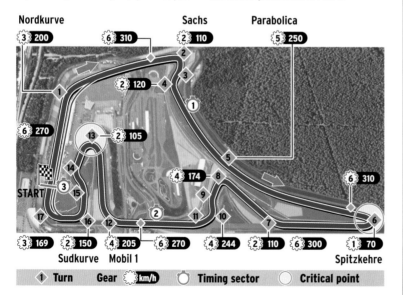

Nordkurve 3 200 | 6 310 | **Sachs** 2 110 | **Parabolica** 5 250
2 120 | 2
6 270 | 2 105 | 13
14
3 START | 15
17 | 16 | 12 | 2 | 11 | 10 | 7 | 6
3 169 | 2 150 | 4 205 | 6 270 | 4 244 | 2 110 | 6 300 | 1 70
Sudkurve Mobil 1 | **Spitzkehre**
4 174 | 8 | 9 | 5 | 6 310 | 1
6 270 (13) | 2 105

1 **Turn** Gear km/h ○ **Timing sector** ○ **Critical point**

2008 POLE TIME: **HAMILTON (McLAREN)**, 1M15.666S, 135.215MPH/217.608KPH
2008 WINNER'S AVERAGE SPEED: 125.076MPH/201.291KPH

2008 FASTEST LAP: **HEIDFELD (BMW SAUBER)**, 1M15.987S, 134.651MPH/216.700KPH
LAP RECORD: **RAIKKONEN (McLAREN)**, 1M14.917S, 138.685MPH/223.182KPH, 2004

HUNGARORING

If there was ever a race for the strategists, then this is it, for the Hungaroring is a track that twists so much, with only one straight, that passing is almost impossible.

On the plus side, the sun almost always shines here, so the televised images look great. There are huge crowds draped over the hillsides of this natural bowl, adding atmosphere. Yet, however you dress it up, this is not a circuit for racing.

The drivers, being drivers, will try, but there is precious little space for getting alongside another driver in an attempt to make a move.

Turn 1 remains the most obvious place, principally at the start of the grand prix, but the advent of KERS last year provided a few more chances during the race when a KERS-equipped car could be driven into the slipstream of another car then use the extra horsepower provided to pull off the move.

Lewis Hamilton even managed to use his KERS to drag past Mark Webber when he got out of shape exiting Turn 1 and then complete the passing move into Turn 2. Take the KERS away, though, and the races will return to being won and lost in the pits.

The fact that a grand prix is held in Hungary may not seem strange now, but it seemed revolutionary when it was invited into the World Championship in 1986 when the country was still behind the Iron Curtain, still under communist rule, but the huge crowds that turned up proved a burning desire to watch this most Western of sports.

INSIDE TRACK

HUNGARIAN GRAND PRIX

Date:	**1 August**
Circuit name:	**Hungaroring Circuit**
Circuit length:	**2.722 miles/4.381km**
Number of laps:	**70**
Telephone:	**00 36 2 844 1861**
Website:	**www.hungaroring.hu**

PREVIOUS WINNERS

1999	**Mika Hakkinen** McLAREN
2000	**Mika Hakkinen** McLAREN
2001	**Michael Schumacher** FERRARI
2002	**Rubens Barrichello** FERRARI
2003	**Fernando Alonso** RENAULT
2004	**Michael Schumacher** FERRARI
2005	**Kimi Raikkonen** McLAREN
2006	**Jenson Button** HONDA
2007	**Lewis Hamilton** McLAREN
2008	**Heikki Kovalainen** McLAREN
2009	**Lewis Hamilton** McLAREN

Formula One and Hungary: Motor racing in Hungary certainly didn't start when it had its first F1 race in 1986. Far from it, as there was much racing there in the pre-communist days, with the main circuit in Budapest's Nepliget Park and Tazio Nuvolari winning the first Hungarian GP for Alfa Romeo in 1936. Years before that, Hungarian driver Ferenc Szisz had the distinction of winning the first ever grand prix, the French, in 1906.

Trickiest corner: Approached at 180mph, Turn 4 is very fast and entered uphill before levelling out on the exit, with an awkward camber that catches out those who enter it too fast.

Do you remember when?: Michael Schumacher put on a masterclass in 1998. He was up against Mika Hakkinen, with the Finn leading away from pole ahead of McLaren team-mate David Coulthard. However, the Finn hadn't counted on Ross Brawn putting Schumacher's Ferrari onto a three-stop strategy. By the time Hakkinen realised what was happening, it was too late, and Schumacher won by nearly 10s.

---

5 105 | **3** 151 | **5** 243 | **6** 249 | **6** 271 | **2** 113 | **3** 132

START

5 241 | **3** 148 | **5** 209 | **7** 281 | **5** 224 | **5** 230 | **2** 93

◆ **Turn**   **Gear** ✳ **km/h**   ○ **Timing sector**   ○ **Critical point**

2009 POLE TIME: **ALONSO (RENAULT)**,
1M21.569S, 120.134MPH/193.337KPH
2009 WINNER'S AVERAGE SPEED:
117.308MPH/188.790KPH 2009

FASTEST LAP: **WEBBER (RED BULL)**,
1M21.931S, 119.612MPH/192.497KPH
LAP RECORD: **M SCHUMACHER (FERRARI)**,
19.071S, 123.828KPH/199.461KPH, 2004

SPA-FRANCORCHAMPS

This circuit is a true piece of art. It's a flat-out blast over hill and down vale, with the forest close enough to the track to enclose it and make it seem even more special.

Ask Formula One drivers their favourite circuit, and the majority will say Spa-Francorchamps. One visit will convince any fan that they are right, for the fast corners are fearsome. There's reward for the brave and even more so for a driver who can combine being gung-ho with an ability to be accurate enough to keep their momentum going.

For years, there was talk of one corner above all others: Eau Rouge. Only the best of the best would consider trying to take it without a lift off the throttle as the cars hit the compression where the downhill run from the La Source hairpin bucked into a steep climb, the drivers having to

twist left and right as they did so. It must have been hard, as even the great Ayrton Senna had to build up to it. Now, though, it's taken flat in top by everyone after being resurfaced. It still makes a great spectacle, though.

Indeed, spectacle is what it's all about at Spa-Francorchamps and admiring the artistic flow that a driver really in control of a car can paint around the dramatic topography.

It's nowhere near as tough as it was, with even Blanchimont now flat-out in top, but even that was a pale shadow of how the track was 40 years ago when it ran into the next valley and was fast, fast, fast.

INSIDE TRACK

BELGIAN GRAND PRIX

Date:	29 August
Circuit name:	Spa-Francorchamps Circuit
Circuit length:	4.352 miles/7.004km
Number of laps:	44
Telephone:	00 32 8727 5138
Website:	www.spa-francorchamps.be

PREVIOUS WINNERS

1998	**Damon Hill** JORDAN
1999	**David Coulthard** McLAREN
2000	**Mika Hakkinen** McLAREN
2001	**Michael Schumacher** FERRARI
2002	**Michael Schumacher** FERRARI
2004	**Kimi Raikkonen** McLAREN
2005	**Kimi Raikkonen** McLAREN
2007	**Kimi Raikkonen** FERRARI
2008	**Felipe Massa** FERRARI
2009	**Kimi Raikkonen** FERRARI

Formula One and Belgium: The greatest Belgian driver was Jacky Ickx, who won eight times and was world title runner-up in 1970, outstripping 1950s racers Paul Frere and Olivier Gendebien, while Thierry Boutsen won thrice in 1989/90. Three circuits have held the Belgian GP. Spa-Francorchamps is the best known, while Nivelles was tried twice and Zolder will always be known as the place where Gilles Villeneuve died in 1982.
Trickiest corner: Now that Eau Rouge has been tamed, it's time that Pouhon picked up the plaudits. If a car is instilling a driver with confidence, this double-apex downhill left can be taken in sixth gear, at 180mph.
Do you remember when?: There was mayhem just after the start in 1998 as the cars fought for track space out of La Source. Coulthard's McLaren snapped sideways and 13 cars became caught up in the chain reaction. The race had to be restarted and ended up with Jordan's first win, with Damon Hill leading home Ralf Schumacher.

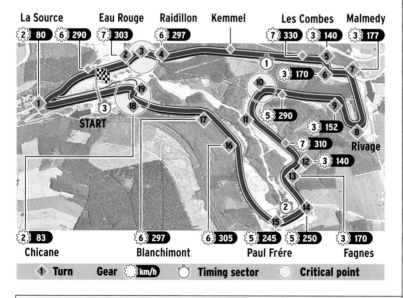

2009 POLE TIME: **FISICHELLA (FORCE INDIA),** 1M46.308S, 147.378MPH/237.182KPH
2009 WINNER'S AVERAGE SPEED: **136.969MPH/220.430KPH 2009**
FASTEST LAP: **VETTEL (RED BULL),** 1M47.263S, 146.065MPH/235.070KPH
LAP RECORD: **VETTEL (RED BULL), 1M47.263S, 146.065MPH/235.070KPH, 2009**

MONZA

There is always action at Monza, whether simply on the opening lap at the first chicane or because someone has excited the fans by doing something special in a Ferrari.

Eagle-eyed television viewers watching the Italian GP will notice when a rear shot is shown of the cars piling into the first chicane that there is something odd on the right-hand side of their screen. Did their eyes deceive them, or was that a banked corner?

Oh yes, it was, for this historic circuit was launched in 1922 with a speed oval running as part of its lap. This dropped from use after Phil Hill won the 1961 Italian GP for Ferrari to become world champion. However, there it lurks, a reminder of when drivers had no choice but to be brave.

The days of great bunches of cars hunting in slipstreaming packs around Monza's endless fast, open sweeps are also behind us, ended when chicanes were inserted for 1972.

These days, the basic shape of this wonderful circuit remains, with no start/finish straight so imbued with character. Anyone lucky enough to sit high in the grandstand opposite the pits is afforded a wonderful view of not only the track but the parkland in which it is set, like a jewel. There was a period when Monza's facilities were shabby chic. In fact, they still lag behind the newer circuits, but charm and history cannot be bought and should never be replaced. This is a track that offers an unbroken link with the sport's past.

INSIDE TRACK

ITALIAN GRAND PRIX

Date:	**12 September**
Circuit name:	**Monza Circuit**
Circuit length:	**3.600 miles/5.793km**
Number of laps:	**53**
Telephone:	**00 39 39 24821**
Website:	**www.monzanet.it**

PREVIOUS WINNERS

2000	**Michael Schumacher**	FERRARI
2001	**Juan Pablo Montoya**	WILLIAMS
2002	**Rubens Barrichello**	FERRARI
2003	**Michael Schumacher**	FERRARI
2004	**Rubens Barrichello**	FERRARI
2005	**Juan Pablo Montoya**	McLAREN
2006	**Michael Schumacher**	FERRARI
2007	**Fernando Alonso**	McLAREN
2008	**Sebastian Vettel**	TORO ROSSO
2009	**Rubens Barrichello**	BRAWN

Formula One and Italy: Italy's love of racing has ensured that there has been a steady stream of drivers, especially when F1 began in 1950 as Alfa Romeo dominated and Giuseppe Farina became the first World Champion. Then Ferrari got going and Alberto Ascari won two titles. However, since 1953, no Italian has been champion. Michele Alboreto came closest when he was second to Alain Prost in 1985. At least the love of Ferrari remains constant, albeit with non-Italians driving. Monza is a near constant, too, but Imola hosted the Italian GP in 1980 before being given its own race, the San Marino GP.

Trickiest corner: Monza is not the scary beast it was when there were no chicanes to break its flow, so the two-part Lesmo corners, both right-handers, are probably the most difficult now.

Do you remember when?: Derek Warwick was a hard man and this was demonstrated in 1990 when he slammed his Lotus into the barriers exiting the Parabolica, inverting it, at the end of the first lap, walked back to the pits and calmly took the spare car for the restart.

Lesmo I Lesmo II Lesmo II

Variante Ascari Parabolica

Roggia Curva Biassono Variante del Rettifilio Rettifilio Tribune

START

◆ Turn	Gear	❄ km/h	⬭ Timing sector	⬭ Critical point

2009 POLE TIME: HAMILTON (McLAREN),
1M24.066S, 154.165MPH/248.104KPH
2009 WINNER'S AVERAGE SPEED:
149.750MPH/241.000KPH

2009 FASTEST LAP: SUTIL (FORCE INDIA),
1M24.739S, 152.923mph/246.106kph
LAP RECORD: BARRICHELLO (FERRARI),
1M21.046S, 159.909MPH/257.349KPH

SINGAPORE

The images that come out of Singapore are something to behold. Not because the track is wildly exceptional, but because the racing action is held under floodlights.

The difference is, well, night and day, the effect of shadow so dramatic. If the race was held in day time, the backdrop would be dramatic, with towering office blocks, an urban park, waterfront and the Anderson Bridge. Yet it's the fact that Singapore has set the ball rolling in running a night race that sets it apart.

The lap starts with a testing left, where passing is possible, although many try to make a pass into Turn 3, where the track doubles back for the blast down to Turn 5 before another largely straight section to Turn 7, one of the best potential passing places.

Ninety degree bends are a regular feature of street circuits and a run of these follow, but the Anderson Bridge provides a landmark, as

does the blast over the Esplanade Bridge and the run through Turns 20 and 21 where the track goes under a grandstand.

The track was modified last year, with tweaks including the pit exit being after the first corner rather than before and the lowering of kerbs plus the flattening of bumps, but its nature remains, as a tricky track.

The grand prix is a huge draw to Singapore, thousands of visitors from overseas pour in, filling hotels, bars, restaurants and shops, and this factor was very much one of the intentions when the hosting of a grand prix was mooted and it explains why the national government agreed to put up finances for 60% of the construction costs.

Formula One and Singapore: For many years, F1's only connection with Singapore was that it was the airport at which the teams and journalists would disembark from their flights to Australia to stretch their legs. However, this finally came to an end when Singapore held its first grand prix towards the end of the 2008 season. When they got off the plane, they could stay off, and everyone involved enjoyed it enormously. Until then, Singapore had produced no drivers of note, but had hosted street races on a circuit laid out centred on its Upper Thomson Road in the 1960s.

Trickiest corner: Turn 1 proved one of the trickiest in the first running of the race, not only on lap 1 as the field attempted to get through this tight right into an esse, but for the rest of the race when they tried to overtake into it after making the dash up the start/finish straight. Made tighter for 2009, it made it less tempting to go for a move, which was less fun, but safer with the walls surrounding its exit.

Do you remember when?: Fernando Alonso appeared to have no chance of winning as he was running 11th in 2008. He then made his first pit stop wildly early, after only 12 laps, and yet he was able to turn it around. Why? Because his Renault team-mate Nelson Piquet Jr then crashed at Turn 17 and famously brought out the safety car before anyone else had pitted, helping Alonso to go on to win.

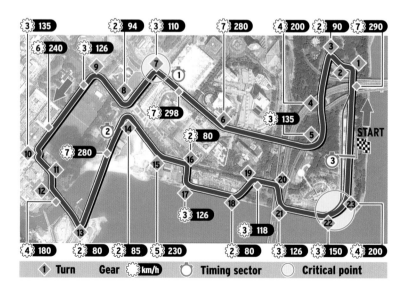

Turn ◆ **Gear** ⚙ km/h **Timing sector** ○ **Critical point** ○

2009 POLE TIME: **HAMILTON (McLAREN),** 1M47.891S, 105.179MPH/169.270KPH
2009 WINNER'S AVERAGE SPEED: 99.323MPH/159.845KPH

2009 FASTEST LAP: **ALONSO (RENAULT),** 1M48.240S, 104.561MPH/168.725KPH
LAP RECORD: **RAIKKONEN (FERRARI),** 1M45.599S, 107.358MPH/172.776KPH

SUZUKA

This great circuit has the hosting rights for the Japanese GP exclusively again after alternating from 2007 with Fuji Speedway. The drivers couldn't be happier as it's a treat.

Honda withdrew from Formula One at the very end of 2008, but it has bragging rights over Toyota, as its circuit, Suzuka, now hosts the Japanese Grand Prix rather than Toyota-owned Fuji Speedway.

Designed by John Hugenholtz, the man who designed Zandvoort in his native Holland, Suzuka opened in 1962 as a test circuit for Honda, but it was soon opened by the car manufacturer for racing, for which racing fans the world over should be extremely grateful.

The reason that Suzuka is considered in the same breath as even Spa-Francorchamps is that it provides drivers with a serious challenge, its mixture of corners including some really fast ones, all overlaid with the extra twist of gradient running from Spoon Curve all the way down to First Curve. Although located within a funfair complex, Mickey Mouse this circuit most certainly is not.

Its trademark corners include the difficult double-right called Degner Curve, the seemingly endless Spoon Curve onto the back straight, the flat-out left kink of 130R and the Casio Triangle at which Ayrton Senna and Alain Prost clashed so famously beneath the giant Ferris Wheel in the heat of their 1989 title battle. A year later, it was at First Curve that they collided...

A unique feature of racing in Japan is the fans who even dress like their heroes out of intense and unwavering respect.

INSIDE TRACK

JAPANESE GRAND PRIX

Date:	10 October
Circuit name:	Suzuka
Circuit length:	3.608 miles/5.806km
Number of laps:	53
Telephone:	00 81 593 783620
Website:	www.suzukacircuit.co.jp

PREVIOUS WINNERS

1998	**Mika Hakkinen** McLAREN
1999	**Mika Hakkinen** McLAREN
2000	**Michael Schumacher** FERRARI
2001	**Michael Schumacher** FERRARI
2002	**Michael Schumacher** FERRARI
2003	**Rubens Barrichello** FERRARI
2004	**Michael Schumacher** FERRARI
2005	**Kimi Raikkonen** McLAREN
2006	**Fernando Alonso** RENAULT
2009	**Sebastian Vettel** RED BULL

Formula One and Japan: No Japanese driver has won a grand prix, but two have made it to the podium. Aguri Suzuki did so in 1990, fittingly at Suzuka, then Takuma Sato finished third in the 2004 US GP for BAR. Fuji was awarded Japan's first World Championship round in 1976. But, after a marshal was killed with the spectator he was trying to move in 1977, there was no race until Suzuka took over in 1987.

Trickiest corner: Before it was made more open, 130R used to be the big one. Now, it's the uphill 'S' Curves that command the most respect. They are taken in fourth and a slip wide in any part of its sequence will result in a driver having to lift and lose momentum.

Do you remember when?: The 1998 title race went to the final round and Mika Hakkinen arrived with a four-point lead over Michael Schumacher. The Ferrari driver qualified on pole, but stalled and had to start from the rear of the grid. He stormed through to third, only to have a tyre blow. He was out and the title was Hakkinen's, who won the race as he pleased.

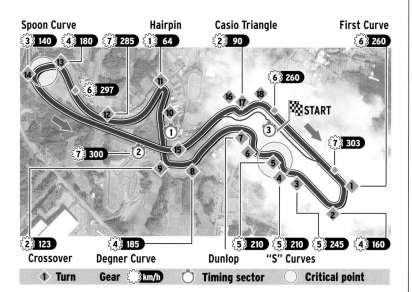

Spoon Curve		Hairpin		Casio Triangle		First Curve
3 140	4 180	7 285	1 64	2 90		6 260

6 297
6 260

START

7 303

7 300

7 300

2 123	4 185	5 210	5 210	5 245	4 160
Crossover	**Degner Curve**	**Dunlop**		**"S" Curves**	

◆ **Turn**   **Gear**   ⚙ **km/h**   ○ **Timing sector**   ○ **Critical point**

2009 POLE TIME: **VETTEL (RED BULL),**
1M32.160S, 140.938MPH/226.817KPH
2009 WINNER'S AVERAGE SPEED:
129.804MPH/208.900KPH

2009 FASTEST LAP: **WEBBER (RED BULL),**
1M32.569S, 140.315MPH/225.815KPH
LAP RECORD: **RAIKKONEN (McLAREN),**
1M31.540S, 141.904MPH/228.373KPH

SOUTH KOREA

Bernie Ecclestone had long wanted a race in Korea and government backing granted last year made this possible, with a rapidly-built circuit bringing F1 to a new audience.

South Korea has been angling to host a grand prix for most of the past decade, with plans for a circuit near Kunsan City to host a grand prix from 1998, but the circuit was never built so that never happened, and nor did plans for a race in the city of Chinae.

However, it was only last autumn that the go-ahead was finally granted for a brand new circuit - the Korean International Circuit - to be built in Yeongam County in the South Cholla province a couple of hundred miles south of capital city Seoul to put South Korea on Formula One's map and give it much-desired prestige alongside neighbouring countries China and Japan.

Pushed ahead by a body called KAVO (the Korea Auto Valley Operation), the circuit only gained the go-ahead when the South Korean government agreed to finance any shortfall.

Built on reclaimed land, the sea-facing circuit is designed unusually to be part permanent (Turn 3 to Turn 12) and part temporary, with the extra loop being added for the grand prix, running along the harbourside to add glamour to Korea's new showcase sporting event.

With grandstand seating for 120,000 people, KAVO is clearly planning on drawing in the crowds to fill the seats, like Japan, and build too many seats, like Shanghai, that remain empty and send out the message that F1 hasn't quite caught the nation's interest.

INSIDE TRACK

SOUTH KOREA GRAND PRIX

Date:	**24 October**
Circuit name:	**Korean International Circuit**
Circuit length:	**3.390 miles/5.450km**
Number of laps:	**57**
Telephone:	**tba**
Website:	**southkoreangrandprix.com**

PREVIOUS WINNERS

Not applicable

Formula One and Korea: Not surprisingly, there is not yet any connection between Korea and Formula One, although the likes of Jenson Button, Nelson Piquet Jr and Lewis Hamilton raced in Korea in their Formula Three days at a circuit at Changwon when it hosted an end-of-season race the weekend after the established race at Macau from 1999 to 2003. Sportscar convert Hwang Jin-Woo raced briefly for South Korea's A1GP team, but Keisuke Kunimoto who has been racing in Japan's Formula Nippon series looks to be the nation's best hope as they cling to the fact that he is half Korean, half Japanese. Behind him on the racing ladder is Sung-Hak "Tom" Mun, who competed in British Formula Renault in 2008.

Most memorable race: This will be the race to build the circuit from scratch in just over a year and a half in time for its grand prix date.

Trickiest corner: Judging by the circuit plans, Turn 3 looks to be the toughest of all, because it's at the end of the longest straight, is sharp and will be where drivers also have to ward off attacks from rivals and yet get a good exit speed.

Where is it?: The circuit is 200 miles south of Seoul, near the city of Yeongan.

Who designed the track?: As soon as the financial plans were put into place, ubiquitous circuit designer Hermann Tilke was called into action and he created the outline of the circuit, as he had for every other grand prix circuit in Asia bar the Japanese ones.

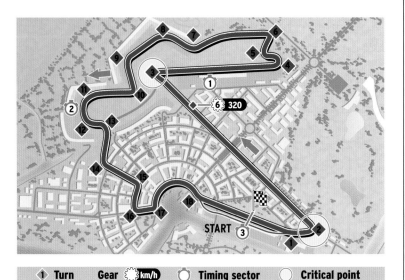

◆ **Turn**   **Gear** ⚙️ **km/h**   ⏱ **Timing sector**   ⚪ **Critical point**

2009 POLE TIME:	2009 FASTEST LAP:
NOT APPLICABLE	**NOT APPLICABLE**
2009 WINNER'S AVERAGE SPEED:	LAP RECORD:
NOT APPLICABLE	**NOT APPLICABLE**

INTERLAGOS

Here is a circuit with a heart that is always packed with people pumped full of passion. It's a natural amphitheatre and the racing fare on offer is never less than theatrical.

Silverstone, Monaco, Spa-Francorchamps and Monza are the only links to the inaugural World Championship remaining. Interlagos, which first hosted a World Championship round in 1973, belongs to the next rank, with Montreal, Hockenheim and Suzuka, and it exudes memories of races past, not just because its facilities look ancient, but because so many of its races have been full of drama.

Sao Paulo is a sprawling city and Interlagos' position in its outskirts has long been overrun. However, from the grandstands on the start/finish straight, fans can still look out across an area of greenery, although there are now factories where there used to be fields.

The feel of the circuit remains, as it is a wonderful, dipping, twisting stretch of tarmac that challenges the drivers. It's not as long as it was, with its original 4.946-mile layout being cut back to its current format in 1990 with the removal of a loop. It retains a wonderful flow, from the dropping away of the first corner into a compression followed by a sharp right-left out of which drivers vie for position to try a passing manoeuvre into Descida do Lago. The drivers then climb to Ferra Dura before going up and down the face of the hill all the way to Juncao, out of which drivers must get the power down early to carry their speed to the first corner and, hopefully, outflank the car ahead.

INSIDE TRACK

BRAZILIAN GRAND PRIX

Date:	7 November
Circuit name:	Interlagos
Circuit length:	2.667 miles/4.292km
Number of laps:	71
Telephone:	00 55 11 813 5775
Website:	www.interlagos.com

PREVIOUS WINNERS

1999	**Mika Hakkinen** McLAREN
2000	**Michael Schumacher** FERRARI
2001	**David Coulthard** McLAREN
2002	**Michael Schumacher** FERRARI
2003	**Giancarlo Fisichella** JORDAN
2004	**Juan Pablo Montoya** WILLIAMS
2005	**Juan Pablo Montoya** McLAREN
2006	**Felipe Massa** FERRARI
2007	**Kimi Raikkonen** FERRARI
2008	**Felipe Massa** FERRARI
2009	**Mark Webber** RED BULL

Formula One and Brazil: Here is a country that started delivering in F1 when Emerson Fittipaldi won titles in 1972 and 1974. Nelson Piquet was champion in 1981, 1983 and 1987. But Ayrton Senna remains Brazil's greatest driver, winning 41 times as he became champion in 1988, 1990 and 1991. Since his death in 1994, Felipe Massa has come closest, just losing out in 2008.

Trickiest corner: The first corner is hard enough when taken one at a time. However, this tight left with a sharp drop from the apex is a perpetual place for trouble on the opening lap when there seem to be more cars than space.

Do you remember when?: At the start of the 1975 GP, as Jean-Pierre Jarier stuck his unfancied Shadow on pole for the opening race in Argentina, but failed to start, then qualified on pole at Interlagos. He was jumped by Brabham's Carlos Reutemann, then got in front after four laps and streaked 30s clear, only for a fuel metering unit to fail with eight laps to go, handing victory to local hero Carlos Pace.

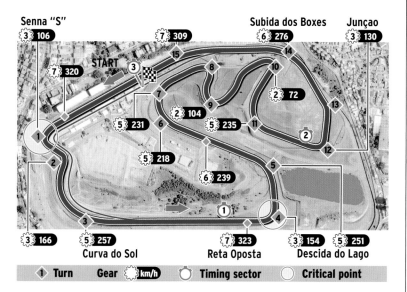

Senna "S" · **Subida dos Boxes** · **Junçao**
START
Curva do Sol · **Reta Oposta** · **Descida do Lago**

◆ **Turn** | **Gear** | km/h | ○ **Timing sector** | ○ **Critical point**

2009 POLE TIME: BARRICHELLO (BRAWN),
1M19.576S, 121.107MPH/194.903KPH
2009 WINNER'S AVERAGE SPEED:
123.451MPH/198.676KPH

2009 FASTEST LAP: WEBBER (RED BULL),
1M13.733S, 130.728MPH/210.387KPH
LAP RECORD: MONTOYA (WILLIAMS),
1M11.473S, 134.837MPH/217.000KPH

YAS MARINA

Singapore brought the first night time grand prix. Abu Dhabi then put on the first day-night race, but its amazing facilities brought much, much more.

Abu Dhabi's Yas Marina circuit is the sort of track of which Formula One impresario Bernie Ecclestone dreamed about: ultra-modern, glamorous and built with no expense spared. Oh, and it's in the right part of the world to capture the key European television market.

From the moment that the plans for Abu Dhabi's circuits were aired, it was clear that neighbouring grand prix host Bahrain was going to feel very much second best once it had been completed. This wasn't going to be a circuit tucked away out on a patch of stony desert. No, Abu Dhabi's was going to be the centrepiece of a swish, high-spending complex garlanded with hotels and marinas, luxury housing, golf courses and the Ferrari World theme park. This was putting Formula One precisely where the big money is.

Whereas the Bahrain circuit is split into two sections, oasis and desert, Abu Dhabi's trumps it by having three definite sections. These are not demarcated by having green grass verges or not, but by track format, with the the first part of the lap being high-speed in nature, the second part a street section, with tighter corners, and the third part a marina section, oddly ducking under a bridge linking the two parts of the luxury Yas Hotel.

There are huge grandstands at the hairpin onto the main straight and at the far end of the straight, with the latter offering views over the best overtaking point on the circuit.

INSIDE TRACK

ABU DHABI GRAND PRIX

Date:	14 November
Circuit name:	Yas Marina
Circuit length:	3.429 miles/5.518km
Number of laps:	56
Telephone:	00 971 4366 2125
Website:	www.abudhabigp.com

PREVIOUS WINNERS

2009   **Sebastian Vettel** RED BULL

Formula One and Abu Dhabi: The short answer to this one is that there was no prior connection between F1 and the United Arab Emirates, of which Abu Dhabi is capital, other than it produces oil and cars use oil. In short, until Bahrain landed a grand prix in 2004, there was no motor racing of note in the Gulf. Dubai followed suit and built its own circuit as it pursued its policy of trying to attract all the world's top sports, but its interest has waned and it stays at sub-F1 level. However, as much as the Arabs like their fast cars, they are not yet in tune with attending races, so crowds stay small.

Trickiest corner: Turn 8 is the hardest, at the end of the long main straight running past the golf course, as drivers not only have to slow their cars from flat-out in top to about 50mph, possibly while being attacked by a rival, but they have to immediately get onto the right line for Turn 9, as exit speed from there dictates their pace down the following straight.

Do you remember when?: Sebastian Vettel won the inaugural race last November after Lewis Hamilton had looked to end the season on a high for McLaren, only to hit brake problems and hand the advantage in this night-day race to Vettel, with Mark Webber having to fight very hard to stop Jenson Button from overhauling him.

Who designed it?: Hermann Tilke's architectural practice enjoyed doing this one, as there was budget aplenty and acceptance of grandiose ideas. They wanted big and bold, and they got it.

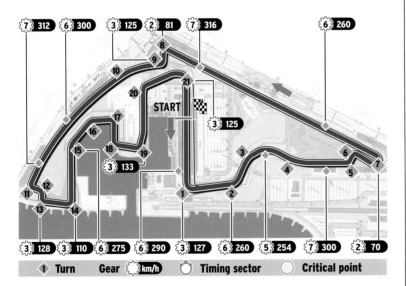

Turn	Gear	km/h	Timing sector	Critical point

2009 POLE TIME: HAMILTON (McLAREN), 1M40.948S, 123.069MPH/198.061KPH
2009 WINNER'S AVERAGE SPEED: 121.036MPH/194.789KPH

2009 FASTEST LAP: VETTEL (RED BULL), 1M40.279S, 123.890MPH/199.383KPH
LAP RECORD: VETTEL (RED BULL), 1M40.279S, 123.890MPH/199.383KPH

The 2009 season provided a real mixing of the teams, as this bunch containing a BMW Sauber, a Renault, a Toro Rosso, a Brawn, a Red Bull and a Force India shows. Hopefully, 2010 will be better still.

REVIEW OF
THE 2009 SEASON

Technical rule changes have often shaken up the order, but never like this. Never have the leading teams been caught on the hop to the extent they were in 2009, and never has a "new" team stepped in and trumped them. This is what happened as Brawn GP, the team formed from the wreckage of Honda, guided Jenson Button to the title.

There has never been a season like this. F1 giants Ferrari and McLaren failed to guess how far they could "maximise" the changes in the rulebook. Brawn GP - born at the 11th hour from the remains of the Honda Racing team after the Japanese manufacturer pulled out as the global economy slumped - Toyota and Williams all got it right by including a double-decked diffuser under their cars. The others protested, claiming these were outside the rules, but the FIA said they weren't, leaving the other seven teams with no option but to redesign their cars to accommodate them.

By the time that they had, for the Spanish GP, Brawn GP had three wins in the bag and Red Bull Racing had scored its first victory.

Such was the shock experienced by Ferrari and McLaren at their lack of pace, that there was talk of both abandoning hope and focusing even that early in the year on their 2010 cars. This wasn't considered by these great teams, though, and they fought back through the year. Indeed, both teams became winners again.

Stranger even than this was that teams' form appeared to ebb and flow from race to race, with the nature of individual circuits

suiting some teams better than others. The Red Bull RB5 became the car of the year, with both Vettel and Mark Webber winning, but the Brawn BGP 001's early season form set the Ross Brawn-led team fair for the constructors' title and its development appeared to suit Rubens Barrichello better than it did team-mate Button, making the Englishman's bid to close out the drivers' title all the more painful. However, he did it in Brazil, with one round still to run.

McLaren's form leapt forward markedly as it introduced much-needed chassis upgrades mid-season at the German GP and reigning champion Lewis Hamilton was the one who carried the team's hopes as Heikki Kovalainen failed to deliver.

Ferrari's challenge was mainly in the hands of 2008 runner-up Felipe Massa, with Kimi Raikkonen looking disinterested, but the Finn responded when the team needed cheering after Massa suffered a head injury in qualifying at the Hungarian GP. Neither stand-in, Luca Badoer or Giancarlo Fisichella, was able to shine.

Toyota had looked as though it might finally challenge for its first win, even with Jarno Trulli and Timo Glock filling the front row in Malaysia, but they weren't bold enough and Button won. It took until the late-season races before they were as competitive again.

Williams promised so much, usually in practice rather than qualifying, and Nico Rosberg drove well, but their return to winning was postponed for another year.

BMW Sauber started with higher hopes and ended with a slam of the door as the German manufacturer pulled out, leaving former owner Peter Sauber trying to orchestrate a return to running as a privateer, provided the other teams would allow it to be the 14th team for 2010 when just 13 teams were guaranteed a place. In between, the team floundered, although progress was made to the point that Robert Kubica finished second in the penultimate race, of the 17-race campaign in Brazil.

Renault had an even worse time, not only being less than competitive but being stung for race-fixing in the 2008 Singapore GP once Nelson Piquet Jr showed how disgruntled he was to have been fired. The punishment? A ban from F1, suspended for two years. Many feared that this would cause Renault to follow BMW out of F1.

Force India didn't have high hopes for the year but came within a blink of becoming winners when an update for the Belgian GP yielded pole for Giancarlo Fisichella and a very close second place right on the tail of Raikkonen's winning Ferrari. Strong form in the next race, at Monza, showed that this was no flash in the pan.

Scuderia Toro Rosso ended the year bottom, but after Sebastien Bourdais was fired the team ended up with two rookie drivers, with flashes of speed shown by Sebastien Buemi.

It all came to a close at F1's most spectacular new circuit, for years, Yas Marina in Abu Dhabi.

AUSTRALIAN GP

Take one team that underachieved through 2008, pull the plug then revive just before the opening race. Include a double diffuser on the new car, monopolise the front row, then reel off a one-two finish. It should never happen, but it did. Enter Brawn GP.

Jenson Button leads away from Sebastian Vettel at the start as Robert Kubica and his team-mate Rubens Barrichello struggle for traction.

The speed of the Brawn BGP 001, a car that was created through 2008 by Honda Racing's design team, had been remarkable in the limited amount of pre-season testing that it managed. Of course, many thought that this was a case of Rubens Barrichello and Jenson Button running light to look fast and thus attract some much-needed sponsors for the team. Wrong, the sacrificing of the 2008 season when it was clear that their car was a dud was simply paying dividends and Ross Brawn and the crew were reaping the benefits.

Key among this, other than the car's long lead time was that Brawn, Toyota and Williams had all plumped for a double diffuser and their rivals were all atwitter, insisting that they were outside the new rules as the upper diffuser was

more than 175mm above the reference plane. However, the FIA rejected their appeal and it was clear that the other seven teams would have considerable rejigging to do.

The pace of the double diffuser gang was good enough to claim the first three places, with Button leading all the way to claim his first win since the 2006 Hungarian GP, with Barrichello second and Toyota's Jarno Trulli third, despite having had to start from the pits along with team-mate Timo Glock as their rear wings were deemed illegal for being too flexible.

Button had made a cracking start from pole, whereas Barrichello had his anti-stall kick in and was swamped before he got going, then clashing with home race hero Mark Webber's Red Bull at Turn 1 after being

nudged by Heikki Kovalainen's McLaren. BMW Sauber's Nick Heidfeld, on the outside, was the next ingredient in this mix-up, with Force India's Adrian Sutil also getting caught up. Barrichello was the lucky one, as he didn't have to pit for repairs, but his hopes of challenging Button were long gone.

Button had made his escape, finishing the opening lap almost 4 seconds clear of Sebastian Vettel's Red Bull. Nico Rosberg was zapped by Felipe Massa's Ferrari around the opening lap, showing the value of using a KERS system as the Brazilian released the extra power harnessed during braking and flew by.

Button was struggling on his final set of tyres, the softer option tyres, and Kubica had the pace to overhaul him. Fortunately for Button, Vettel was between the two and kept the Pole at bay, with the pair coming together at Turn 4 on lap 56 of 58. The BMW Sauber then slammed off the circuit, while Vettel attempted to complete the race with his front left wheel hanging off, for which he was fined $50,000. Barrichello said thank you and moved up to second.

Brawn could not have asked for a better start, and Honda's executives must have experienced conflicting emotions, having thrown away the chance to achieve their goal by quitting. What should have been their car was now fitted with a Mercedes engine and was at the opposite end of the field to the end it had occupied as the 2008 season came to a close.

As ever with F1, there was controversy, and it involved an incident between Trulli and Lewis Hamilton in the aftermath of the Vettel/ Kubica clash when the safety car was deployed. The pair were running third and fourth when Trulli ran wide at the penultimate corner and Hamilton had little choice but to go past as the Toyota bounced over the grass. What followed was that he slowed and let the Italian back ahead, which he needn't have done. As a result, Trulli was penalized 25 seconds for overtaking on the track behind the safety car, dropping him to an eventual 12th. However, the matter didn't end there and Hamilton was later disqualified for lying to the stewards, with Trulli reinstated.

MELBOURNE – ROUND 01

Date: **29 March 2009**   Laps: **58**   Distance: **191.110 miles/307.562km**
Weather: **Sunny and hot**

RACE RESULT

Position	Driver	Team	Result	Stops	Qualifying Time	Grid
1	Jenson Button	Brawn	1h34m15.784s	2	1m26.202s	1
2	Rubens Barrichello	Brawn	1h34m16.591s	2	1m26.505s	2
3	Jarno Trulli	Toyota	1h34m17.388s	2	1m27.127s	19**
D	Lewis Hamilton	McLaren*	1h34m17.700s	2	no time	18***
4	Timo Glock	Toyota	1h34m20.219s	2	1m62.975s	20**
5	Fernando Alonso	Renault*	1h34m20.663s	2	1m25.605s	10
6	Nico Rosberg	Williams	1h34m21.506s	2	1m26.973s	5
7	Sebastien Buemi	Toro Rosso	1h34m21.788s	2	1m26.503s	13
8	Sebastien Bourdais	Toro Rosso	1h34m22.082s	2	1m26.964s	17
9	Adrian Sutil	Force India	1h34m22.119s	2	1m26.742s	16
10	Nick Heidfeld	BMW Sauber*	1h34m22.869s	3	1m25.504s	9
11	Gincarlo Fisichella	Force India	1h34m23.158s	2	1m26.677s	15
12	Mark Webber	Red Bull	57 laps	2	1m27.246s	8
13	Sebastian Vettel	Red Bull	56 laps/accident	2	1m26.830s	3
14	Robert Kubica	BMW Sauber	55 laps/accident	2	1m26.914s	4
15	Kimi Raikkonen	Ferrari*	55 laps/differential	4	1m27.163s	7
R	Felipe Massa	Ferrari*	45 laps/upright	2	1m27.033s	6
R	Nelson Piquet Jr	Renault*	24 laps/brakes	1	1m26.598s	14
R	Kazuki Nakajima	Williams	17 laps/accident	0	1m25.607s	11
R	Heikki Kovalainen	McLaren*	0 laps/accident damage	0	1m25.726s	12

FASTEST LAP: ROSBERG, 1M27.706S, 135.252MPH/217.667KPH ON LAP 48
RACE LEADERS: BUTTON 1-58
* RUNNING WITH KERS ** STARTED FROM THE PIT LANE. *** FIVE-PLACE GRID PENALTY

TALKING POINT: BRAWN MAKES VICTORIOUS DEBUT

With the global recession starting to bite, it came as little surprise that some manufacturer teams looked at their involvement in F1 as 2008 came to a close. That Honda pulled the plug still came as something of a shock, but the fact that the team born from its wreckage, Brawn GP, managed to pull off a one-two result on its debut was remarkable. This wasn't just a simple case of renaming, as had happened many times in recent years to the team that was once Jordan. It was also a case of a team that was languishing at the tail of the field being transformed over the course of a - much disrupted - winter into a winning outfit in a metamorphosis the like of which F1 has never seen.

Winner Button and runner-up Barrichello pose with the first of the new team's trophies.

MALAYSIAN GP

Jenson Button came out on top as Sepang was hit by its second massive storm in three days. The first, though, hit McLaren, with the team brought back in front of the FIA stewards to explain discrepancies in what they told them at the Australian GP.

A tropical downpour brought this race to a halt and so only half points were awarded as less than 75% of the planned race distance had been covered. However, even that couldn't wipe the smile off the faces of the Brawn GP crew as Jenson Button made it two wins from two.

The images that were beamed around the globe after the race had been brought to a halt after 32 laps were confusing. The red flag had been brought out as cars were aquaplaning everywhere, but confusion reigned as to what would happen next, and when. Eventually, after the drivers sat on the starting grid for a very long time, the whole thing was called off as darkness approached, making the 2009

Malaysian GP the third shortest since the World Championship began.

Many pointed fingers at the fact that the race had been moved back two hours from its traditional starting time so that it would fit better with European waking hours, and thus moved itself to the time of day at which thunderstorms traditionally hit.

Of the race itself, Button started from pole position ahead of the Toyotas of Jarno Trulli and Timo Glock. Nico Rosberg was fourth and the German made the best start of all to put his Williams into the lead before Turn 1.

Button was not so quick off the mark and he had to fight hard with Trulli on the dash to the

first turn, losing out and then finding himself on the outside line for the corner. With less grip here, Button lost a further place to Renault's fast-starting Fernando Alonso who had shot up from ninth on the grid.

Knowing Alonso's car was carrying more fuel, Button had to get past and duly did at Turn 13. Others would spend longer finding a way by, with team-mate Rubens Barrichello next to do so two laps later into Turn 14, only to have Alonso out-accelerate him down the straight before making the pass stick into Turn 1.

Nine laps later, Kimi Raikkonen relegated the Spanish driver further, followed by Red Bull Racing's Mark Webber doing the same.

It's red lights on - meaning the race has been stopped – and umbrellas up. But, with light fading, there was no time for a restart.

Race leader Rosberg was the first to call at the pits. Storm clouds were approaching, but no rain had arrived. So there was no choice but to fit another set of dry-weather tyres. Trulli pitted two laps later, but it was still impossible to fit wet tyres in anticipation of rain. So Button assumed the lead and was able to run two laps further still before making his pit stop, two laps in which he flew and was able to emerge effectively in the lead as he was behind only Barrichello who pitted a lap later.

The rain was holding off, but Ferrari put wet weather tyres on Raikkonen's car. Rain did arrive, but not before the Finn had destroyed them on the dry track. So, Button waited until rain finally arrived three laps after his first stop and drove beautifully to extend his lead over Rosberg before he pitted again for wets.

Glock alone opted for intermediate tyres and shot up the order, reaching second by lap 28.

Then rain turned to torrent and Button was at the helm when the officials decided that it was too wet to continue. The timing of his eventual change to full wets was unfortunate for Glock as Nick Heidfeld moved up to second, thanks to pitting just once. Glock usurped him immediately, but the red flag was shown and with results having to be declared at the end of the previous lap, that left him third, with Trulli fourth just ahead of Barrichello.

SEPANG - ROUND 02

Date: **5 April 2009** Laps: **31** Distance: **106.777 miles/171.841km**
Weather: **Dry then very wet**

RACE RESULT

Position	Driver	Team	Result	Stops	Qualifying Time	Grid
1	**Jenson Button**	Brawn	55m30.622s	4	1m15.181s	1
2	**Nick Heidfeld**	BMW Sauber*	55m53.344s	1	1m34.769s	10
3	**Timo Glock**	Toyota	55m54.135s	3	1m35.690s	3
4	**Jarno Trulli**	Toyota	56m16.795s	4	1m35.273s	2
5	**Rubens Barrichello**	Brawn	56m17.982s	4	1m35.651s	9**
6	**Mark Webber**	Red Bull	56m22.955s	4	1m35.757s	5
7	**Lewis Hamilton**	McLaren*	56m31.355s	3	1m34.905s	12
8	**Nico Rosberg**	Williams	56m42.198s	4	1m35.750s	4
9	**Felipe Massa**	Ferrari*	56m47.554s	3	1m35.642s	16
10	**Sebastien Bourdais**	Toro Rosso	57m12.786s	3	1m35.431s	15
11	**Fernando Alonso**	Renault*	57m20.044s	3	1m37.659s	8
12	**Kazuki Nakajima**	Williams	57m26.752s	3	1m34.788s	11
13	**Nelson Piquet Jr**	Renault*	57m27.335s	3	1m35.708s	17
14	**Kimi Raikkonen**	Ferrari*	57m53.463s	3	1m36.170s	7
15	**Sebastian Vettel**	Red Bull	30 laps	4	1m35.518s	13***
16	**Sebastien Buemi**	Toro Rosso	30 laps	2	1m36.107s	20
17	**Adrian Sutil**	Force India	30 laps	2	1m35.918s	19
18	**Giancarlo Fisichella**	Force India	29 laps	1	1m35.908s	18
R	**Robert Kubica**	BMW Sauber	1 lap/engine	0	1m36.106s	6
R	**Heikki Kovalainen**	McLaren*	0 laps/accident	0	1m34.924s	14

FASTEST LAP: BUTTON, 1M36.641S, 101.143MPH/162.774KPH ON LAP 18
RACE LEADERS: ROSBERG 1-15, TRULLI 16, BUTTON 17-19 & 21-31; BARRICHELLO 20
* RUNNING WITH KERS ** 5-PLACE GRID PENALTY *** 10-PLACE GRID PENALTY

TALKING POINT: HAMILTON AND McLAREN COME UNDER FIRE

When Lewis Hamilton threatens to quit F1, you know something diabolical has occurred. Yet this is what he told FIA president Max Mosley on the Saturday at Sepang. This was due to being hauled back in front of the FIA two days before to explain why he told the press one thing in Australia about his pass on Trulli while the safety car was circulating and subsequent surrender of third place, then the stewards something different. It appeared he and sporting director Dave Ryan had lied and not only was he disqualified but Ryan fired, after 35 years with McLaren. Hamilton held a conference in which he said he had been instructed not to tell the truth, and would never make that mistake again.

Lewis Hamilton will never have felt as much discomfort facing the press as he did at Sepang.

CHINESE GP

Just as at the Italian GP at Monza in 2008, if it's wet, very wet, who do you call? Why, Sebastian Vettel. And, just as he did for the Scuderia Toro Rosso sister team, he gave Red Bull Racing its maiden victory, with Mark Webber making it a one-two result.

This was the first sign that newboys Brawn GP were going to have a fight on their hands, as Red Bull Racing clearly now had a challenger in its Adrian Newey-designed and Renault-powered RB5.

This was shown clearly in qualifying when Sebastian Vettel grabbed pole position by 0.2s, with team-mate Mark Webber third behind Renault's Fernando Alonso, then put on another masterclass in the race to win by 11 seconds from Webber to take not just the team's first win, but its first one-two. If ever there was a driver who repaid his mentor's support, Vettel is that man, as this result meant that he had given Red Bull drinks magnate a first victory for both of him teams: Scuderia Toro Rosso and now Red Bull Racing.

For the record, Jenson Button, winner of the first two rounds for Brawn GP, qualified only fifth, behind team-mate Rubens Barrichello, then raced to third place, but was 45 seconds adrift of the beaming, effervescent Vettel.

The key to this turnaround in form was the rain, and there was lots of it. In fact, so much so that the race had to take its start with the safety car leading the field around.

In the dry, the Brawns had the edge on performance, but Christian Horner and his engineers masterminded the decision to run their cars with a light fuel load to ensure that they would be on the front of the grid. Had the race been run in the dry, they would probably have been outrun by the Brawn

drivers. But it wasn't, and in the wet, their RB5 was the car to have, with the Brawn BGP 001 clearly no match as it failed to get sufficient heat into its tyres to challenge. In fact, it was no contest, such was the Red Bulls' superiority.

The safety car stayed at the front of the field for the first eight laps, leaving all the drivers to go racing on a circuit whose puddles they had grown accustomed to. One driver was caught out by the safety car's withdrawal, though, and this was Alonso who had had to pit for fuel and new tyres, as his second place on the grid had been achieved by running incredibly light. So he rejoined at the back, along with Nico Rosberg who had also pitted under the safety car, albeit

Sebastian Vettel splashes around in the lead ahead of his Red Bull Racing team-mate Mark Webber and Rubens Barrichello's Brawn.

simply to change race strategy to suit the conditions. Neither would go on to score.

Leading was the best place to be, and Vettel used his advantage of not being blinded by spray to pull clear, with the Brawns dropping back from Webber's wake, falling away in third and fourth.

One of the most bizarre reasons for the Brawns' troubles in the wet was that their 11th hour reprieve after Honda's withdrawal was that the BGP 001 had never run in the wet in its limited testing before the start of the season. On the day, though, Button reckoned that he did well just keeping the car on the circuit. Barrichello finished another 19 seconds back.

Of the rest, Lewis Hamilton had a couple of spins, and Heikki Kovalainen, for once, came out as the better placed of the pair as McLaren bagged fifth and sixth.

Timo Glock wasn't far behind them, but Toro Rosso rookie Sebastien Buemi remarkably finished in the points for the second time in his three outings, not putting a foot wrong in truly difficult conditions and again showing up his more experienced team-mate Sebastien Bourdais.

Actually, there was one slip, and that was clipping Vettel under the safety car, but Buemi got away with that...

SHANGHAI - ROUND 03

Date: **19 April 2009** Laps: **56** Distance: **189.680 miles/305.250km**
Weather: **Heavy rain**

RACE RESULT

Position	Driver	Team	Result	Stops	Qualifying Time	Grid
1	Sebastian Vettel	Red Bull	1h57m43.485s	2	1m36.184s	1
2	Mark Webber	Red Bull	1h57m54.455s	2	1m36.466s	3
3	Jenson Button	Brawn	1h58m28.460s	2	1m36.532s	5
4	Rubens Barrichello	Brawn	1h58m47.189s	2	1m36.493s	4
5	Heikki Kovalainen	McLaren*	1h58m48.587s	1	1m36.032s	12
6	Lewis Hamilton	McLaren*	1h58m55.351s	1	1m38.595s	9
7	Timo Glock	Toyota	1h58m57.961s	1	1m36.066s	19**
8	Sebastien Buemi	Toro Rosso	1h58m59.924s	2	1m39.321s	10
9	Fernando Alonso	Renault	1h59m07.794s	2	1m36.381s	2
10	Kimi Raikkonen	Ferrari	1h59m15.235s	1	1m38.089s	8
11	Sebastien Bourdais	Toro Rosso	1h59m17.641s	1	1m36.906s	15
12	Nick Heidfeld	BMW Sauber*	1h59m19.319s	1	1m35.975s	11
13	Robert Kubica	BMW Sauber	1h59m30.338s	2	1m36.966s	17***
14	Giancarlo Fisichella	Force India	55 laps	2	1m37.672s	20
15	Nico Rosberg	Williams	55 laps	3	1m37.397s	7
16	Nelson Piquet Jr	Renault	54 laps	3	1m36.908s	16
17	Adrian Sutil	Force India	50 laps	3	1m37.669s	18
R	Kazuki Nakajima	Williams	43 laps/transmission	3	1m36.193s	14
R	Felipe Massa	Ferrari	20 laps/electrics	0	1m36.033s	13
R	Jarno Trulli	Toyota	18 laps/crash damage	0	1m36.835s	6

FASTEST LAP: BARRICHELLO, 1M52.592S, 108.298MPH/174.289KPH ON LAP 42
RACE LEADERS: VETTEL 1-15, 20-37 & 41-56; BUTTON 16-19 & 40; WEBBER 38-39
* RUNNING WITH KERS ** 5-PLACE GRID PENALTY *** STARTED FROM THE PIT LANE

TALKING POINT: RON DENNIS HANDS OVER CONTROL

When you've built an empire, it must be incredibly hard to hand it over, yet this is what McLaren's Ron Dennis did before the season's third race. He was planning to go, but the moment that Martin Whitmarsh was given full control of the group's racing team was forced by the lies that Lewis Hamilton and sporting director Dave Ryan told the FIA stewards after the Australian GP. Many felt that the sudden move was a peace offering to the FIA, something that would appeal to its president Max Mosley, with whom Dennis had a prickly relationship. Dennis said that he would concentrate on McLaren's Automotive Group and the building of a new supercar from the ultra-modern McLaren Technical Centre.

Whitmarsh became the absolute commander of McLaren's racing after Dennis's withdrawal.

BAHRAIN GP

The Toyotas led away, but it was a Brawn in front when it mattered, with Jenson Button cruising to his third victory from four starts as the various fuel strategies unfolded, aided by a feisty pass on Lewis Hamilton, showing searing form in scorching conditions.

Lagging behind the Toyotas in the early running, Sebastian Vettel leads Jenson Button and Lewis Hamilton, but it was to be Button's day.

The ever-changing face of Formula One resulted in Toyotas filling the front row of the grid, with Jarno Trulli edging Timo Glock for pole position. But, analysis of how much fuel their TF109s had been carrying revealed that they had gambled, run light. Their car weights, published post-qualifying for the first time in 2009 were 648.5kg and 643kg respectively. Behind them on the grid, Sebastian Vettel had qualified third for Red Bull Racing, weighing 659kg and Jenson Button fourth for Brawn at 652.5kg, identical to the weight of Lewis Hamilton's McLaren that would start fifth and 3.5kg lighter than his own team-mate Rubens Barrichello who would start sixth.

True to their lighter weight, the Toyotas led down to the first corner, with Trulli failing to repel an attack from Glock who knew he had to hit the front to make the most of his lighter fuel load. Once clear, he rocketed away, with Hamilton having made the most of his MP4-24's KERS to blast Button and Vettel. Indeed, the German was the chief loser, falling to fifth at Turn 2 as Button held his line to dive up the inside for fourth.

Hamilton then made a move on Trulli and powered past into Turn 4, only to run wide and let Trulli dive back into second place.

Button knew that he had to pass Hamilton if he wanted to keep his winning run going. And this he did as they raced onto lap 2, even with Hamilton able to reload his extra KERS horsepower as they crossed the start/finish line. By slotting himself into the McLaren's slipstream, Button did just enough to negate the extra 60bhp or so and was perfectly placed to make a dive up the inside into Turn 1. It was tight, but it worked in the sort of move that Formula One fans the world over lust after.

Now Button had to tackle the Toyotas, but he knew that they would be pitting way before him. And so they did, with Glock pulling in from the lead on lap 11 then Trulli two laps later. Button stayed out until lap 16. Vettel, frustrated by failing to get past Hamilton in the opening laps, went on until lap 20 before he made his first stop, but his inability to put the McLaren behind him was to scupper any chance of victory.

By the time the first stops were out of the way, Button was in front, Trulli second and Vettel right behind him and being held up. Without the electrifying pace on the less favoured medium tyre, Trulli wasn't able to do enough and knew that his hopes of glory were but dust when he was the first of this trio to make his second stop. He knew that the super-soft tyres for the final stint would give him an advantage as his rivals would have to do their enforced stint on the mediums, but the damage was done. Toyota had blown its chance as it had been worried about a heavy fuel load for the longer middle stint destroying super-soft tyres. Instead, their drivers found the mediums offered little grip. Paddock experts reckoned they should have hedged their bets and run one of their drivers on super-softs in that middle stint.

With a 10s lead before his final stop, Button had the race under control and Vettel, who came out of his final stop ahead of Trulli, was unable to do anything about it and indeed had to keep an eye on his mirrors as Trulli, now on the super-softs was pressing.

They finished: Button, Vettel, Trulli, with Glock struggling so badly on the mediums that he fell to seventh place. Behind Hamilton, three-stopping Barrichello finished a distant fifth and Kimi Raikkonen able to give Ferrari its first points of the season in sixth place.

BAHRAIN - ROUND 04
Date: **26 April 2009** Laps: **57** Distance: **191.530 miles/308.238km**
Weather: **Hot and dry**

RACE RESULT

Position	Driver	Team	Result	Stops	Qualifying Time	Grid
1	**Jenson Button**	Brawn	1h31m48.182s	2	1m34.044s	4
2	**Sebastian Vettel**	Red Bull	1h31m55.369s	2	1m34.105s	3
3	**Jarno Trulli**	Toyota	1h31m57.352s	2	1m33.431s	1
4	**Lewis Hamilton**	McLaren*	1h32m10.278s	2	1m34.196s	5
5	**Rubens Barrichello**	Brawn	1h32m25.961s	3	1m34.239s	6
6	**Kimi Raikkonen**	Ferrari*	1h32m30.239s	2	1m35.380s	10
7	**Timo Glock**	Toyota	1h32m31.062s	2	1m33.712s	2
8	**Fernando Alonso**	Renault*	1h32m40.957s	2	1m34.578s	7
9	**Nico Rosberg**	Williams	1h32m46.380s	2	1m35.134s	9
10	**Nelson Piquet Jr**	Renault*	1h32m53.331s	2	1m33.941s	15
11	**Mark Webber**	Red Bull	1h32m55.823s	2	1m34.038s	18
12	**Heikki Kovalainen**	McLaren*	1h33m06.006s	2	1m33.242s	11
13	**Sebastien Bourdais**	Toro Rosso	1h33m06.987s	2	1m34.159s	20
14	**Felipe Massa**	Ferrari*	56 laps	3	1m34.818s	8
15	**Giancarlo Fisichella**	Force India	56 laps	2	1m33.910s	17
16	**Adrian Sutil**	Force India	56 laps	2	1m33.722s	19**
17	**Sebastien Buemi**	Toro Rosso	56 laps	2	1m33.753s	16
18	**Robert Kubica**	BMW Sauber*	56 laps	2	1m33.487s	13
19	**Nick Heidfeld**	BMW Sauber*	56 laps	2	1m33.562s	14
R	**Kazuki Nakajima**	Williams	48 laps/oil pressure	2	1m33.348s	12

FASTEST LAP: TRULLI, 1M34.556S, 128.059MPH/206.091KPH ON LAP 10
RACE LEADERS: GLOCK 1-10; TRULLI 11-12; BUTTON 13-15, 22-37 & 41-57; VETTEL 16-19 & 38-40; RAIKKONEN 20-21
* RUNNING WITH KERS ** 3-PLACE GRID PENALTY FOR BLOCKING

TALKING POINT: FERRARI VOWS THAT IT WILL IMPROVE

Three points from four races is not the tally you expect from Ferrari and so it came as no surprise when sporting director Stefano Domenicali pledged not to abandon development of the F60 in favour of the team's 2010 challenger. A double diffuser was promised for the Spanish GP and Domenicali said that the team's lack of results was not down to disorganisation, countering a charge from former Ferrari World Champion Niki Lauda who accused the team of a jumbled "spaghetti culture". Ferrari president Luca di Montezemolo said most of the blame should be aimed at badly written technical rules, the introduction of KERS and having started the F60 too late as it focused on trying to win both titles.

Racing chief Stefano Domenicali talks to Rob Smedley as the team plans its fightback.

SPANISH GP

Every year, teams say "let's see what happens in Barcelona", when their first updates are fitted after the flyaways. By the end of the race, Brawn GP was still smiling, but one of its drivers, Rubens Barrichello, was not, feeling that he should have been the winner.

Jenson Button's facial expression on the podium says it all as he savours a 14-point championship lead. Rubens Barrichello wasn't so happy.

Rubens Barrichello is a driver known for his cheery countenance. However, after spending most of the close-season looking as though he had no ride for 2009 following Honda's withdrawal, you'd think that he would be beaming. After all, here he was, not only still in Formula One, but with the pace-setting car.

Yet he was livid after flagfall, convinced that Brawn GP had changed his team-mate Jenson Button from a three-stop strategy to a two-stopper specifically to assist the Briton to move ahead of him and then go on to win.

As we would see later in the campaign, this wouldn't be the only time that Barrichello felt the team had kept him from victory.

Button had qualified on pole, just 0.133s ahead of Sebastian Vettel, showing that Red Bull Racing really was going to be Brawn GP's main rival, and was fast closing in. Indeed, the German had set his lap time carrying an extra 5.5kg of fuel. Barrichello was another 0.1s back in third, with Felipe Massa an improved fourth thanks to his Ferrari now sporting a double diffuser, shading Mark Webber.

For McLaren and BMW Sauber – second and third overall in 2008 – Spain brought only pain, as their best positions on the grid were only 14th and 10th respectively.

Barrichello was first to reach Turn 1, slipstreaming his team-mate then diving past at the final instant. With more fuel on board, this looked as though he held the winning cards.

Conversely, Vettel's hopes of glory in the dry after wet wins at Monza and Shanghai, appeared to have been scuppered as Massa used his KERS to move into third place.

Before the drivers could settle, the safety car was out after Jarno Trulli clattered into Adrian Sutil's Force India after being forced off by Nico Rosberg then firing back onto the track in the path of Sutil and the Toro Rossos. With one lap down, four cars were out of the running.

When the safety car withdrew, Fernando Alonso gave the home fans something to cheer about as he slipstreamed past Webber to take fifth, only to have the Australian use his slipstream to go back by before Turn 1.

It was the timing of the pit stops that was

to cause Barrichello such anger. The team calculated that Button, who was going to pit before Barrichello, would return to the track behind Rosberg. So, instead, they fuelled him so that he would need to come in just once more. This was to stop Button from losing ground, but Barrichello would only see it afterwards as one adopted to help Button win, at his expense.

Barrichello was able to return ahead of Rosberg, who would be stopping way later on his two-stop run, so all seemed good for the Brazilian. The trouble was, as he led up to his second pit stop on lap 31, he wasn't fast enough and Button's speed with a heavier fuel load was more impressive. To compound this, Barrichello became ragged on his third set of tyres and his advantage ebbed away. Their relative positions became clear when Button emerged from his second pit stop and, two laps later, Barrichello came back from his third and was 7s behind. The margin opened out to 13s, Barrichello seemingly spending those laps convinced that there was a conspiracy against him.

There was also a change of places between the Red Bulls, with Webber being given a bigger fuel load at his first stop and using it to leapfrog Vettel and Massa. The Ferrari would fall away in its final stint, Massa having to nurse it around after not enough fuel was put in, and so Alonso claimed fifth place before flagfall.

BARCELONA - ROUND 05

Date: **10 May 2009**   Laps: **66**   Distance: **190.825 miles/307.104km**
Weather: **Dry and bright**

RACE RESULT

Position	Driver	Team	Result	Stops	Qualifying Time	Grid
1	**Jenson Button**	Brawn	1h37m19.202s	2	1m20.527s	1
2	**Rubens Barrichello**	Brawn	1h37m32.258s	3	1m20.762s	3
3	**Mark Webber**	Red Bull	1h37m33.126s	2	1m21.049s	5
4	**Sebastian Vettel**	Red Bull	1h37m38.143s	2	1m20.660s	2
5	**Fernando Alonso**	Renault	1h38m02.368s	2	1m21.392s	8
6	**Felipe Massa**	Ferrari*	1h38m10.029s	2	1m20.934s	4
7	**Nick Heidfeld**	BMW Sauber	1h38m11.514s	2	1m20.676s	13
8	**Nico Rosberg**	Williams	1h38m24.413s	2	1m22.558s	9
9	**Lewis Hamilton**	McLaren*	65 laps	2	1m20.805s	14
10	**Timo Glock**	Toyota	65 laps	2	1m21.247s	6
11	**Robert Kubica**	BMW Sauber	65 laps	2	1m22.685s	10
12	**Nelson Piquet Jr**	Renault	65 laps	2	1m20.604s	12
13	**Kazuki Nakajima**	Williams	65 laps	3	1m20.531s	11
14	**Giancarlo Fisichella**	Force India	65 laps	4	1m22.204s	20
R	**Kimi Raikkonen**	Ferrari*	17 laps/hydraulics	0	1m21.291s	16
R	**Heikki Kovalainen**	McLaren*	7 laps/gearbox	0	1m21.675s	18
R	**Jarno Trulli**	Toyota	0 laps/accident	0	1m21.254s	7
R	**Sebastien Buemi**	Toro Rosso	0 laps/accident	0	1m21.067s	15
R	**Sebastien Bourdais**	Toro Rosso	0 laps/accident	0	1m21.300s	17
R	**Adrian Sutil**	Force India	0 laps/accident	0	1m21.742s	19

FASTEST LAP: BARRICHELLO, 1M22.762S, 125.844MPH/202.527KPH ON LAP 28
RACE LEADERS: BARRICHELLO 1-19, 21-31 & 49-50; MASSA 20; BUTTON 32-48 & 51-66
* RUNNING WITH KERS

TALKING POINT: BMW SAUBER TUMBLES DOWN THE ORDER

Having finished third, not far behind Ferrari and McLaren in 2008, BMW Sauber had high hopes. The team was confident that its KERS-fitted cars would be on the pace. But they weren't. Qualifying in the top half of the grid would be considered an achievement. In Barcelona, even with the introduction of an aero upgrade that modified the wings plus the sidepods, Heidfeld advanced from 13th to seventh, but this raised the team's tally only to six points, leaving them still seeking downforce to help the cars stop graining their tyres. The team even elected to drop KERS, in order to accommodate more aerodynamic sidepods. All hopes were being pinned on a double diffuser for the Turkish GP.

BMW Sauber dices with Ferrari. But, unlike in 2008, this was for midfield positions.

MONACO GP

The team principals met in Monaco to discuss the future of F1, but one glance at the form of Jenson Button and Brawn GP showed that this combination was very much F1's present as the English driver led all the way from pole position for his fifth win of 2009.

Brawns to the fore, again, as Jenson Button leads Rubens Barrichello and Ferrari's Kimi Raikkonen into Ste Devote on the opening lap.

It didn't take a genius to notice that a pattern was emerging as 2009 unfolded. Sure, Brawn GP was taking the wins, and it was Jenson Button not team-mate Rubens Barrichello who was doing the winning. However, there was another element to this pattern, and this was that Button was peaking at the right time. Barrichello would often have the legs on him through practice, then Button would put it all together in qualifying, take pole position and carry that advantage into the race.

This must have driven Barrichello to despair, and Button did it at Monaco. In fact, Button left his brinksmanship to the very end, only getting it all together on his final run to nab pole.

To make matters worse for Barrichello, who had a near identical fuel load, he was demoted to third by Kimi Raikkonen whose Ferrari came within 0.025s of pole but at least gave Ferrari its first front row start of the year.

Button would have been worried about the getaway ability of the Finn's Ferrari with the extra 80bhp or so provided by its KERS, but the short approach to the first corner, Ste Devote, was always going to limit that. Yet, the Brawns were among only five cars that went onto the grid on the softer tyre, the Ferrari team not yet confident that their cars wouldn't destroy theirs too soon. And this was what enabled Button to counter the Ferrari KERS threat.

Not only did Button reach Ste Devote first, but Barrichello got his Mercedes power down well to slot into second place behind him.

While the first three drivers eased clear, Sebastian Vettel soon rooted his tyres, his Red Bull RB5 clearly less than happy on a circuit without high-speed corners, and found Felipe Massa right on his tail. The Ferrari driver tried to pass him into the harbourfront chicane after a dab of KERS through the tunnel. He was rebuffed. Next time around, he tried again, but was again given no room and this time shot wide, ran through the chicane, and came out ahead. He had to give the position back to Vettel but found himself in a position where

Nico Rosberg was able to dive past as well.

The Williams driver then put pressure on Vettel, eventually forcing the Red Bull to let him through into the chicane, with Massa benefiting from Vettel being off line and passing him into Tabac. Vettel's run got worse, as he was brought in early for his pit stop then tried too hard on his return and crashed at Ste Devote.

Vettel wasn't the first driver to retire from the race, though, as Sebastien Buemi rammed his Toro Rosso into the back of Nelson Piquet Jr's Renault at the same corner.

It was at this point that Barrichello started to struggle in second, as his super soft tyres offered ever less grip, and so he dropped back from Button, by more than a second per lap. His first pit stop couldn't come soon enough.

None of this affected leader Button, as he had two stints on the regular tyre to come. He duly pitted from the lead on lap 19 then returned in the lead and was headed only when he came in for his second pit stop, when Raikkonen led for a single lap. Once back in front, though, he led all the way to the finish, ecstatic at the fifth win of his campaign, by 7.666s from Barrichello, who was far happier on the regular tyre.

Raikkonen and Massa made it a three-four finish for Ferrari, while Mark Webber made it up to fifth, gaining ground over Rosberg by daring to run a longer final stint on super softs.

MONACO - ROUND 06

Date: **24 May 2009** Laps: **78** Distance: **161.850 miles/260.473km**
Weather: **Warm and bright**

RACE RESULT

Position	Driver	Team	Result	Stops	Qualifying Time	Grid
1	**Jenson Button**	Brawn	1h40m44.282s	2	1m14.902s	1
2	**Rubens Barrichello**	Brawn	1h40m51.948s	2	1m15.077s	3
3	**Kimi Raikkonen**	Ferrari*	1h40m57.724s	2	1m14.927s	2
4	**Felipe Massa**	Ferrari*	1h40m59.392s	2	1m15.437s	5
5	**Mark Webber**	Red Bull	1h41m00.012s	2	1m15.653s	8
6	**Nico Rosberg**	Williams	1h41m17.868s	2	1m15.455s	6
7	**Fernando Alonso**	Renault	1h41m22.121s	2	1m16.009s	9
8	**Sebastien Bourdais**	Toro Rosso	1h41m47.424s	1	1m16.281s	14
9	**Giancarlo Fisichella**	Force India	1h41m49.322s	1	1m16.146s	13
10	**Timo Glock**	Toyota	77 laps	1	1m16.788s	20**
11	**Nick Heidfeld**	BMW Sauber	77 laps	1	1m16.264s	16
12	**Lewis Hamilton**	McLaren*	77 laps	2	1m16.264s	19***
13	**Jarno Trulli**	Toyota	77 laps	2	1m16.548s	18
14	**Adrian Sutil**	Force India	77 laps	2	1m16.545s	15
R	**Kazuki Nakajima**	Williams	76 laps/accident	2	1m17.344s	10
R	**Heikki Kovalainen**	McLaren*	51 laps/accident	1	1m15.516s	7
R	**Robert Kubica**	BMW Sauber	28 laps/brakes	1	1m16.405s	17
R	**Sebastian Vettel**	Red Bull	15 laps/accident	1	1m15.271s	4
R	**Nelson Piquet Jr**	Renault	10 laps/crash damage	0	1m15.837s	12
R	**Sebastien Buemi**	Toro Rosso	10 laps/accident	0	1m15.833s	11

FASTEST LAP: MASSA, 1M15.154S, 99.418MPH/159.998KPH ON LAP 50
RACE LEADERS: 1-51 & 53-78; RAIKKONEN 52
* RUNNING WITH KERS ** STARTED FROM THE PIT LANE *** 5-PLACE GRID PENALTY

TALKING POINT: TOP TEAMS LOOK TO SIGN BUTTON FOR 2010

Seemingly on the scrapheap as 2008 drew to a close after Honda pulled the plug on his ride, Jenson Button's five wins from the first six starts made him F1's hottest property. Unsurprisingly, as other top teams circled, Brawn GP, was working in earnest to hang on to his services. Without a big sponsor coming on board, Ross Brawn's team looked unlikely to keep hold of the 29-year-old English driver for the rest of his three-year contract, especially as Button will be looking to recoup the drop in salary he accepted to help the team out in its struggle to get onto the grid for 2009. After all the hard work he had put in to help the team turn around, it was going to be a tough decision for Button.

Button can't help but smile at the turnaround in his fortunes from the dark days of 2008.

TURKISH GP

Another grand prix, another victory for Jenson Button. However, this was a real scrap as his Brawn was pushed hard all the way by Red Bull Racing's Sebastian Vettel and the German was left to rue a slip-up when leading Button halfway around the opening lap.

Sebastian Vettel leads away, but a slip half way around the lap let Jenson Button through to lead. Jarno Trulli leads Mar Webber and the rest.

Sebastian Vettel stuck his Red Bull RB5 on pole position in Turkey. This he had done before, but never in the dry, and so it was plain for all to see that Red Bull Racing was fulfilling its promise and was now Brawn GP's main rival.

Taking into account fuel load in qualifying, it was going to be mighty close spread across the grand prix distance, as his 0.1s advantage came with a fuel load that was 6kg heavier. Red Bull Racing team chief Christian Horner said that their calculations suggested he would have a 2.5s advantage after the final round of pit stops. Not a lot, but enough.

What Vettel absolutely had to do was to ensure that he took the lead at the start of the race, which he did. But then he blew it.

Coming out of Turn 10, with Button's Brawn right on his tail, Vettel ran wide over the kerbs on the corner's exit after trying to carry too much speed into Turn 9 and thus missing his turn-in point. Not waiting for a second, Button was through into the lead in a flash and could now run the race on his own terms.

Button would have liked to take the lead off the line at the start, but the even positions on the grid - those lining up second, fourth, sixth and so on - always have a problem at Istanbul Park as their stretch of track is dusty. Indeed, Button was just as concerned about keeping team-mate Rubens Barrichello behind him. This he did, by heading straight across to the right to slot in front of the Brazilian.

Button needn't have worried, though, as Barrichello suffered another poor getaway and was swamped, completing the first lap in 12th, his afternoon ruined as he was now stuck behind slower cars. The frustration would get to him and there were contretemps with Heikki Kovalainen, with Barrichello spinning, and Adrian Sutil as he forced his way past. Eventually, he parked up with gearbox failure.

Another frustrated driver was Mark Webber, who had hoped to stick with the lead pair, but had been beaten to Turn 1 by Jarno Trulli's Toyota. That order was to change before the lap was out, with Trulli skating wide at Turn 9.

By the first round of pit stops, Button was 6s clear of Vettel, and stayed out longer. It was only after the stops that Brawn realised, judging by the amount of fuel that Vettel had had put in, that he was going to be running a three-stop stategy and that, to make it work, he was going to have to pass Button on the track. This was going to be nigh on impossible, as Button was having a day of days, later saying that he thought his car's handling was "outrageous." It was to prove the highpoint of the relationship of Button and his car, and it went downhill from here.

Button headed Vettel after those first stops, but was running with a heavier fuel load, as he planned to stop just once more, and delayed Vettel, with only one failed dive up the inside into the final corner to show for it. All the time that Vettel was behind Button, though, he was running beneath the pace that he needed to make his strategy work.

This also favoured team-mate Webber who would be stopping just twice, with Webber moving into second when Vettel made his extra stop. There was nothing that the Australian could do about Button, though, who backed off to save his engine and yet still won easily.

Trulli did just enough to repel Nico Rosberg's efforts, with the second Williams driver, Kazuki Nakajima, being thwarted in his bid for points, when a jammed wheelnut at his final pit stop cost him seventh place.

ISTANBUL PARK - ROUND 07
Date: **7 June 2009** Laps: **58** Distance: **192.388 miles/309.619km**
Weather: **Very hot and bright**

RACE RESULT

Position	Driver	Team	Result	Stops	Qualifying Time	Grid
1	**Jenson Button**	Brawn	1h26m24.848s	2	1m28.421s	2
2	**Mark Webber**	Red Bull	1h26m31.562s	2	1m28.613s	4
3	**Sebastian Vettel**	Red Bull	1h26m32.309s	3	1m28.316s	1
4	**Jarno Trulli**	Toyota	1h26m52.691s	2	1m28.666s	5
5	**Nico Rosberg**	Williams	1h26m56.387s	2	1m29.191s	9
6	**Felipe Massa**	Ferrari*	1h27m04.844s	2	1m28.858s	7
7	**Robert Kubica**	BMW Sauber	1h27m11.095s	2	1m29.357s	10
8	**Timo Glock**	Toyota	1h27m11.807s	2	1m27.795s	13
9	**Kimi Raikkonen**	Ferrari*	1h27m15.094s	2	1m28.815s	6
10	**Fernando Alonso**	Renault	1h27m27.268s	2	1m29.075s	8
11	**Nick Heidfeld**	BMW Sauber	1h27m29.175s	2	1m27.521s	11
12	**Kazuki Nakajima**	Williams	1h27m31.224s	2	1m27.629s	12
13	**Lewis Hamilton**	McLaren*	1h27m45.302s	1	1m28.318s	16
14	**Heikki Kovalainen**	McLaren*	57 laps	2	1m28.207s	14
15	**Sebastien Buemi**	Toro Rosso	57 laps	2	1m28.708s	18
16	**Nelson Piquet Jr**	Renault	57 laps	2	1m28.582s	17
17	**Adrian Sutil**	Force India	57 laps	2	1m28.391s	15
18	**Sebastien Bourdais**	Toro Rosso	57 laps	1	1m28.918s	20
R	**Rubens Barrichello**	Brawn	47 laps/gearbox	2	1m28.579s	3
R	**Giancarlo Fisichella**	Force India	4 laps/brakes	0	1m28.717s	19

FASTEST LAP: BUTTON, 1M27.579S, 136.342MPH/219.422PH ON LAP 40
RACE LEADERS: BUTTON 1-17 & 19-58; WEBBER 18
* RUNNING WITH KERS

TALKING POINT: McLAREN FALLS FURTHER FROM THE PACE

McLaren's season went from bad to worse in Turkey and it came away with no points for the third race in a row. With its cars qualifying 14th and 16th, the extent of the problem was clear. What was harder to identify was how to fix the problem that left its MP4-24s off the pace on circuits with high-speed corners. The clearest evidence came through Turn 8, where it found itself 9mph slower than the Force India, a car using the same engine. Announcing that the team's hopes of retaining the title were now over, many thought that all focus would be thrown at its 2010 car, especially with the ban on in-season testing, although it's hard to imagine McLaren turning its back on a problem.

Smiles were few and far between in the McLaren camp as Hamilton and Kovalainen struggled.

BRITISH GP

Those expecting yet another win for Brawn and Jenson Button were disappointed as cooler temperatures prevented the white cars getting heat into their tyres. Instead, Red Bull Racing set the pace, and Sebastian Vettel headed home a one-two result.

Sebastian Vettel leads Rubens Barrichello into Copse, followed by Mark Webber, Kazuki Nakajima, Kimi Raikkonen and Jarno Trulli.

How long a year must have felt for Lewis Hamilton when he arrived at Silverstone for his third British GP. In 2007 and 2008, he was the hero, feted at every turn, yet here he was, still well supported, but a sideshow in the Jenson Button parade.

As events unfolded through practice then qualifying, neither of the British drivers would have much to smile about, as Button just couldn't get heat into his tyres and would line up sixth. For once, team-mate Rubens Barrichello had the upper hand, starting second behind the weekend's dominant driver, Sebastian Vettel, and just edging out the second Red Bull, Mark Webber's.

For Hamilton, it was even worse and his qualifying position, 19th, was the worst of his

career. It made little difference that he was promoted one place on the grid when Adrian Sutil dropped to last place as he was starting in a new car after his major shunt at Abbey.

Once the five red lights on the gantry had been extinguished to signal the start of the race, it was all Vettel, with Webber losing ground as he was stuck behind Barrichello's Brawn although plainly faster.

And so Vettel was able to dictate the race as he pleased, leading all the way until lap 44 before Webber had three laps at the front after Vettel's second pit stop, then made his own second visit to the pits and dropped back to second, eventually finishing 15s adrift, cursing having not been able to pass Barrichello at the start.

At the end, Vettel got right onto the wavelength of the British crowd, saying that looking at their response, and remembering how they used to go wild for Nigel Mansell, that he half wished he was an Englishman.

It really was a case of Red Bull Racing against the rest. Barrichello finished in third place, but he finished the race fully 26s down on Webber who had got ahead by staying out a lap longer before their first pit stops and then streaking away. Sporting a far bigger smile at flagfall was Felipe Massa, for he had had a strong run to fourth for Ferrari from eighth on the grid. Most of his ground was made by being the last to make his first pit stop, and he ran fifth after that, behind Rosberg, who he demoted by again stopping later for the second round of pit stops.

Button was tripped by Jarno Trulli who was slow off the grid in front of him and thus losing a place to Nico Rosberg. The Williams driver passed Trulli's Toyota further around the lap. With both Ferrari drivers using their KERS to good effect, Button found himself down in ninth. He was brought in on the same lap as Trulli, and so made to trail him through the second stint as well, albeit with Trulli just squeezing out ahead of Raikkonen as they re-emerged. The one good turn for Button was that he had been fuelled for a long middle stint, pitted several laps after Trulli and Raikkonen, and so got past both.

Having qualified an encouraging fifth fastest for Williams and jumped Trulli at the start, Kazuki Nakajima found himself at the sharp end of the field for once, but he was the first of the chasing pack to pit and fell to ninth, then to 11th after his second pit stop.

Hamilton ended up 16th, but at least he entertained the crowd in a fabulous tussle with Fernando Alonso and Robert Kubica. The battle might have been over 13th place, but it was no holds barred in the early laps. They weren't gunning for victory, but they still had their pride. Hamilton ended up lapped, after a spin at Vale, but entertained the crowd after the finish with some doughnut spins.

SILVERSTONE – ROUND 08

Date: **21 June 2009**   Laps: **60**   Distance: **191.640 miles/308.415km**
Weather: **Warm and bright**

RACE RESULT

Position	Driver	Team	Result	Stops	Qualifying Time	Grid
1	Sebastian Vettel	Red Bull	1h22m49.328s	2	1m19.509s	1
2	Mark Webber	Red Bull	1h23m04.516s	2	1m19.868s	3
3	Rubens Barrichello	Brawn	1h23m30.503s	2	1m19.856s	2
4	Felipe Massa	Ferrari*	1h23m34.371s	2	1m18.927s	11
5	Nico Rosberg	Williams	1h23m35.243s	2	1m20.361s	7
6	Jenson Button	Brawn	1h23m35.613s	2	1m20.289s	6
7	Jarno Trulli	Toyota	1h23m57.635s	2	1m20.091s	4
8	Kimi Raikkonen	Ferrari*	1h23m58.950s	2	1m20.715s	9
9	Timo Glock	Toyota	1h23m59.151s	2	1m20.490s	8
10	Giancarlo Fisichella	Force India	1h24m00.850s	2	1m19.802s	16
11	Kazuki Nakajima	Williams	1h24m03.351s	2	1m20.216s	5
12	Nelson Piquet Jr	Renault	59 laps	1	1m19.392s	14
13	Robert Kubica	BMW Sauber	59 laps	2	1m19.308s	12
14	Fernando Alonso	Renault	59 laps	2	1m20.741s	10
15	Nick Heidfeld	BMW Sauber	59 laps	2	1m19.448s	15
16	Lewis Hamilton	McLaren	59 laps	2	1m19.917s	18
17	Adrian Sutil	Force India	59 laps	1	1m19.909s	20**
18	Sebastien Buemi	Toro Rosso	59 laps	2	1m20.236s	19
R	Sebastien Bourdais	Toro Rosso	37 laps/crash damage	2	1m19.898s	17
R	Heikki Kovalainen	McLaren	36 laps/crash damage	2	1m19.353s	13

FASTEST LAP: VETTEL, 1M20.735S, 142.422MPH/229.206KPH ON LAP 16
RACE LEADERS: VETTEL 1-44 & 48-60; WEBBER 45-47
* RUNNING WITH KERS ** STARTED FROM THE PIT LANE

TALKING POINT: F1 BREAKAWAY THREAT BECOMES REAL

Fans came in droves to what could be the final British GP at Silverstone, but left confused as to whether they would be spectating here, at Donington Park or not in Britain at all in 2010. What had caused this disquiet was that FOTA had announced a breakaway series as it disagreed with F1's governance and the direction of FIA proposals. FOTA wanted all rule changes to be devised by the Technical Working Group rather than by the FIA president, also aiming for the FIA International Court of Appeal to be replaced by an independent body. FOTA said that it would organise its own series, chiefly using circuits dropped by F1, including Adelaide, Kyalami and, fittingly, Silverstone.

Renault chief Flavio Briatore was among the FOTA chiefs who announced a breakaway series.

GERMAN GP

The speed has been there but never the equipment, until 2009, and so Mark Webber finally scored a hugely popular first grand prix win. Even so, the battling Australian had to show his tenacity to win despite having to lose time serving a drivethrough penalty.

Sebastian Vettel dominated the British GP, but he had to play a supporting role when he reached home ground as Red Bull Racing team-mate Mark Webber was in the driving seat at the Nurburgring once he managed to dislodge Rubens Barrichello from the lead.

By race's end, the early-pitting Brazilian driver had tumbled to fifth place and the Australian was victor by 9.2s over Vettel who could only offer his congratulations.

First things first, Webber secured his first ever pole position. Importantly, he achieved this with a heavy fuel load. In fact, Barrichello's Brawn carried fully 14kg less, and this would surely have him pitting earlier. Webber, being Webber, wanted to keep Barrichello behind him at the start, so that he could control events, but it all got hairy as they piled into the tightening right-hander.

Webber not only had to defend from Barrichello but from Lewis Hamilton's KERS-boosted McLaren that was rocketing up on his left, up from a greatly improved fifth on the grid. Webber came across on Barrichello, hitting his front left wheel.

Fortunately, both continued, but the stewards were later to decide that the contact was avoidable and so hit Webber with a stop-go penalty.

Webber's rough ride wasn't over, either, as he pinged across and hit Hamilton's right rear tyre, puncturing it. The McLaren driver then had to crawl back around the remaining 90% of the lap and so dropped right to the tail of the field on a day on which he'd hoped updates on the car would have guided him back to the points for the first time since the fourth round in Bahrain.

It wasn't all bad news for McLaren, as Heikki Kovalainen slotted into third place behind Barrichello and Webber. He wasn't able to challenge them, but for those stuck behind the Finn's silver car there was only frustration. Jenson Button passed Felipe Massa to lead the group delayed in the McLaren's wake. But, of course, all the time, Barrichello and Webber pulled further clear.

In fact, they were so far clear that Webber was able to take his drivethrough penalty and emerge still ahead of Kovalainen.

In fact, he came back out in the lead, as Barrichello had come in at the same time and taken on fuel. Worse still for Barrichello, compatriot Felipe Massa had yet to pit and moved into a temporary second place, having gained places when Kovalainen and Button pitted before him.

Mark Webber's maiden victory propelled him to third place in the drivers' championship table and was met with universal adulation.

Now Webber had to fly, as he still had to make what would be his scheduled first stop. He drove them like qualifying laps and came out in eighth place after his pit stop. Importantly, though, he had been fuelled for a long middle stint, and this would be key to his recovery.

Barrichello resumed the lead when Massa finally called at the pits, but he knew that the time lost behind the red car had cost him, as he was running a three-stop strategy. The race was coming back to Webber and, indeed, he rose to second as those ahead of him made their stops. Then, when Barrichello made the second of his three stops, he hit the front again. And there he stayed.

Vettel also made a late second pit stop and this tactic worked well for him too, as he went on to finish in second place with Massa's Ferrari 6s behind in third.

Nico Rosberg used a long first stint to work his way forward from 15th and took an eventual fourth, leading the Brawns and Fernando Alonso home

Adrian Sutil should have finished among the points scorers for Force India, but he clashed with Kimi Raikkonen's Ferrari after leaving the pits and that dropped him down the order.

NURBURGRING - ROUND 09

Date: **12 July 2009**   Laps: **60**   Distance: **191.940 miles/308.898km**
Weather: **Sunny but cool**

RACE RESULT

Position	Driver	Team	Result	Stops	Qualifying Time	Grid
1	Mark Webber	Red Bull	1h36m43.310s	3	1m32.230s	1
2	Sebastian Vettel	Red Bull	1h36m52.562s	2	1m32.480s	4
3	Felipe Massa	Ferrari*	1h36m59.216s	2	1m34.574s	8
4	Nico Rosberg	Williams	1h37m04.409s	2	1m42.859s	15
5	Jenson Button	Brawn	1h37m07.009s	3	1m32.473s	3
6	Rubens Barrichello	Brawn	1h37m07.778s	3	1m32.357s	2
7	Fernando Alonso	Renault	1h37m08.198s	2	1m42.318s	12
8	Heikki Kovalainen	McLaren*	1h37m42.002s	2	1m33.859s	6
9	Timo Glock	Toyota	1h37m44.767s	1	1m32.423s	20**
10	Nick Heidfeld	BMW Sauber	1h37m45.235s	2	1h42.310s	11
11	Giancarlo Fisichella	Force India	1h37m45.637s	2	1m32.402s	18
12	Kazuki Nakajima	Williams	1h37m46.186s	2	1m42.500s	13
13	Nelson Piquet Jr	Renault	1h37m51.638s	2	1m34.803s	10
14	Robert Kubica	BMW Sauber	1h37m52.865s	2	1m31.190ds	16
15	Adrian Sutil	Force India	1h37m55.251s	3	1m34.316s	7
16	Sebastien Buemi	Toro Rosso	1h38m13.535s	2	1m32.251s	17
17	Jarno Trulli	Toyota	1h38m14.280s	3	1m42.771s	14
18	Lewis Hamilton	McLaren*	59 laps	2	1m32.616s	5
R	Kimi Raikkonen	Ferrari*	34 laps/radiator	1	1m34.710s	9
R	Sebastien Bourdais	Toro Rosso	18 laps/hydraulics	0	1m33.559s	19

FASTEST LAP: ALONSO, 1M33.365S, 123.341MPH/198.498KPH ON LAP 49
RACE LEADERS: BARRICHELLO 1-14 & 25-31; WEBBER 15-19, 32-43 & 45-60; MASSA 20-24; VETTEL 44
* RUNNING WITH KERS ** DENOTES THREE-PLACE PENALTY, STARTED FROM PIT LANE

TALKING POINT: WEBBER STILL RECOVERING FROM BROKEN LEGS

Watching Webber's ever-improving form and now this, his first F1 win, it was easy to forget that he had broken his right leg by crashing his bicycle into a 4WD vehicle during his own charity triathlon at the start of the close-season. This injury limited his testing, so he had been playing catch up to team-mate Vettel, and yet this win took him to within 1.5 points of the German, with both closing in on points leader Button. In the lead-in to the German GP Mark had had titanium screws removed from his right leg. And, although he prefers not to mention any pain he'd been enduring, lest it gave encouragement to his rivals, you can be sure that each piece of metal reinforcement removed must be a relief.

Sebastian Vettel offers his congratulations to Mark Webber after his maiden victory.

HUNGARIAN GP

There were two massive stories from the Hungaroring. Firstly, news of Felipe Massa suffering career-threatening head injuries when hit by a spring in qualifying. Secondly, McLaren was back, as Lewis Hamilton hit form to score the first win of his title defence.

Lewis Hamilton lines up Mark Webber before passing him and going on to his first 2009 win.

Hungaroring as it was deprived of Hungary's normal soaring summer temperatures that many had said would help them get the heat into their tyres that the drivers needed for grip. Jenson Button would line up eighth, Rubens Barrichello 12th.

As predicted, bearing in mind how light his Renault was, Alonso did enough at the start to lead the field away. But it was open warfare behind him as Hamilton and Ferrari's Kimi Raikkonen used their KERS to great effect at the start, both diving past a slow-starting Vettel and then Hamilton lunging past Webber for second into Turn 1. But then he ran wide and Webber reclaimed the position.

Behind them, Raikkonen had to lift off the throttle to avoid Webber and clattered into Vettel, causing suspension damage.

Hamilton had his dander up after losing his narrowly-gained second place, though, and chased after Webber before demoting him into Turn 2 on lap 5 in a move of exceptional bravado, leaving Webber to come under attack next from Raikkonen's Ferrari.

Now Hamilton had to consider Alonso, but the leader was clearly on a three-stop strategy as he had run so light in qualifying. As the McLaren driver was planning to stop twice, he knew that he now had the race under control.

Sure enough, Alonso came in for his first stop after just 12 laps, but his race for points was then ruined when his right front wheel wasn't secured properly after being changed and came off around his out lap. This was to lead to the FIA banning the team from the European GP, although this was later reversed and the team fined instead.

Hamilton then led the race as he pleased all the way to the finish for the first win of

Felipe Massa was fortunate to escape with his life after suffering head injuries when an 800g spring fell off the suspension of Rubens Barrichello's Brawn that had been lapping several seconds ahead of him in the final qualifying session (see sidebar).

It seemed almost incidental that Fernando Alonso was fastest in that final qualifying session to grab pole position for Renault. As you might have guessed, though, the Spaniard

set his time carrying next to no fuel. Sebastian Vettel would start the race alongside him, albeit having lapped just a fraction slower with fully 17.5kg more fuel on board.

Red Bull team-mate Mark Webber would start from third, with McLaren's continued improvement in form leading to Lewis Hamilton qualifying fourth and Heikki Kovalainen sixth, sandwiching Nico Rosberg.

Brawn GP was in all sorts of trouble at the

his title defence. He was understandably delighted, and McLaren's day became better still when Kovalainen finished fifth.

Raikkonen also gave Ferrari, still stunned after Massa's accident, something to smile about by beating Webber to second thanks to a frantic incident in the pit lane. The Australian and Finn pitted together, but Webber tried to leave before the lollipop was raised, hesitated then all but got waved out into the Ferrari's path, with Raikkonen just squeezing through.

Ten seconds further back, Rosberg scored his second straight fourth place for Williams.

Button was able to finish only seventh but still led the title race, although his advantage was down to 18.5 points, now over Webber after Vettel's failure to score.

Nineteen-year-old Spanish driver Jaime Alguesuari made history when he replaced Sebastien Bourdais at Toro Rosso by becoming the youngest ever F1 driver, beating Mike Thackwell's record of 19 years and 182 days, set in Canada for Tyrrell in 1980, by 57 days. The British F3 Champion was scorned for his lack of F1 experience, which amounted to three sessions of straightline testing, thanks to the in-season testing ban. However, he performed with aplomb and his only real problem was being very tired in the final half dozen laps as his neck muscles suffered.

HUNGARORING - ROUND 10

Date: **26 July 2009**   Laps: **70**   Distance: **190.540 miles/306.645km**
Weather: **Hot and dry**

RACE RESULT

Position	Driver	Team	Result	Stops	Qualifying Time	Grid
1	**Lewis Hamilton**	McLaren*	1h38m23.876s	2	1m21.839s	4
2	**Kimi Raikkonen**	Ferrari*	1h38m35.405s	2	1m22.468s	7
3	**Mark Webber**	Red Bull	1h38m40.762s	2	1m21.741s	3
4	**Nico Rosberg**	Williams	1h38m50.843s	2	1m21.890s	5
5	**Heikki Kovalainen**	McLaren*	1h38m58.268s	2	1m22.095s	6
6	**Timo Glock**	Toyota	1h38m59.113s	2	1m21.242s	13
7	**Jenson Button**	Brawn	1h39m18.964s	2	1m22.511s	8
8	**Jarno Trulli**	Toyota	1h39m32.048s	2	1m21.082s	11
9	**Kazuki Nakajima**	Williams	1h39m32.650s	2	1m22.835s	9
10	**Rubens Barrichello**	Brawn	1h39m33.132s	2	1m21.222s	12
11	**Nick Heidfeld**	BMW Sauber	1h39m34.488s	2	1m21.738s	15
12	**Nelson Piquet Jr**	Renault	1h39m35.388s	2	1m21.389s	14
13	**Robert Kubica**	BMW Sauber	1h39m37.922s	2	1m21.901s	18
14	**Giancarlo Fisichella**	Force India	69 laps	2	1m21.807s	16
15	**Jaime Alguersuari**	Toro Rosso	69 laps	2	1m22.359s	19
16	**Sebastien Buemi**	Toro Rosso	69 laps	2	1m21.002s	10
R	**Sebastian Vettel**	Red Bull	29 laps/suspension	2	1m21.607s	2
R	**Fernando Alonso**	Renault	15 laps/fuel pump	2	1m21.569s	1
R	**Adrian Sutil**	Force India	1 lap/water temperature	0	1m21.868s	17
NS	**Felipe Massa**	Ferrari*	Driver injury	-	no time	-

FASTEST LAP: WEBBER, 1M21.931S, 119.612MPH/192.497KPH ON LAP 65
RACE LEADERS: RACE LEADERS: ALONSO 1-11; HAMILTON 12-20, 22-70; KOVALAINEN 21
* RUNNING WITH KERS

TALKING POINT: MASSA SURVIVES BEING HIT ON THE HEAD

F1 is given a jolt every now and then that emphasises that it never can be an entirely safe sport. Felipe Massa was running behind Rubens Barrichello in qualifying when a spring bounced up and clattered into his helmet, leaving him stunned as his Ferrari careered into a tyrewall. Not surprisingly, there were fears, as this followed a week after Henry Surtees - son of 1964 F1 World Champion John Surtees - was killed when a wheel struck him on the head in an F2 race at Brands Hatch. Luckily, Massa would escape with a fractured skull, and talk of him losing sight in his left eye proved erroneous, although it took several days before Massa was released from hospital in Budapest and sent home to Brazil.

With Massa already on his way to hospital, his battered Ferrari is delivered back to the pits.

EUROPEAN GP

All but five years had passed between this vital victory for Rubens Barrichello and his previous one, for Ferrari, and it fired him back into the championship battle as his Brawn GP team-mate Jenson Button lost ground at the start and fell to seventh place.

Jenson Button was the man for Brawn in the first half of the season, but Rubens Barichello's first win for five years put him into the mix.

Rubens Barrichello is an extremely emotional individual: he cries when he wins and fumes when he doesn't. He's a good friend too, as shown by the message atop his helmet, offering supported to injured compatriot Felipe Massa. One look at how people from teams the length of the pit lane, and most notably Ferrari, came out to greet him as he drove into the pits after winning from Lewis Hamilton demonstrated his popularity.

The only people who didn't feel too inclined to applaud him were McLaren, as they were preparing to be questioned by the media about whether their pit stop fumble at Lewis Hamilton's final pit stop cost the British driver victory. Afterwards, the McLaren management said that they didn't have

the pace to win, but the fact that the tyres were brought out as Hamilton's car came to a standstill was a fiasco. This happened as a decision had been made to keep him out for an extra lap of his middle stint, and he had saved fuel accordingly. The decision was then reversed, for fear that he might not have enough fuel, and he dived for the pits, only to be told to stay out, just as he had peeled into the pit entry lane. Too late! And so he caught his tyre men on the hop and seconds were lost as they struggled to remove the tyre blankets, wiping out Hamilton's pre-stop lead of 3.6s. Commendably, Hamilton kept his cool and said finishing second wasn't so bad if you consider the mess they had been in at the start of the season.

Hamilton had started from pole, with team-mate Heikki Kovalainen tucking in behind him. With the Valencia street circuit so narrow and overtaking all but impossible for the drivers whose cars are not KERS-equipped, Turn 2 offers a rare passing opportunity after the field has blasted through the Turn 1 kink. Several moves were made, with Sebastien Buemi's Toro Rosso's nose shattering after clipping Timo Glock's left rear tyre. Renault's rookie Romain Grosjean got caught up and had his front wing clattered by Jarno Trulli, while Ferrari stand-in Luca Badoer had the first of the spins that were to mark his F1 return. The next would happen on lap 2...

Jenson Button's race had already been compromised as he tried to get past Sebastian

Vettel's Red Bull, but Vettel was so intent on keeping Kimi Raikkonen's KERS-boosted Ferrari behind that he pulled towards the pit wall, forcing Button to back off, losing further places to Nico Rosberg and Fernando Alonso. With overtaking all but impossible, his chance of a big points haul was compromised.

Button and Alonso then had a good scrap, but soon afterwards Button was radioed to give a place back to Mark Webber, as he had gained it on the opening lap by cutting the chicane. His hopes of not losing any more ground to Red Bull's racers had been spiked, but salvation came when Vettel suffered another engine failure and Webber drifted away, falling to an eventual ninth.

Hamilton pitted from the lead on lap 16, Kovalainen from second a lap later, while Barrichello stayed out five laps longer than Hamilton before he made his first stop.

Then came the mix-up at Hamilton's second pit stop and Barrichello was only sure that he had done enough to take the lead going into the final stint when he pitted three laps later and emerged in front. The Brazilian then controlled the race and took the win that triggered the full flow of emotions as Ross Brawn congratulated him over the radio, describing it as being like the old days, when they won races together for Ferrari.

VALENCIA - ROUND 11

Date: **23 August 2009** Laps: **57** Distance: **191.919 miles/308.864km**
Weather: **Very hot and sunny**

RACE RESULT

Position	Driver	Team	Result	Stops	Qualifying Time	Grid
1	**Rubens Barrichello**	Brawn	1h35m51.289s	2	1m39.563s	3
2	**Lewis Hamilton**	McLaren*	1h35m53.647s	2	1m39.498s	1
3	**Kimi Raikkonen**	Ferrari*	1h36m07.283s	2	1m40.144s	6
4	**Heikki Kovalainen**	McLaren*	1h36m11.321s	2	1m39.532s	2
5	**Nico Rosberg**	Williams	1h36m12.159s	2	1m40.185s	7
6	**Fernando Alonso**	Renault	1h36m19.033s	2	1m40.236s	8
7	**Jenson Button**	Brawn	1h36m26.202s	2	1m39.821s	5
8	**Robert Kubica**	BMW Sauber	1h36m27.956s	2	1m40.512s	10
9	**Mark Webber**	Red Bull	1h36m36.199s	2	1m40.239s	9
10	**Adrian Sutil**	Force India	1h36m39.224s	2	1m38.846s	12
11	**Nick Heidfeld**	BMW Sauber	1h36m40.111s	2	1m38.826s	11
12	**Giancarlo Fisichella**	Force India	1h36m54.903s	1	1m39.531s	16
13	**Jarno Trulli**	Toyota	1h36m55.816s	1	1m39.807s	18
14	**Timo Glock**	Toyota	1h37m17.808s	3	1m38.991s	13
15	**Romain Grosjean**	Renault	1h37m23.063s	3	1m39.040s	14
16	**Jaime Alguersuari**	Toro Rosso	56 laps	2	1m39.925s	19
17	**Luca Badoer**	Ferrari*	56 laps	3	1m41.413s	20
18	**Kazuki Nakajima**	Williams	54 laps/car damage	2	1m39.795s	17
R	**Sebastien Buemi**	Toro Rosso	41 laps/brakes	2	1m39.514s	15
R	**Sebastian Vettel**	Red Bull	23 laps/engine	2	1m39.789s	4

FASTEST LAP: GLOCK, 1M38.683S, 122.837MPH/197.687KPH ON LAP 55
RACE LEADERS: HAMILTON 1-15, 21-36; KOVALAINEN 16; BARRICHELLO 17-20, 37-57
* RUNNING WITH KERS

TALKING POINT: BADOER STRUGGLES AFTER 10 YEARS AWAY

There was one rookie in Valencia, Renault's Grosjean, but many treated Ferrari's Badoer, a driver with 48 grand prix starts, as a rookie too as he'd not raced in F1 for 10 years since leaving Minardi. It wasn't as though he'd got out of the F1 loop, having been pounding around Ferrari's Fiorano test track in support of Michael Schumacher's title challenges. When Massa was hurt, Schumacher elected to come back from three years of retirement, but his neck was still too weak after falling off his motorbike. So, loyalty was rewarded, and the 38-year-old Italian – Formula 3000 champion in 1992 – was presented with a chance to end a record he hates: the most grands prix without scoring.

Luca Badoer gathers his thoughts as he waits to start his Ferrari from the back of the grid.

BELGIAN GP

Kimi Raikkonen scored his fourth win at Spa and there was a first lap crash that took out Jenson Button and Lewis Hamilton, but the big news was that Giancarlo Fisichella not only scored Force India's first points, but crossed the line just 1s behind Raikkonen.

From whichever angle you looked at it, this was a topsy-turvy event. The practice sessions had teams bouncing up and down the timesheets, with no pattern emerging. Then qualifying was all a-jumble. Just ask Jenson Button and Lewis Hamilton who were eliminated in the second qualifying session, along with Fernando Alonso, leaving even the sport's experts scratching their heads.

When fuel loads were taken into account, it was clear that Giancarlo Fisichella had taken pole for Force India by running with a light fuel load. Rubens Barrichello, in fourth, had carried even less. Jarno Trulli and Nick Heidfeld, second and third on the grid, were due to make their first pit stop two or even three laps later. Yet, it was Sebastian Vettel,

who had qualified down in eighth place, who had the best speed on adjusted times.

Fisichella led away under sunny skies, knowing that he was going to have to make good his escape and not be impeded if he wanted to have a chance of a famous result.

Behind him, Trulli bent his front wing against Heidfeld at La Source, while Robert Kubica dived past his team-mate around the outside. Damage could have been worse, as Barrichello failed to get away and was nearly hit by several cars as they jinked around him.

Going up the hill to Les Combes, Raikkonen displayed the advantage of the extra power provided by KERS and got a good tow before bursting past Kubica for second place, albeit running over the grass at the right-left esse.

Those further back were not so lucky and the sequence of events that accounted for four cars was triggered by Romain Grosjean hitting Button into a spin. In attempting to avoid the melee, Hamilton was hit hard by Jaime Alguersuari. All were out on the spot.

The safety car was triggered and this helped Raikkonen to close onto Fisichella's tail then use his KERS simply to blast into the lead on the climb to Les Combes when they were released on lap 5. And that was that, despite Fisichella being able to stick to his tail like a limpet right the way to the finish. Unfortunately, they were both on the very same strategy, so they pitted together at both stops, and Fisichella never had clear track to try to eke out an advantage.

This was a sight no one thought they would ever see: Force India's Giancarlo Fisichella pushing Ferrari's Kimi Raikkonen hard for victory.

Vettel ran a very different race to the lead duo, making his first stop later and so leapfrogging past the BMW Saubers to finish third, with Heidfeld frustrated at not being able to overhaul Kubica.

Stopping even later than Vettel was Alonso, but his hopes that his one-stop strategy would fire him up the order ended when there was a problem with his left front wheel and, after a slow lap, he retired.

Barrichello did well to make it back to seventh behind the one-stopping Heikki Kovalainen and at least take two points out of Button's lead, reducing it to 16. Had he not all but stalled at the start, then had to pit to have debris cleared from his sidepods after going off at Les Combes on lap 1, he would have taken a bigger bite into his defeat to Button who acknowledged that his first non-finish hadn't been as costly as it might have been.

Mark Webber should have been right in the mix after running in fifth place, but he was again flagged out away from his pit stop into trouble, all but pushing Heidfeld into the pit wall. In trying to save him a fraction of a second and keep him ahead of the German, the team earned him a drivethrough penalty and cost Webber a point score as he could make it back only to ninth, right on the tail of Nico Rosberg's Williams.

SPA-FRANCORCHAMPS - ROUND 12

Date: **30 August 2009** Laps: **44** Distance: **191.491 miles/308.175km**
Weather: **Dry & bright**

Position	Driver	Team	Result	Stops	Qualifying Time	Grid
1	**Kimi Raikkonen**	Ferrari*	1h23m50.995s	2	1m46.633s	6
2	**Giancarlo Fisichella**	Force India	1h23m51.934s	2	1m46.308s	1
3	**Sebastian Vettel**	Red Bull	1h23m54.879s	2	1m46.761s	8
4	**Robert Kubica**	BMW Sauber	1h24m00.961s	2	1m46.586s	5
5	**Nick Heidfeld**	BMW Sauber	1h24m02.271s	2	1m46.500s	3
6	**Heikki Kovalainen**	McLaren*	1h24m23.758s	1	1m45.259s	15
7	**Rubens Barrichello**	Brawn	1h24m26.456s	2	1m46.513s	4
8	**Nico Rosberg**	Williams	1h24m27.203s	2	1m47.362s	10
9	**Mark Webber**	Red Bull	1h24m27.954s	3	1m46.788s	9
10	**Timo Glock**	Toyota	1h24m32.485s	2	1m46.677s	7
11	**Adrian Sutil**	Force India	1h24m33.631s	2	1m45.119s	11
12	**Sebastien Buemi**	Toro Rosso	1h24m37.101s	2	1m45.951s	16
13	**Kazuki Nakajima**	Williams	1h24m45.236s	1	1m46.307s	18
14	**Luca Badoer**	Ferrari*	1h25m33.172s	1	1m46.957s	20
R	**Fernando Alonso**	Renault	26 laps/brakes	1	1m45.136s	13
R	**Jarno Trulli**	Toyota	21 laps/crash damage	2	1m46.395s	2
R	**Lewis Hamilton**	McLaren*	0 laps/accident	0	1m45.122s	12
R	**Jenson Button**	Brawn	0 laps/accident	0	1m45.251s	14
R	**Jaime Alguersuari**	Toro Rosso	0 laps/accident	0	1m46.032s	17
R	**Romain Grosjean**	Renault	0 laps/accident	0	1m46.359s	19

FASTEST LAP: VETTEL, 1M47.263S, 146.065MPH/235.069KPH ON LAP 38
RACE LEADERS: FISICHELLA 1-4; RAIKKONEN, 5-14, 18-31, 36-44; VETTEL 15-16, 32-35; ROSBERG 17
* RUNNING WITH KERS

TALKING POINT: FIA PUTS RENAULT UNDER INVESTIGATION

If Renault thought that it had got off without punishment when its ban from contesting the European GP – for allowing Alonso's car to leave a pit stop without a wheel fully secured – had been lifted, it appeared to be heading for far greater trouble when news broke at Spa that it was under investigation again. This time, the FIA announced it would be looking into the way in which it won the 2008 Singapore GP, when a crash by Nelson Piquet Jr brought out the safety car just after Fernando Alonso had pitted, thus handing him the lead, which he held to the finish. Conspiracy theories had abounded, but the trigger for the belated FIA investigation came after Piquet Jr was fired from the team.

This accident for Nelson Piquet Jr in the 2008 Singapore GP came under renewed scrutiny.

ITALIAN GP

This is the grand prix in which F1's balance of power slipped back to Brawn GP as Rubens Barrichello led home Jenson Button for a one-two at the same time as Red Bull Racing tumbled down the order, emphasizing how there was not one dominant team in 2009.

Back on a track that suited his car, Rubens Barrichello led Jenson Button home after running a one-stop strategy and playing a waiting game.

There will always be certain circuits that suit one team over another and Red Bull Racing arrived at Monza knowing that the classic circuit's layout was one on which it was unlikely to shine, as it lacked the long, fast corners through which its RB5 shines. On top of that, it arrived, knowing that it had precious few Renault engines left that they could use without taking a penalty. To be quick in a straight line, the team had to take off the wing angle that would help it around the corners, and that reduced it to a supporting role.

After qualifying, Sebastian Vettel and Mark Webber were ninth and 10th. Their rivals from Brawn were fifth and sixth, Rubens Barrichello

ahead of Jenson Button. However, the Brawn camp was confident that their chances were better than that when fuel strategy was taken into consideration.

So it proved, as the first three on the grid - Lewis Hamilton's McLaren, Adrian Sutil's ever-improving Force India and Kimi Raikkonen's Ferrari - were going to pit twice, although this still left Heikki Kovalainen's one-stopping McLaren ahead of the Brawns on the grid.

Hamilton, using his KERS to good effect, took the lead at the start and resisted a challenge from Raikkonen, but what gave the Brawn drivers hope was that Kovalainen was slow off the line and blew his chance of victory.

Barrichello passed him into the first chicane, then Button got by at the second Lesmo. Within a lap, the Finn had lost two more places, to Vitantonio Liuzzi - in for Giancarlo Fisichella at Force India when his compatriot transferred to Ferrari - and Fernando Alonso.

Red Bull's duo failed to gain from this, and Webber was already out, having clashed with Robert Kubica at the first chicane.

Hamilton made good his escape, but the question was whether he would be able to open out a large enough gap to make his two-stop strategy work. It would take a while to find out.

Hamilton had a lead of 17s when he pitted and slotted back in to third behind Barrichello and Button once fellow two-stoppers Raikkonen and Sutil had pitted. It was still hard to gauge whether Hamilton had a winning tactic or not. The Brawns made their only pit stops just after mid-distance, and had to hope that they had done enough so that Hamilton would re-emerge behind them after his second stop. This came on lap 34 and the signals were in the laps before then that it would take a superhuman run to enable him to come out ahead. And so it proved, with Barrichello and Button already past pit exit before he came out again. His hope now rested on catching Button, who was 4s ahead, and overhauling him with a deft touch of KERS. As the laps came down, so did the gap, and Button defended with aplomb, only for Hamilton to make a mistake at the first Lesmo on the final lap, crashing into the barriers as he tried to gain a superior exit speed to help him make a passing move into the Ascari chicane. Thus Brawn collected its first one-two since Monaco, this time with Barrichello in front.

Raikkonen was elevated to a distant third, chased home for the second race in a row by a Force India, this time with Sutil right on his tail. New team-mate Liuzzi might have finished sixth or higher, but a driveshaft failed. Meanwhile, Fisichella's maiden run for Ferrari was less successful and he ended up ninth, rueing qualifying outside the top 10.

MONZA – ROUND 13
Date: **13 September 2009** Laps: **53** Distance: **190.779 miles/307.029km**
Weather: **Dry and bright**

Position	Driver	Team	Result	Stops	Qualifying Time	Grid
1	**Rubens Barrichello**	Brawn	1h16m21.706s	1	1m25.015s	5
2	**Jenson Button**	Brawn	1h16m24.572s	1	1m25.030s	6
3	**Kimi Raikkonen**	Ferrari*	1h16m52.370s	2	1m24.523s	3
4	**Adrian Sutil**	Force India	1h16m52.837s	2	1m24.261s	2
5	**Fernando Alonso**	Renault*	1h17m20.888s	1	1m25.072s	8
6	**Heikki Kovalainen**	McLaren*	1h17m22.399s	1	1m24.845s	4
7	**Nick Heidfeld**	BMW Sauber	1h17m44.118s	1	1m24.275s	15
8	**Sebastian Vettel**	Red Bull	1h17m47.113s	1	1m25.180s	9
9	**Giancarlo Fisichella**	Ferrari*	1h17m48.562s	1	1m23.901s	14
10	**Kazuki Nakajima**	Williams	1h19m03.869s	1	1m24.074s	17
11	**Timo Glock**	Toyota	1h19m05.631s	1	1m24.036s	16
12	**Lewis Hamilton**	McLaren*	52 laps/accident	2	1m24.066s	1
13	**Sebastien Buemi**	Toro Rosso	52 laps/pulled in	1	1m24.220s	19
14	**Jarno Trulli**	Toyota	52 laps	1	1m23.611s	11
15	**Romain Grosjean**	Renault*	52 laps	1	1m23.728s	12
16	**Nico Rosberg**	Williams	51 laps	3	1m24.121s	18
R	**Vitantonio Liuzzi**	Force India	22 laps/transmission	0	1m25.043s	7
R	**Jaime Alguersuari**	Toro Rosso	19 laps/gearbox	1	1m24.951s	20**
R	**Robert Kubica**	BMW Sauber	15 laps/oil leak	1	1m23.866s	13
R	**Mark Webber**	Red Bull	0 laps/accident	0	1m25.314s	10

FASTEST LAP: SUTIL, 1M24.739S, 152.930MPH/246.117KPH ON LAP 63
RACE LEADERS: HAMILTON 1-15 & 30-34; RAIKKONEN 16-19 & 35-37; BARRICHELLO 20-29 & 38-53
* RUNNING WITH KERS ** STARTED FROM THE PITLANE

TALKING POINT: RENAULT ENGINE'S ARE RED BULL'S ACHILLES HEEL

Red Bull's star had shone so brightly as Vettel and Webber won races and took the fight to Brawn's Button and Barrichello. However, as they closed in, a cloud appeared, and the spectre was that of Renault engine failures. A rule specified that teams could change a driver's engine eight times without penalty, but would be hit with a 10-place grid demotion on any subsequent occasions, Red Bull's Christian Horner was torn between going for glory and getting the drivers to hold back a few revs to ensure greater engine life. This was just what they didn't need as they considered how best to outscore the Brawns. Team owner Dietrich Mateschitz said that the grid penalty was inevitable with four races still to run.

The Renault V8 engine in the rear of the Red Bull RB5s had failed a few times too many.

SINGAPORE GP

Lewis Hamilton dominated from pole position to atone for his last lap accident at Monza, but the story line focused on the fact that Jenson Button was able to rise from 11th to fifth and even nick a point off title challenging team-mate Rubens Barrichello.

Lewis Hamilton was all but untouchable in the second Singapore night race and would have won by more but for a safety car intervention.

The 2009 season was a strange one from the outset. If you had a double diffuser at the opening round, you were onto a good thing. For the other seven teams, the year was going to be about playing catch up. Despite dark days of despair at Woking and Maranello, you always felt that they would make it in the end. They both got onto the top step of the podium by late summer, but it was McLaren in the driving seat as the season wound down. Well, Lewis Hamilton at least as Heikki Kovalainen continued to be some way adrift, claiming the deficit was because the car hadn't been developed to suit his driving style.

And so Hamilton proved in the Singapore night race. He qualified on pole position, and had not only the advantage of his KERS for a

quick blast towards the tricky first corner, but knew that as long as he reached Turn 1 first he ought to be in control for the remainder of the race as the next four cars on the grid ought to be making their first pit stop before he made his, as they had qualified their cars with lighter fuel loads.

As far as the battle for title honours was concerned, Jenson Button started from down in 11th, but this was less of a disaster than it might have been as team-mate and rival Rubens Barrichello was lining up immediately ahead, in ninth, having been demoted five places on the grid for his car having had a gearbox change.

Hamilton duly did what he had to do and was chased not by second fastest qualifier Sebastian Vettel, but by Nico Rosberg who

made a fine start from third on the grid.

What happened in their wake shuffled the race order, with Mark Webber running wide when trying to demote a fast-starting Fernando Alonso, and Timo Glock nipped past the Spaniard as well. A few laps later, Webber was instructed by race control to give up the places he had gained by making use of an area beyond the track. He didn't like it, but he had to.

This increased the gap between the breakaway trio of Hamilton, who was controlling the race comfortably – even though he had to work through a sequence of radio instructions to reset a pump that had failed and forced him to switch off his KERS – Rosberg and Vettel.

Rosberg's race was ruined when he made

his first pit stop, as he ran wide over the white line at pit exit and collected a drivethrough penalty. Then out came the safety car after Adrian Sutil had spun trying to pass Jaime Alguersuari then spun his car around, straight into the path of Nick Heidfeld's BMW Sauber. This meant that the pit lane was closed and also that the field bunched up. It cost Rosberg, big time, as otherwise he could have made his stop and still slotted back in ahead of Glock, to be third. Instead, he rejoined in 14th place.

When racing again, Hamilton had Vettel right on his tail, and Glock behind him. But Vettel pitted way seven laps before Hamilton needed to make his second stop, with Glock lasting another six laps and thus emerging in what would become second as Vettel was given a drivethrough penalty for speeding in the pit lane. The German's penalty dropped him to fourth behind Alonso. No-one could match Hamilton though, and he raced away to win by just under 10s from Glock.

Third place for Alonso was a welcome boost for troubled Renault (see box-out), while the most important move further back was when Barrichello stalled at his second pit stop and that was enough for Button to take fifth and thus extend his lead to 15 points rather than see it come down.

SINGAPORE - ROUND 14
Date: **27 September 2009** Laps: **61** Distance: **191.972 miles/308.950km**
Weather: **Hot and dark**

Position	Driver	Team	Result	Stops	Qualifying Time	Grid
1	**Lewis Hamilton**	McLaren*	1h56m06.337s	2	1m47.891s	1
2	**Timo Glock**	Toyota	1h56m15.971s	2	1m49.180s	6
3	**Fernando Alonso**	Renault	1h56m22.961s	2	1m49.054s	5
4	**Sebastian Vettel**	Red Bull	1h56m26.598s	3	1m48.204s	2
5	**Jenson Button**	Brawn	1h56m36.352s	2	1m47.141s	11
6	**Rubens Barrichello**	Brawn	1h56m38.195s	2	1m48.828s	9**
7	**Heikki Kovalainen**	McLaren*	1h56m42.494s	2	1m49.778s	8
8	**Robert Kubica**	BMW Sauber	1h57m01.391s	2	1m49.514s	7
9	**Kazuki Nakajima**	Williams	1h57m02.391s	2	1m47.013s	10
10	**Kimi Raikkonen**	Ferrari*	1h57m05.229s	2	1m47.177s	12
11	**Nico Rosberg**	Williams	1h57m06.114s	3	1m48.348s	3
12	**Jarno Trulli**	Toyota	1h57m19.346s	2	1m47.413s	14
13	**Giancarlo Fisichella**	Ferrari*	1h57m26.227s	2	1m48.350s	17
14	**Vitantonio Liuzzi**	Force India	1h57m39.839s	2	1m48.792s	19
R	**Jaime Alguersuari**	Toro Rosso	47 laps/brakes	2	1m48.340s	16
R	**Sebastien Buemi**	Toro Rosso	47 laps/gearbox	3	1m47.369s	13
R	**Mark Webber**	Red Bull	45 laps/brakes	2	1m48.722s	4
R	**Adrian Sutil**	Force India	23 laps/brakes	1	1m48.231s	15
R	**Nick Heidfeld**	BMW Sauber	19 laps/accident	0	1m49.307s	20***
R	**Romain Grosjean**	Renault	3 laps/brakes	0	1m48.544s	18

FASTEST LAP: ALONSO, 1M48.240S, 104.56IMPH/168.275KPH ON LAP 53
RACE LEADERS: HAMILTON 1-46, 51-61; ALONSO 47-50
* RUNNING WITH KERS ** FIVE-PLACE GRID PENALTY FOR GEARBOX CHANGE *** PUT TO BACK OF GRID AS CAR UNDERWEIGHT

TALKING POINT: A NEW ORDER AT RENAULT

With team principal Flavio Briatore and executive director of engineering Pat Symonds having been banished from F1 for their part in "Crashgate" in the 2008 Singapore GP, and sponsor ING demanding to be removed from the car, there was a new look to the beleaguered Renault team. Technical director Bob Bell stepped into the breach and ran the show. The rest of the team kept their heads down and worked away, raised their eyes to the sky in incredulity when Romain Grosjean crashed in practice at the same corner as Nelson Piquet Jr had 12 months earlier to trigger the furore. Yet, they then got their reward when Alonso came through for third place in the race. This was racing, not politics.

Following "Crashgate 2008", Bob Bell (left) found himself at the helm of the Renault F1 team.

JAPANESE GP

Most of the talk ahead of the Japanese GP was about how Jenson Button could clinch the drivers' title at Suzuka, and he did move a small step closer to doing so, but Sebastian Vettel put himself back into the hunt with a flawless victory for Red Bull.

A lot of the talk as the teams arrived at Suzuka was how Button was looking ever more fragile. Then the talk after Sebastian Vettel controlled the race was how the German might be the one to beat him to the crown rather than Button's team-mate Rubens Barrichello.

The gap between Button and Vettel had fallen to 16 points, with 20 to play for, and Red Bull Racing's principal Christian Horner was talking of how the momentum was with Vettel, and how Lewis Hamilton had squandered a 17-points advantage in the final two races of 2007 to lose the title to Kimi Raikkonen.

Vettel qualified on pole, as everyone revelled in returning to this real drivers' circuit with its revamped facilities. Better still, his fuel load was heavier than his rivals'.

Hamilton made a bid for the lead, from third on the grid, but the run to the first corner at Suzuka is a short one and he couldn't quite get enough extra oomph from his McLaren's KERS. He got past Jarno Trulli's Toyota and ran alongside Vettel, but was on the outside line and so had to slot into second place.

If all was OK at the front, it wasn't at the back. Sebastien Buemi stalled but fortunately was missed. Mark Webber had to start from the pit lane after a new chassis was required following a shunt at Degner that forced him to miss qualifying. Within a lap, he was in the pits as his headrest had come loose. And he was in again the lap after that, for the same repair. Then, on lap 4, he picked up a puncture, turning his race into a test session.

Timo Glock didn't even get to start. Unwell on the Friday, he was replaced by Kamui Kobayashi. On Saturday, he crashed, gashed a leg and it was decided he wouldn't race.

Vettel soon put clear air between himself, Hamilton and Trulli. They, in turn, left the rest of the field in their wake.

Title protagonists Barrichello and Button were among a quintet of drivers who were put back five places on the grid for not slowing for yellow flags that were shown in the final qualifying session after Buemi crashed his Toro Rosso, meaning that they had to start sixth and 10th.

Things got worse immediately for Button as he lost a place to Heikki Kovalainen, but he got past Robert Kubica into the chicane on

Victory for Sebastian Vettel kept him in the hunt for the drivers' title, but Jenson Button made sure he scored to edge closer to the crown.

lap 3, which was crucial as the BMW Sauber was carrying far more fuel. Barrichello, who was Button's sole focus, remained in sixth, but was able to turn faster laps.

However, Button was then gifted two places when Adrian Sutil, frustrated by being delayed by Kovalainen, and mindful that he would be pitting before the Finn, made a move into the chicane. He appeared to have the line, but Kovalainen refused to cede, their cars touched and Sutil spun. Button didn't need to be asked twice and dived through.

There was nothing that Hamilton or Trulli could do about Vettel as he drove a stunning race, but the Toyota driver was desperate to give Toyota a good race in Japan and he got ahead at the second round of pit stops, helped when Hamilton had a problem leaving his stop and coasted for 100m down the pit lane before his engine fired again and he went back out to finish in third place.

BMW Sauber's Nick Heidfeld lost fourth to Raikkonen thanks to a jammed wheelnut at his second stop. Nico Rosberg also demoted him thanks to making his second pit stop as the safety car came out after Jaime Alguersuari crashed at fearsome 130R.

Seventh and eighth places for Barrichello and Button left Brawn half a point shy of claiming the constructors' crown.

SUZUKA - ROUND 15

Date: **4 October 2009**   Laps: **53**   Distance: **191.224 miles/307.746km**
Weather: **Warm & bright**

RACE RESULT

Position	Driver	Team	Result	Stops	Qualifying Time	Grid
1	Sebastian Vettel	Red Bull	1h28m20.443s	2	1m32.160s	1
2	Jarno Trulli	Toyota	1h28m25.320s	2	1m32.220s	2
3	Lewis Hamilton	McLaren	1h28m26.915s	2	1m32.395s	3
4	Kimi Raikkonen	Ferrari	1h28m28.383s	2	1m32.980s	5
5	Nico Rosberg	Williams	1h28m29.236s	2	1m31.482s	7
6	Nick Heidfeld	BMW Sauber	1h28m29.952s	2	1m32.945s	4
7	Rubens Barrichello	Brawn	1h8m31.084s	2	1m32.660s	6**
8	Jenson Button	Brawn	1h28m31.917s	2	1m32.962s	10**
9	Robert Kubica	BMW Sauber	1h28m32.220s	2	1m32.341s	9
10	Fernando Alonso	Renault	1h28m33.508s	1	1m31.638s	16**
11	Heikki Kovalainen	McLaren	1h28m34.178s	2	No time	11***
12	Giancarlo Fisichella	Ferrari	1h28m35.039s	2	1m31.704s	14
13	Adrian Sutil	Force India	1h28m35.402s	2	1m32.466s	8**
14	Vitantonio Liuzzi	Force India	1h28m36.177s	2	1m32.087s	18
15	Kazuki Nakajima	Williams	1h28m38.416s	1	1m31.718s	15
16	Romain Grosjean	Renault	52 laps	1	1m32.073s	17
17	Mark Webber	Red Bull	51 laps	5	No time	19****
R	Jaime Alguersuari	Toro Rosso	43 laps/accident	2	No time	12
R	Sebastien Buemi	Toro Rosso	11 laps/clutch	0	No time	13**
NS	Timo Glock	Toyota	Leg injury	-	No time	

FASTEST LAP: WEBBER, 1M32.569S, 140.326MPH/225.833KPH ON LAP 50
RACE LEADERS: VETTEL 1-53
* RUNNING WITH KERS ** GRID PENALTY FOR NOT SLOWING UNDER YELLOWS *** 5-PLACE PENALTY FOR GEARBOX CHANGE
**** NEW CHASSIS SO HAD TO START FROM PIT LANE

TALKING POINT: THE DONINGTON PARK SAGA RUNS AND RUNS

There was considerable surprise in July 2008 when Bernie Ecclestone awarded Donington Park the right to host the British GP from 2010, for 17 years. Few thought it had the money to finance the changes to bring it up to F1 standards. On top of this, the news that the finance was expected to come from a debenture scheme at a time the world economy was in freefall didn't seem encouraging. The rumours that it would crash grew through 2009, to the point in October that it had missed its final deadline to prove that the finances were in place and that the construction work could be completed. Silverstone fretted in the sidelines, seeking a multi-year deal before stepping back into the breach.

Excavation continued at Donington Park, but the finances still remained in short supply.

BRAZILIAN GP

Button had fought to keep his nerves in check for a full month, tried to ignore the criticism, then produced the drive of a true champion to tiger up the field to claim fifth place and with it the world title on a day when Red Bull's Mark Webber dominated.

The cork is out of the bottle, the pressure is clearly released and it's celebration time for Jenson Button after a magnificent charge up to fifth.

Qualifying badly had become Jenson Button's bane. So, when heavy rain threatened to bring qualifying to a premature end, with Button sixth, he'd have been happy with that. But the rain subsided enough for the session to be continued and he missed the top 10 cut. His nightmare had come true. He would start 14th.

At least he was in good company, for both Sebastian Vettel and Lewis Hamilton had found their cars to handle more like boats and would start 15th and 17th.

The home crowd went wild when qualifying was over, for Rubens Barrichello had given his title challenge a gargantuan fillip by hurling his Brawn around fastest. He knew that nothing less than victory would do in front of his fans.

On race day, though, it wasn't his dream that would come true, but Button's, and this wasn't without a magnificent, aggressive drive from the Englishman, fighting his way up to fifth with a drive that silenced his army of critics who'd been saying that he had lost his bottle as he found the Brawn no longer to be the best car.

The first corner, with its blind entry and steep drop away always provides fireworks, and many felt that Button was a prime candidate to get caught up in them. This time, the drivers behaved, until Turn 2 where Vettel pitched Kovalainen's McLaren into a spin, putting Giancarlo Fisichella's Ferrari onto the grass.

Then Kimi Raikkonen bent his front wing on Webber's Red Bull on the sprint to Descida do Lago. He'd have to pit for a new one.

Just behind that, coming out of Turn 5, Jarno Trulli tried to go around the outside of Adrian Sutil, was squeezed onto the grass or ran out of space, according to who you talked to, and slammed into the barriers, with Sutil collecting Fernando Alonso. With debris on the track, the safety car was scrambled.

It might have been calm at the front, as Barrichello led Webber around, with a gap before Nico Rosberg. But the first lap action wasn't over, as Hamilton came in for a crafty pit stop to change off the unloved super soft tyres, while both Raikkonen and Kovalainen pitted for repairs. Kovalainen rushed to get back out, but took his fuel hose with him, leaking fuel that ignited when Raikkonen drove over it.

The driver making the most ground, crucially, was Button, who knew he had to quickly pass several cars ahead of him that were due to pit after he was. Romain Grosjean was passed with aplomb into Turn 4, then fought back but came again to take eighth out of Turn 5. Kazuki Nakajima was next, and he was passed into Turn 1 with some great late braking.

Then came Kamui Kobayashi on his debut for Toyota. He was impressive but, as Button would describe him later "crazy." It took until lap 24 and the whoop Button emitted when he finally passed him said it all.

Barrichello led until his first stop. But, with Webber staying out six laps longer, it was always likely he'd take the lead, and he did.

Robert Kubica also outran Barrichello, and the local hero faded to the point at which he was fourth and knew Button would be champion, even before getting a puncture.

Webber went on peerlessly to victory, with Kubica second and Hamilton up from the tail to third, with the field bunched after a late-race safety car after Kazuki Nakajima littered the track after hitting Kobayashi. Vettel finished fourth, leaving fifth-placed Button to run around embracing the entire paddock.

INTERLAGOS – ROUND 16

Date: **18 October 2009** Laps: **71** Distance: **190.101 miles/305.939km**
Weather: **Warm and cloudy**

RACE RESULT

Position	Driver	Team	Result	Stops	Qualifying Time	Grid
1	Mark Webber	Red Bull	1h32m23.081s	2	1m19.668s	2
2	Robert Kubica	BMW Sauber	1h32m30.707s	2	1m20.631s	8
3	Lewis Hamilton	McLaren	1h32m42.025s	2	1m25.192s	17
4	Sebastian Vettel	Red Bull	1h32m42.733s	2	1m25.009s	15
5	Jenson Button	Brawn	1h32m52.086s	2	1m22.504s	14
6	Kimi Raikkonen	Ferrari	1h32m56.421s	2	1m20.168s	5
7	Sebastien Buemi	Toro Rosso	1h32m59.072s	2	1m20.250s	6
8	Rubens Barrichello	Brawn	1h33m08.535s	3	1m19.576s	1
9	Kamui Kobayashi	Toyota	1h33m26.405s	2	1m21.960s	11
10	Giancarlo Fisichella	Ferrari	1h33m33.746s	1	1m40.703s	19
11	Vitantonio Liuzzi	Force India	1h33m34.469s	3	no time	20*
12	Heikki Kovalainen	McLaren	1h33m36.580s**	3	1m25.052s	16
13	Romain Grosjean	Renault	70 laps	2	1m22.477s	13
14	Jaime Alguersuari	Toro Rosso	70 laps	2	1m22.231s	12
R	Kazuki Nakajima	Williams	30 laps/accident	1	1m20.674s	9
R	Nico Rosberg	Williams	27 laps/gearbox	1	1m20.326s	7
R	Nick Heidfeld	BMW Sauber	21 laps/out of fuel	1	1m25.515s	18
R	Adrian Sutil	Force India	0 laps/accident	0	1m19.912s	3
R	Jarno Trulli	Toyota	0 laps/accident	0	1m20.097s	4
R	Fernando Alonso	Renault	0 laps/accident	0	1m21.422s	10

FASTEST LAP: WEBBER, 1M13.733S, 130.728MPH/210.386KPH ON LAP 25
RACE LEADERS: BARRICHELLO 1-20; WEBBER 21-71
* FIVE-PLACE GRID PENALTY FOR GEARBOX CHANGE. ** INCLUDING 25S PENALTY FOR UNSAFE RELEASE FROM PIT STOP

TALKING POINT: FIRST BACK-TO-BACK BRITISH CHAMPS IN 40 YEARS

Britain's lead in the table for the country with the most World Champions stretched further when Jenson Button crossed the finish line in Brazil. In so doing, the Brawn driver became the 10th British driver to be World Champion. However, by following on from Lewis Hamilton's title-winning year in 2008, they became the first British duo to win the world title in consecutive year since Graham Hill and Jackie Stewart pulled off this trick for Lotus then Matra in 1968 and 1969 respectively. Since Mike Hawthorn scored Britain's first world title in 1958, the other nine drivers have added 16 further world titles, with Brazil the next most successful nation, with three drivers sharing eight world titles.

Jackie Stewart, shown at Monaco in 1969, was the previous Briton to make it two on the trot.

ABU DHABI GP

Red Bull Racing dominated the first race on Abu Dhabi's spectacular Yas Marina circuit, with Sebastian Vettel nabbing second spot in the rankings in a race that Lewis Hamilton was tipped to win until a brake problem forced his McLaren into a rare retirement.

It really was a brave new world when Hamilton and Vettel lined up on the front row in fading afternoon light for Abu Dhabi's inaugural grand prix.

Abu Dhabi's prodigious wealth was on clear display when Formula 1 came to this gulf state for the first time. Its Yas Marina circuit, which was just part of a spectacular sporting complex, was the most extravagant facility yet to host a grand prix.

It had seemed through qualifying that the honours in front of the sheiks would certainly be going to Lewis Hamilton and McLaren, as a fitting reward for their considerable effort to haul their car not only up to being competitive, but to being the pace-setter.

However, that was not to be and the pole-setter struggled to open out the gap he needed to come out of the first of his two pit stops still in front of Sebastian Vettel who would be pitting two laps later. Hamilton had

been forced into a time-consuming run wide at Turn 17 before the pit stop and, straight after it, the outgoing World Champion was back in the pits, his car waved straight into its garage. Team data had indicated what Hamilton knew: his car had a braking problem and the team decided that it wasn't safe to go on.

So, having dropped his team-mate, Vettel had the race in his pocket.

Indeed, he was helped after the second round of pit stops when insufficient fuel had gone into Mark Webber's Red Bull and so he had to go on an economy run and this set up the most exciting moment of an otherwise lifeless race as newly crowned champion Jenson Button closed in.

Button had started fifth, but moved past

team-mate Rubens Barrichello before the end of the opening lap after the Brazilian had lost part of his front wing when Webber drove across it after having been squeezed to the outside going into the first corner by Vettel.

Button closed in fast and looked to be close enough in the final two laps to make a move stick. Twice he nosed his Brawn in front, but never on the right side to take the place into the next corner as Webber defended stoutly and held onto second place. Barrichello was a short distance behind in fourth.

The race was notable for being the final one for BMW Sauber, although it may return in a different guise. Whatever happens, Nick Heidfeld was delighted to send the Swiss team out with a good result, finishing fifth and later being presented with his car.

One of the most interesting feature of the last two races of 2009, Brawn's title double aside, was the form of Toyota stand-in Kamui Kobayashi. Experienced drivers had struggled, like Giancarlo Fisichella and Luca Badoer, when swapping to another car and suffering from a lack of testing, but Kobayashi simply got stuck in and shone. He passed Kimi Raikkonen on the opening lap and this elevated him to 11th. So what you might think, but this meant that he was first of the one-stoppers. Team-mate Jarno Trulli was ahead, running the supposedly superior two-stop strategy, but such was Kobayashi's determined push that he was in front when Trulli returned from his second stop, racing on to finish in sixth place.

The final point went to a driver who ended the year in style: Toro Rosso's Sebastien Buemi. He'd scored in Brazil and now again here, forcing those who hadn't heard of him before his graduation to reconsider their opinion thanks to the way he'd kept the likes of the more experienced Nico Rosberg behind him and repelled an attack from the highly-rated Robert Kubica as well.

That brought the 2009 World Championship to a close, after an enthralling season that truly flipped F1's form book onto its head.

YAS MARINA - ROUND 17
Date: **1 November 2009** Laps: **55** Distance: **189.810 miles/305.470km**
Weather: **Very hot and dry**

RACE RESULT

Position	Driver	Team	Result	Stops	Qualifying Time	Grid
1	Sebastian Vettel	Red Bull	1h34m03.414s	2	1m41.615s	2
2	Mark Webber	Red Bull	1h34m21.271s	2	1m41.726s	3
3	Jenson Button	Brawn	1h34m21.881s	2	1m41.892s	5
4	Rubens Barrichello	Brawn	1h34m26.149s	2	1m41.786s	4
5	Nick Heidfeld	BMW Sauber	1h34m29.667s	2	1m42.343s	8
6	Kamui Kobayashi	Toyota	1h34m31.757s	1	1m40.777s	12
7	Jarno Trulli	Toyota	1h34m37.780s	2	1m41.897s	6
8	Sebastien Buemi	Toro Rosso	1h34m44.708s	2	1m42.713s	10
9	Nico Rosberg	Williams	1h34m49.355s	2	1m42.583s	9
10	Robert Kubica	BMW Sauiber	1h34m51.594s	2	1m41.992s	7
11	Heikki Kovalainen	McLaren	1h34m56.212s	1	1m40.983s	18*
12	Kimi Raikkonen	Ferrari	1h34m57.731s	1	1m40.726s	11
13	Kazuki Nakajima	Williams	1h35m03.253s	1	1m41.148s	13
14	Fernando Alonso	Renault	1h35m13.101s	1	1m41.667s	15
15	Vitantonio Liuzzi	Force India	1h35m37.864s	1	1m41.701s	16
16	Giancarlo Fisichella	Ferrari	54 laps	2	1m42.184s	20
17	Adrian Sutil	Force India	54 laps	2	1m41.863s	17
18	Romain Grosjean	Renault	54 laps	1	1m41.950s	19
R	Lewis Hamilton	McLaren	20 laps/brakes	1	1m40.948s	1
R	Jaime Alguersuari	Toro Rosso	18 laps/gearbox	0	1m41.689s	14

FASTEST LAP: VETTEL 1M40.279S, 123.893MPH/199.387KPH ON LAP 54
RACE LEADERS: HAMILTON 1-16; VETTEL 17-55
* FIVE-PLACE GRID PENALTY FOR GEARBOX CHANGE

TALKING POINT: TOM WHEATCROFT DIES

It was a terrible week for Donington Park. First of all Simon Gillett failed in his attempt to raise the money to host the British GP from 2010. Then, and far sadder, came the news on race morning at Abu Dhabi that Tom Wheatcroft had died, aged 87. Wheatcroft had watched grands prix there in the 1930s and his passion for racing was so strong that he restored the circuit after a near 30-year break in the late 1970s, also building a museum to house his ever-growing collection of grand prix cars that went on to become the largest in the world. His greatest day came in 1993 when Donington Park hosted the European GP and Ayrton Senna scored a famous win in treacherous conditions for McLaren.

Donington Park owner Tom Wheatcroft celebrates Ayrton Senna's stunning victory in 1993.

Brawn GP goes crazy after the Brazilian GP as Rubens Barrichello, Ross Brawn, new World Champion Jenson Button et al celebrate an extraordinary double success.

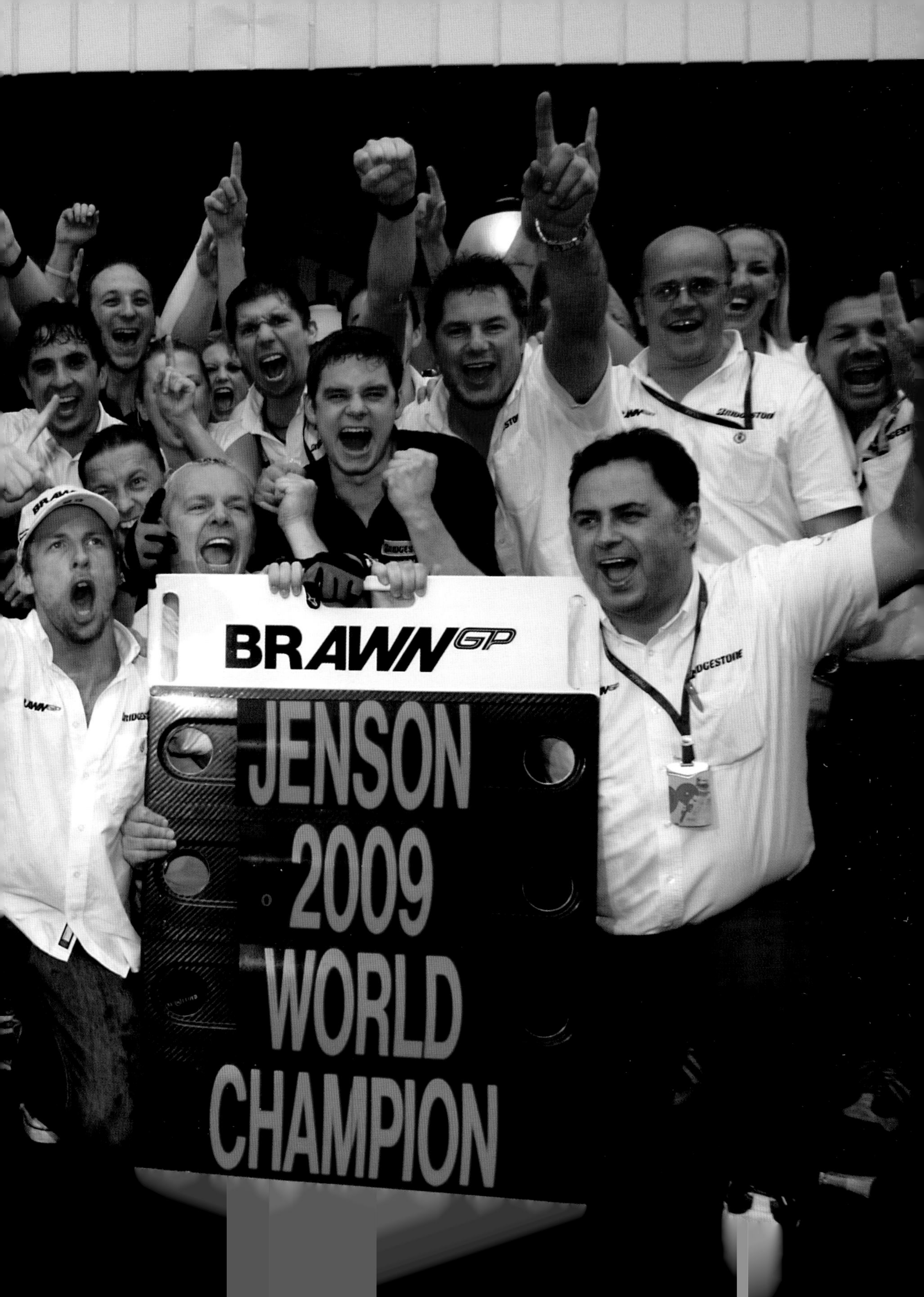
BRAWN GP
JENSON
2009
WORLD
CHAMPION

FINAL RESULTS 2009

	DRIVER	NAT.		ENGINE	R1	R2	R3	R4
1	JENSON BUTTON	GBR	🇬🇧	BRAWN-MERCEDES BGP 001	1P	1PF	3	1
2	SEBASTIAN VETTEL	GER		RED BULL-RENAULT RB5	13	15	1P	2
3	RUBENS BARRICHELLO	BRA	🇧🇷	BRAWN-MERCEDES BGP 001	2	5	4F	5
4	MARK WEBBER	AUS		RED BULL-RENAULT RB5	12	6	2	11
5	LEWIS HAMILTON	GBR	🇬🇧	McLAREN-MERCEDES MP4-24	D4	7	6	4
6	KIMI RAIKKONEN	FIN	🇫🇮	FERRARI F60	15	14	10	6
7	NICO ROSBERG	GER		WILLIAMS-TOYOTA FW31	6F	8	15	9
8	JARNO TRULLI	ITA	🇮🇹	TOYOTA TF109	3	4	R	3PF
9	FERNANDO ALONSO	SPA		RENAULT R29	5	11	9	8
10	TIMO GLOCK	GER		TOYOTA TF109	4	3	7	7
11	FELIPE MASSA	BRA	🇧🇷	FERRARI F60	R	9	R	14
12	HEIKKI KOVALAINEN	FIN	🇫🇮	McLAREN-MERCEDES MP4-24	R	R	5	12
13	NICK HEIDFELD	GER		BMW SAUBER F1.09	10	2	12	19
14	ROBERT KUBICA	POL		BMW SAUBER F1.09	14	R	13	18
15	GIANCARLO FISICHELLA	ITA	🇮🇹	FORCE INDIA-FERRARI VJM02	11	18	14	15
				FERRARI F60	-	-	-	-
16	SEBASTIEN BUEMI	SUI	🇨🇭	TORO ROSSO-FERRARI STR4	7	16	8	17
17	ADRIAN SUTIL	GER		FORCE INDIA-FERRARI VJM02	9	17	17	16
18	KAMUI KOBAYASHI	JPN	●	TOYOTA TF109	-	-	-	-
19	SEBASTIEN BOURDAIS	FRA	🇫🇷	TORO ROSSO-FERRARI STR4	8	10	11	13
20	KAZUKI NAKAJIMA	JAP	●	WILLIAMS-TOYOTA FW31	R	12	R	R
21	NELSON PIQUET JR	BRA	🇧🇷	RENAULT R29	R	13	16	10
22	VITANTONIO LIUZZI	ITA	🇮🇹	FORCE INDIA-MERCEDES VJM02	-	-	-	-
23	ROMAIN GROSJEAN	FR/SUI	🇫🇷🇨🇭	RENAULT R29	-	-	-	-
24	JAIME ALGUERSUARI	SPA		TORO ROSSO-FERRARI STR4	-	-	-	-
25	LUCA BADOER	ITA	🇮🇹	FERRARI F60	-	-	-	-

SCORING

				(RACE RESULTS FOR BOTH DRIVERS, ie. FIRST AND SECOND LISTED AS 1/2, WITH THE TEAM'S BETTER RESULT LISTED FIRST)			
		1	BRAWN-MERCEDES	1/2	1/5	3/4	1/5
		2	RED BULL-RENAULT	12/13	6/15	1/2	2/11
1st	10 points	3	McLAREN-MERCEDES	D/R	7/R	5/6	4/12
2nd	8 points	4	FERRARI	15/R	9/14	10/R	6/14
3rd	6 points	5	TOYOTA	3/4	3/4	7/R	3/7
4th	5 points	6	BMW SAUBER	10/14	2/R	12/13	18/19
5th	4 points	7	WILLIAMS-TOYOTA	6/R	8/12	15/R	9/R
6th	3 points	8	RENAULT	5/R	11/13	9/16	8/10
7th	2 points	9	FORCE INDIA-MERCEDES	9/11	17/18	14/17	15/16
8th	1 point	10	TORO ROSSO-FERRARI	7/8	10/16	8/11	13/17

SYMBOLS AND GRAND PRIX KEY

ROUND 1 .... AUSTRALIAN GP
ROUND 2 .... MALAYSIAN GP
ROUND 3 .... CHINESE GP
ROUND 4 .... BAHRAIN GP
ROUND 5 .... SPANISH GP
ROUND 6 .... MONACO GP
ROUND 7 .... TURKISH GP
ROUND 8 .... BRITISH GP
ROUND 9 .... GERMAN GP
ROUND 10 .... HUNGARIAN GP
ROUND 11 .... EUROPEAN GP
ROUND 12 .... BELGIAN GP
ROUND 13 .... ITALIAN GP
ROUND 14 .... SINGAPORE GP
ROUND 15 .... JAPANESE GP
ROUND 16 .... BRAZILIAN GP
ROUND 17 .... ABU DHABI GP

D DISQUALIFIED **F** FASTEST LAP **NC** NOT CLASSIFIED **NS** NON-STARTER **P** POLE POSITION **R** RETIRED **W** WITHDREW

R5	R6	R7	R8	R9	R10	R11	R12	R13	R14	R15	R16	R17	TOTAL POINTS
1P	1P	1F	6	5	7	7	R	2	5	8	5	3	95
4	R	3P	1PF	2	R	R	3F	8	4	1P	4	1F	84
2F	2	R	3	6	10	1	7	1	6	7	8P	4	77
3	5	2	2	1P	3F	9	9	R	R	17F	1F	2	69.5
9	12	13	16	18	1	2P	R	12P	1P	3	3	RP	49
R	3	9	8	R	2	3	1	3	10	4	6	12	48
8	6	5	5	4	4	5	8	16	11	5	R	9	34.5
R	13	4	7	17	8	13	R	11	12	2	R	7	32.5
5	7	10	14	7F	RP	6	R	5	3F	10	R	14	26
10	10	8	9	9	6	14F	10	14	2	NS	-	-	24
6	4F	4	3	NS	-	-	-	-	-	-	-	-	22
R	R	14	R	8	5	4	6	6	7	11	12	11	22
7	11	11	15	10	11	11	5	7	R	6	R	5	19
11	R	7	13	14	13	8	4	R	8	9	2	10	17
14	9	R	10	11	14	12	2P	-	-	-	-	-	
-	-	-	-	-	-	-	-	9	13	12	10	16	8
R	R	15	18	16	16	R	12	13	R	R	7	8	6
R	14	17	17	15	R	10	11	4F	R	13	R	17	5
-	-	-	-	-	-	-	-	-	-	-	9	6	3
R	8	18	R	R	-	-	-	-	-	-	-	-	2
13	15	12	11	12	9	18	13	10	9	15	R	13	0
12	R	16	12	13	12	-	-	-	-	-	-	-	0
-	-	-	-	-	-	R	14	14	11	15	-	-	0
-	-	-	-	-	15	R	15	R	16	13	18	-	0
-	-	-	-	-	15	16	R	R	R	R	14	R	0
-	-	-	-	-	-	17	14	-	-	-	-	-	0

R5	R6	R7	R8	R9	R10	R11	R12	R13	R14	R15	R16	R17	TOTAL POINTS
1/2	1/2	1/R	3/6	5/6	7/10	1/7	7/R	1/2	5/6	7/8	5/8	3/4	172
3/4	5/R	2/3	1/2	1/2	3/R	9/R	3/9	8/R	4/R	1/17	1/4	1/2	153.5
9/R	12/R	13/14	16/R	8/18	1/5	2/4	6/R	6/12	1/7	3/11	3/12	11/R	71
6/R	3/4	6/9	4/8	3/R	2/NS	3/17	1/14	3/9	10/13	4/12	6/10	12/16	70
10/R	10/13	4/8	7/9	9/17	6/8	13/14	10/R	11/14	2/12	2/NS	9/R	6/7	59.5
7/11	11/R	7/11	13/15	10/14	11/13	8/11	4/5	7/R	8/R	6/9	2/R	5/10	36
8/13	6/15	5/12	5/11	4/12	4/9	5/18	8/13	10/16	9/11	5/15	R/R	9/13	34.5
5/12	7/R	10/16	12/14	7/13	12/R	6/15	R/R	5/15	3/R	10/16	13/R	14/18	26
14/R	9/14	17/R	10/17	11/15	14/R	10/12	2/11	4/R	14/R	13/14	11/R	15/17	13
R/R	8/R	15/18	18/R	16/R	15/16	16/R	12/R	13/R	R/R	R/R	7/14	8/R	8

2010 FILL-IN CHART

	DRIVER	TEAM	Round 1 – 14 Mar BAHRAIN GP	Round 2 – 28 Mar AUSTRALIAN GP	Round 3 – 4 Apr MALAYSIAN GP	Round 4 – 18 Apr CHINESE GP	Round 5 – 9 May SPANISH GP	Round 6 – 16 May MONACO GP	Round 7 – 30 May TURKISH GP
1	JENSON BUTTON	McLaren							
2	LEWIS HAMILTON	McLaren							
3	NICO ROSBERG	Mercedes							
4	MICHAEL SCHUMACHER	Mercedes							
5	SEBASTIAN VETTEL	Red Bull							
6	MARK WEBBER	Red Bull							
7	FELIPE MASSA	Ferrari							
8	FERNANDO ALONSO	Ferrari							
9	RUBENS BARRICHELLO	Williams							
10	NICO HULKENBERG	Williams							
11	ROBERT KUBICA*	Renault							
12	BERTRAND BAGUETTE*	Renault							
14	ADRIAN SUTIL	Force India							
15	VITANTONIO LIUZZI	Force India							
16	SEBASTIEN BUEMI	Toro Rosso							
17	JAIME ALGUERSUARI*	Toro Rosso							
18	JARNO TRULLI	Lotus							
19	HEIKKI KOVALAINEN	Lotus							
20	PEDRO DE LA ROSA*	Campos Meta							
21	BRUNO SENNA	Campos Meta							
22	JONATHAN SUMMERTON*	US F1							
23	JOSE MARIA LOPEZ*	US F1							
24	TIMO GLOCK	Virgin							
25	LUCAS DI GRASSI	Virgin							
26	NICK HEIDFELD*	Sauber							
27	KAMUI KOBAYASHI	Sauber							

SCORING SYSTEM: 10, 8, 6, 5, 4, 3, 2, 1 POINTS
FOR THE FIRST EIGHT FINISHERS IN EACH GRAND PRIX

* Leading candidates at the time of going to press at the start of 2010.

Round 8 – 13 Jun CANADIAN GP	Round 9 – 27 Jun EUROPEAN GP	Round 10 – 11 Jul BRITISH GP	Round 11 – 25 Jul GERMAN GP	Round 12 – 1 Aug HUNGARIAN GP	Round 13 – 29 Aug BELGIAN GP	Round 14 – 12 Sept ITALIAN GP	Round 15 – 26 Sept SINGAPORE GP	Round 16 – 10 Oct JAPANESE GP	Round 17 – 24 Oct KOREAN GP	Round 18 – 7 Nov BRAZILIAN GP	Round 19 – 14 Nov ABU DHABI GP	POINTS TOTAL

Fernando Alonso's Renault career has come to a stop, but the team is carrying on under new ownership into 2010.

The publishers would like to thank the following sources for their kind permission to reproduce the pictures in this book. The page numbers for each of the photographs are listed below, giving the page on which they appear in the book and any location indicator (T-top, B-bottom).

LAT Photographic: 62-63, 63T, 91, 117, 119, 121; /A1GP: 54; /Charles Coates: 9, 10, 14, 18, 20, 25, 26, 34, 37, 38, 45, 51, 53, 56, 63B, 85, 89, 95, 99, 106, 116, 122-123; /Glenn Dunbar: 8, 12, 16, 22, 64-65, 92, 94, 96, 102, 108, 109, 114, 118, 120; /Steve Etherington: 6-7, 28, 32, 35, 46, 48, 98, 100, 101, 105, 107; /Andrew Ferraro: 13, 19, 23, 24, 29, 39, 47, 49, 50, 55, 57, 58, 59, 97, 103, 110, 112, 113, 115; /Alastair Staley: 11, 15, 27, 31, 41, 62T, 90; /Steven Tee: 2-3, 4, 17, 21, 30, 33, 36, 42, 60-61, 86-87, 88, 93, 104, 128; /Kevin Wood: 43

Press Association Images: /Sutton Images: 111

Sutton Images: 40, 44, 52

Every effort has been made to acknowledge correctly and contact the source and/or copyright holder of each picture and Carlton Books Limited apologises for any unintentional errors or omissions that will be corrected in future editions of this book.